Fodor's
Italian for Travelers

Fodor's
Italian for Travelers

PHRASEBOOK DICTIONARY

From the editors of

LIVING LANGUAGE®
A Random House Company

Fodor's Travel Publications, Inc.
New York • Toronto • London • Sydney • Auckland
Visit us on the Web at http://www.fodors.com/

PREVIOUSLY PUBLISHED AS *LIVING LANGUAGE TRAVELTALK™ ITALIAN*

Acknowledgments
Cover photo: Dave G. Houser/Corbis
Photo researcher: Jolie Novak
Cover design: Guido Caroti

Special Sales
Fodor's Travel Publications are available at special discounts for bulk purchases (100 copies or more) for sales promotions or premiums. Special editions, including personalized covers, excerpts of existing guides, and corporate imprints, can be created in large quantities for special needs. For more information, write to Special Marketing, Fodor's Travel Publications, 201 East 50th St., New York, NY 10022. Inquiries from Canada should be sent to Random House of Canada Ltd., Marketing Department, 1265 Aerowood Drive, Mississauga, Ontario L4W 1B9. Inquiries from the United Kingdom should be sent to Fodor's Travel Publications, 20 Vauxhall Bridge Rd., London, England SW1V 2SA.

Printed in the United States
10

CONTENTS

PREFACE

You don't need to know Italian to get along in Italy. The 2,200 Italian phrases in this guide will see you through almost every situation you encounter as a tourist. Each expression is followed by a phonetic transcription, and all you have to do to make yourself understood is to read the phonetics as you would any English sentence. You don't even need *Fodor's Italian for Travelers* cassette, on which native speakers pronounce the guide's key Italian dialogues, although the cassette will help you polish your pronunciation.

Before you start practicing, familiarize yourself with the main features of the guide:

Pronunciation Guide   The transcription system for this volume is presented in this section through the use of simple English examples and explanations. Reading through it first will enable you to use the phrases in subsequent chapters with full confidence that your pronunciation will be understood.

Chapter 1: Useful Expressions   Many common phrases are likely to be used quite frequently in a variety of contexts. For your convenience, these phrases have been grouped together in one brief chapter.

Chapters 2–13   From arrival at the airport to saying farewell to new friends, *Fodor's Italian for Travelers* provides a comprehensive resource for every important context of your visit.

Sample Dialogues   Beginning most chapters, these give you a sense of how the language sounds in conversation.

Travel Tips and Cultural Highlights Interspersed throughout the chapters is solid information on cultural attractions from Fodor's resident-writers to help you get the most out of your visit.

General Information To ease your transition into a new setting, the guide includes legal holidays, metric conversion tables, important signs, common abbreviations, and clothing and shoe-size conversion charts.

Two-Way 1,600-Word Dictionary For easy reference, all key words in the book appear here, grouped in English-Italian and Italian-English sections. Both sections include the phonetic transcription of each Italian word and phrase to help you pronounce them.

Grammar in Brief This concise section summarizes Italian grammar for those who want to understand the structure of the language and begin to learn it on their own.

ABOUT THE ITALIAN LANGUAGE

Italian belongs to the family of Romance languages—along with French, Spanish, Portuguese, and Rumanian. These languages are all basically variations of the spoken Latin of the Roman Empire.

Before its official unification in 1861, Italy was a geographic entity of loosely knit city-states and regions, each with its own dialect. Various conquerors throughout the centuries, such as the Greeks, Saracens, French, and Germans, left their mark on these dialects. Today's standard Italian, understood throughout the country, originated in Florence, an influential cultural center.

PRONUNCIATION GUIDE

Each English word or phrase in this book is presented with an Italian translation. An easy-to-follow phonetic transcription guides you to the correct pronunciation of the Italian word. You do not need any previous knowledge of Italian. Just read the phonetics as you would read English and you will be speaking comprehensible Italian.

You may use this phrasebook by itself, but the *Italian for Travelers* cassette will help you learn how to pronounce words more accurately. Just listen and repeat after the native speakers.

PRONUNCIATION CHART

The pronunciation chart below is your guide to the phonetic transcriptions used in this book. With practice, you will become more and more familiar with these sounds. Eventually, you will be able to read Italian words without the help of this guide. Three points should be emphasized about pronouncing Italian:

1. Italian spelling is more consistent than English spelling, and therefore it is easier to tell how a word should be pronounced, once you learn the sounds.
2. Pay special attention to the vowel sounds. They vary from English pronunciation. It is crucial to learn the Italian vowel pronunciation to make yourself understood.
3. Italian vowels are more flat than in English. The *o* sound, for instance, does not carry the *w* sound that usually accompanies it in English.

In this phonetic system, the stressed syllables are capitalized.

Vowels

Italian Spelling	Approximate Sound in English	Phonetic Symbol	Example (Phonetic Transcription)
a	f<u>a</u>ther	ah	**banana** (bah-NAH-nah)
e	m<u>e</u>t	eh	**breve** (BREH-veh)
i	mach<u>i</u>ne	ee	**vino** (VEE-noh)

3

| o | hope | oh | **moto** (MOH-toh) |
| u | rule | oo | **fumo** (FOO-moh) |

Vowel Combinations

Diphthongs A diphthong is a double vowel combination that produces a single sound. Here is a list of frequent diphthongs and their pronunciation:

Italian Spelling	Approximate Sound in English	Phonetic Symbol	Example (Phonetic Transcription)
ai	ripe	ahy	**daino** (DAHY-noh)
au	now	ow	**auto** (OW-toh)
ei	may	ay	**sei** SAY(stressed)
eu	—	ehoo	**neutro** (NEHOO-troh)
ia	yarn	yah	**italiano** (ee-tahl-YAH-noh)
ie	yet	yeh	**miele** (MYEH-leh)
io	yodel	yoh	**campione** (kahm-PYOH-neh)
iu	you	yoo	**fiume** (FYOO-meh)
oi	soy	oy	**poi** (poy)
ua	wand	wah	**quando** (KWAHN-doh)
ue	wet	weh	**questo** (KWEH-stoh)
uo	war	woh	**suono** (SWOH-noh)
ui	sweet	wee	**guido** (GWEE-doh)

Words that begin, incorporate, or end in *cia, cie, cio, ciu, gia, gie, gio, giu, scia, scie, scio,* or *sciu* are pronounced as follows: if the *i* is stressed, the two vowels are pronounced separately as in *farmacia* (fahr-mah-CEE-ah), *bugia* (boo-GEE-ah), *scia* (SHEE-ah). If the *i* is not stressed, follow this chart for pronunciation:

Italian Spelling	Phonetic Symbol	Example (Phonetic Transcription)
cia	chah	**ciambella** (chahm-BEHL-lah)
cie	cheh	**cielo** (CHEH-loh)

cio	choh	**cioccolata** (choh-koh-LAH-tah)
ciu	choo	**ciuffo** (CHOOF-foh)
gia	jah	**giacca** (JAHK-kah)
gie	jeh	**ciliegie** (chee-LYEH-jeh)
gio	joh	**giovane** (JOH-vah-neh)
giu	joo	**giusto** (JOO-stoh)
scia	shah	**fasciare** (fah-SHAH-reh)
scie	sheh	**scienza** (SHEHN-tsah)
scio	shoh	**sciopero** (SHOH-peh-roh)
sciu	shoo	**sciupare** (shoo-PAH-reh)

Hiatus A hiatus is a double vowel combination whose sounds are pronounced separately, rather than elided.

Italian Spelling	Example (Phonetic Transcription)
ae	**maestro** (mah-EH-stroh)
au	**paura** (pah-OO-rah)
ea	**reato** (reh-AH-toh)
ia	**bugia** (boo-JEE-ah)
oa	**boato** (boh-AH-toh)
oe	**poeta** (poh-EH-tah)
ue	**bue** (BOO-eh)

Identical Vowels Any same two vowels must be pronounced separately, with the stress on the first vowel:

Italian Spelling	Example (Phonetic Transcription)
ee	**idee** (ee-DEH-eh)
ii	**addii** (ahd-DEE-ee)
oo	**zoo** (DZOH-oh)

Triphthongs A triphthong is a combination of three vowels:

Italian Spelling	Example (Phonetic Transcription)
aia	**baia** (BAH-yah)
aio	**saio** (SAH-yoh)
iei	**miei** (mee-AY)
uio	**buio** (BOO-yoh)
uoi	**buoi** (boo-OY)

Consonants

Italian Spelling	Approximate Sound in English
b/d/f/k/l/m/n/p/q/t/v	similar to English

Italian Spelling	Approximate Sound in English	Phonetic Symbol	Example (Phonetic Transcription)
c (before e/i)	chin	ch	cena (CHEH-nah) cibo (CHEE-boh)
c (before a/o/u)	catch	k	caffè (kahf-FEH) conto (KOHN-toh) cupola (KOO-poh-lah)
ch (with e/i)	can	k	amiche (ah-MEE-keh) chilo (KEE-loh)
g (before e/i)	jelly	j	gente (JEHN-teh) gita (JEE-tah)
g (before a/o/u)	gold	g	gala (GAH-lah) gondola (GOHN-doh-lah) gusto (GOO-stoh)
gh	get	g	spaghetti (spah-GET-tee) ghiotto (GYOHT-toh)
	ghost	gh	funghi (FOON-ghee)
gl (plus vowel followed by consonant)	globe	gl	globo (GLOH-boh) negligente (neh-glee-JEHN-teh)
gli	scallion	lyee	gli (lyee)
glia		lyah	famiglia (fah-MEE-lyah)
glie		lyeh	moglie (MOH-lyeh)
glio		lyoh	aglio (AH-lyoh)

6

gn	ca<u>ny</u>on	ny	**Bologna** (Boh-LOH-nyah)
h	silent	—	**hotel** (oh-TEHL)
r	trilled	r	**rumore** (roo-MOH-reh)
s (generally)	<u>s</u>et	s	**pasta** (PAH-stah)
s (between two vowels and before b/d/ g/l/m/n/v/r)	<u>z</u>ero	z	**rosa** (ROH-zah) **sbaglio** (<u>Z</u>BAH-lyoh)
sc (before e/i)	fi<u>sh</u>	sh	**pesce** (PEH-sheh) **sci** (shee)
sc (before a/o/u)	<u>sc</u>out	sk	**scala** (SKAH-lah) **disco** (DEE-skoh)
sch (with e/i)	<u>sk</u>y	sk	**pesche** (PEH-skeh) **fischi** (FEE-skee)
z (generally like ts)	pi<u>ts</u>	ts	**zucchero** (TSOOK-keh-roh) **grazie** (GRAH-tsyeh)
z (sometimes like dz)	toa<u>ds</u>	dz	**zingaro** (DZEEN-gah-roh) **zanzara** (dzahn-DZAH-ra-h)

Double Consonants

All consonants, except h, can be doubled. They have a much more forceful sound than single consonants. The sound is slightly prolonged. Note the difference in pronunciation between single and double consonants:

nono (NOH-<u>n</u>oh) and **nonno** (NOH<u>N</u>-noh)
fato (FAH-<u>t</u>oh) and **fatto** (FAH<u>T</u>-toh)
babbo (BAH<u>B</u>-boh)
mamma (MAH<u>M</u>-mah)
gatto (GAH<u>T</u>-toh)

ELISION

Certain words, especially articles and prepositions, drop the final vowel when the next sound begins with a vowel:

lo studente (loh stoo-DEHN-teh)
but **l'amico** (lah-MEE-koh)
una matita (OO-nah mah-TEE-tah)
but **un'amica** (oo-nah-MEE-kah)
di Francia (dee FRAHN-chah)
but **d'Italia** (dee-TAH-lyah)

Stress
Italian words are usually (but not always) stressed on the next-to-the-last syllable. An accent grave (`) is only used when the stress is on the final vowel of a word, such as *città* (cheet-TAH), *falò* (fah-LOH), *caffè* (kahf-FEH).

Capitals
Many words that are capitalized in English are not in Italian. Days, months, seasons, proper adjectives (except when used as plural nouns, e.g., the Italians) and titles such as Mr., Mrs., Miss, Dr., and Prof.:

Sunday	**domenica** (doh-MEH-nee-kah)
January	**gennaio** (jehn-NAH-yoh)
Spring	**la primavera** (lah pree-mah-VEH-rah)
She is Italian.	**È italiana.** (eh ee-tah-LYAH-nah)
Prof. Rossi	**Il prof. Rossi.** (eel proh-fehs-SOHR ROHS-see)

Italian Alphabet
The Italian alphabet has twenty-one letters plus five found in foreign words:

A	ah	**G**	jee	**N**	EHN-neh	**S**	EHS-seh
B	bee	**H**	AHK-kah	**O**	oh	**T**	tee
C	chee	**I**	ee	**P**	pee	**U**	oo
D	dee	**L**	EHL-leh	**Q**	koo	**V**	voo
E	eh	**M**	EHM-meh	**R**	EHR-reh	**Z**	DZEH-tah
F	EHF-feh						

Foreign Letters
J	ee LOON-gah	**W**	DOHP-pyah voo	**Y**	ee GREH-kah *(or)*
K	KAHP-pah	**X**	eeks		EEP-see-lohn

8

1/USEFUL EXPRESSIONS

COURTESY

Please.	**Per piacere.**	pehr pyah-CHEH-reh
	(or) Per favore.	pehr fah-VOH-reh
Thank you.	**Grazie.**	GRAH-tsyeh
You're welcome.	**Prego.**	PREH-goh
I'm sorry.	**Mi dispiace.**	mee dee-SPYAH-cheh
Sorry (excuse me).	**Scusi.**	SKOO-zee
Excuse me (may I get through?).	**Permesso.**	pehr-MEHS-soh
It doesn't matter.	**Non importa.**	nohn eem-POHR-tah
	(or) Di niente.	dee NYEHN-teh

GREETINGS

Good morning.	**Buon giorno.**	bwon JOHR-noh
Good afternoon.		
Good evening.	**Buona sera.**	bwoh-nah SEH-rah
Good night.	**Buona notte.**	bwoh-nah NOHT-teh
Good-bye (formal).	**Arrivederci.**	ahr-ree-veh-DEHR-chee
Hello/Good-bye (informal).	**Ciao.**	chow
See you soon.	**A presto.**	ah PREH-stoh
See you later.	**A più tardi.**	ah pyoo TAHR-dee
See you tomorrow.	**A domani.**	ah doh-MAH-nee
Let's go!	**Andiamo!**	ahn-DYAH-mohl

APPROACHING SOMEONE FOR HELP

Excuse me,	**Mi scusi,**	mee SKOO-zee,
• Sir.	• **signore.**	• see-NYOH-reh
• Madam/Mrs.	• **signora.**	• see-NYOH-rah
• Miss/Ms.	• **signorina.**	• see-nyoh-REE-nah
Do you speak English?	**Parla inglese?**	PAHR-lah een-GLEH-zeh?
Do you understand English?	**Capisce l'inglese?**	kah-PEE-sheh leen-GLEH-zeh?
Yes./No.	**Sì./No.**	see/noh

9

I'm sorry.	Desolato (-a)* (or) Mi dispiace.	deh-zoh-LAH-toh (-tah) mee dee-SPYAH-cheh
I am a tourist.	Sono turista #	SOH-noh too-REE-stah
I don't speak Italian.	Non parlo italiano.	nohn PAHR-loh ee-tah-LYAH-noh
I speak very little.	Lo parlo poco.	loh PAHR-loh POH-koh
I understand a little.	Capisco un po'.	kah-PEE-skoh oon poh
Please speak more slowly.	Per favore, parli più adagio.	pehr fah-VOH-reh, PAHR-lee pyoo ah-DAH-joh
Please repeat.	Per favore, ripeta.	pehr fah-VOH-reh, ree-PEH-tah
May I ask a question?	Posso fare una domanda?	POHS-soh FAH-reh OO-nah doh-MAHN-dah?
Could you please help me?	Può aiutarmi, per favore?	pwoh ah-yoo-TAHR-mee, pehr fah-VOH-reh?
Okay./Sure.	D'accordo.	dahk-KOHR-doh
Of course.	Certamente.	cher-tah-MEHN-teh
Where is . . . ?	Dov'è . . . ?	doh-VEH?
Where is the bathroom?	Dov'è la toeletta?†	doh-VEH lah toh-eh LEHT-tah?
Thank you very much.	Molte grazie. (or) Mille grazie.	MOHL-teh GRAH-tsyeh MEEL-leh GRAH-tsyeh

*In Italian, adjectives agree in gender and number with the nouns they modify. *Desolato* is the masculine form and *desolata* is the feminine form. Herein, the feminine endings will appear in parentheses.

#Although there are a few exceptions (*turista*, for example), in Italian most nouns and adjectives end in -*o* in the masculine singular and in -*a* in the feminine singular. There are also several nouns ending in -*e* that are either masculine or feminine singular. The gender has to be learned. In the plural, -*o* becomes -*i*, -*a* becomes -*e*, and -*e* becomes -*i* for both genders. See also Chapter 15, "Grammar in Brief," regarding the gender and number of nouns and adjectives.

†Toilette, or *il gabinetto*, refers to public bathrooms. At someone's home, you would ask *"Dov'è il bagno?"* (doh-VEH eel BAH-nyoh?)

10

QUESTION WORDS

Who?	**Chi?**	kee?
What?	**Che cosa?**	keh KOH-sah
Why?	**Perché?**	pehr-KEH?
When?	**Quando?**	KWAHN-doh?
Where?	**Dove?**	DOH-veh?
How?	**Come?**	KOH-meh?
How much?	**Quanto?**	KWAHN-toh?

NUMBERS

Take the time to learn how to count in Italian. You will find that knowing the numbers will make everything easier during your trip.

0	zero	DZEH-roh
1	uno	OO-noh
2	due	DOO-eh
3	tre	treh
4	quattro	KWAHT-troh
5	cinque	CHEEN-kweh
6	sei	SEH-ee
7	sette	SEHT-teh
8	otto	OHT-toh
9	nove	NOH-veh
10	dieci	DYEH-chee
11	undici	OON-dee-chee
12	dodici	DOH-dee-chee
13	tredici	TREH-dee-chee
14	quattordici	kwaht-TOHR-dee-chee
15	quindici	KWEEN-dee-chee
16	sedici	SEH-dee-chee
17	diciassette	dee-chahs-SEHT-teh
18	diciotto	dee-CHOHT-toh
19	diciannove	dee-chahn-NOH-veh
20	venti	VEHN-tee
21	ventuno	vehn-TOO-noh
22	ventidue	vehn-tee-DOO-eh
23	ventitrè	vehn-tee-TREH
24	ventiquattro	vehn-tee-QWAHT-troh
25	venticinque	vehn-tee-CHEEN-kweh

26	**ventisei**	vehn-tee-SAY
27	**ventisette**	vehn-tee-SEHT tch
28	**ventotto**	vehn-TOHT toh
29	**ventinove**	vehn-tee-NOH-veh
30	**trenta**	TREHN-tah
40	**quaranta**	kwah-RAHN-tah
50	**cinquanta**	cheen-KWAHN-tah
60	**sessanta**	sehs-SAHN-tah
70	**settanta**	seht-TAHN-tah
80	**ottanta**	oh-TAHN-tah
90	**novanta**	noh-VAHN-tah
100	**cento**	CHEHN-toh
101	**centouno**	chehn-toh-OO-noh
102	**centodue**	chehn-toh-DOO-eh
110	**centodieci**	chehn-toh-DYEH-chee
120	**centoventi**	chehn-toh-VEHN-tee
200	**duecento**	dweh-CHEHN-toh
300	**trecento**	treh-CHEHN-toh
400	**quattrocento**	kwaht-troh-CHEHN-toh
500	**cinquecento**	cheen-kweh-CHEHN-toh
600	**seicento**	say-CHEHN-toh
700	**settecento**	seht-teh-CHEHN-toh
800	**ottocento**	oh-toh-CHEHN-toh
900	**novecento**	noh-veh-CHEHN-toh
1,000 (1.000)*	**mille**	MEEL-leh
1,100	**millecento**	meel-leh-CHEHN-toh
1,200	**milleduecento**	meel-leh-dweh-CHEHN-toh
2,000	**duemila**	dweh-MEE-lah
3,000	**tremila**	treh-MEE-lah
10,000	**diecimila**	dyeh-chee-MEE-lah
50,000	**cinquantamila**	cheen-kwahn-tah-MEE-lah
100,000	**centomila**	chehn-toh-MEE-lah
1,000,000	**un milione**	oon mee-LYOH-neh
1,000,000,000	**un miliardo**	oon mee-LYAHR-doh

*The plural of *mille* is *mila*. In Italian, the use of commas and decimal points are the reverse of how they are used in English. For example, 10,000 would be written 10.000, and 5.4 would be written 5,4 and pronounced "CHEEN-kweh VEER-goh-lah KWAHT-troh."

Ordinal Numbers*

first	**primo**	PREE-moh
second	**secondo**	seh-KOHN-doh
third	**terzo**	TEHR-tsoh
fourth	**quarto**	KWAHR-toh
fifth	**quinto**	KWEEN-toh
sixth	**sesto**	SEH-stoh
seventh	**settimo**	seht-TEE-moh
eighth	**ottavo**	oht-TAH-voh
ninth	**nono**	NOH-noh
tenth	**decimo**	DEH-chee-moh
eleventh	**undicesimo**	oon-dee-CHEH-zee-moh
twentieth	**ventesimo**	vehn-TEH-zee-moh
hundredth	**centesimo**	chehn-TEH-zee-moh

*Ordinal numbers agree in gender with the nouns they modify. For example, *la Quinta Strada* (lah KWEEN-tah STRAH-dah), Fifth Avenue, and *le prime notizie* (leh PREE-meh noh-TEE-tsyeh), the first news.

QUANTITIES

once	**una volta**	OO-nah VOHL-tah
twice	**due volte**	DOO-eh VOHL-teh
whole	**intero**	een-TEH-roh
half	**mezzo**	MEHD-dzoh
half of	**metà**	meh-TAH dee
a half hour	**mezz'ora**	mehd-DZOH-rah
a third	**un terzo**	oon TEHR-tsoh
a quarter	**un quarto**	oon KWAHR-toh
two-thirds	**due terzi**	DOO-eh TEHR-tsee
percent	**per cento**	pehr CHEHN-toh
a lot of	**molto**	MOHL-toh
a little	**poco**	POH-koh
a little of	**un po' di**	oon POH dee
a few	**alcuni**	ahl-KOO-nee
half a kilo of	**mezzo chilo di**	MEHD-dzoh KEE-loh dee
enough	**abbastanza**	ahb-bah-STAHN-tsah
that's enough!	**basta!**	BAH-stah
too much	**troppo**	TROHP-poh
too little	**troppo poco**	TROHP-poh POH-koh

13

a glass of	**un bicchiere di**	oon beek-KYEH-reh dee
a cup of	**una tazza di**	OO-nah TAHT-tsah dee
a dozen of	**una dozzina di**	OO-nah dohd-DZEE-nah dee

DIALOGUE: AT THE BANK (*IN BANCA*)

Cliente:	**Vorrei cambiare mille dollari.**	vohr-RAY kahm-BYAH-reh MEEL-leh DOHL-lah-ree
Cassiere:	**Certamente. Il cambio oggi è a milletrecento lire. Sono un milione e trecentomila lire.**	cher-tah-MEHN-teh. eel KAHM-byoh OHD-jee eh ah meel-leh-treh-CHEHN-toh LEE-reh. SOH-noh oon mee-LYOH-neh eh treh-CHEHN-toh MEE-lah LEE-reh
Cliente:	**Va bene. Ecco i travellers cheques.**	vah BEH-neh. EHK-koh ee TREH-vehl-lehr checks
Cassiere:	**Li firmi, per favore.**	lee FEER-mee pehr fah-VOH-reh
Cliente:	**D'accordo. Eccoli, e questo è il mio passaporto.**	dahk-KOHR-doh. EHK-koh-lee, eh KWEH-stoh eh eel MEE-oh pahs-sah-POHR-toh
Cassiere:	**Grazie. Ecco i Suoi soldi.**	GRAH-tsyeh. EHK-koh ee soo-OY SOHL-dee

- -

Customer:	I would like to change one thousand dollars.
Teller:	Certainly, sir. The rate is 1,300 lire to the dollar today. That would be one million, three hundred thousand lire.
Customer:	Fine. Here are my traveler's checks.
Teller:	Would you please sign them?
Customer:	Of course. Here they are, and this is my passport.
Teller:	Thank you. Here's your money.

ABOUT THE CURRENCY

In Italy, the currency is the *lira* (LEE-rah). Its sign is L. or Lit. You will find the best exchange rates at banks, which are open weekdays, with slight regional variations, between 8:30 A.M. and 1:30 P.M. and between 2:30 or 2:45 P.M. to 3:30 or 3:45 P.M. Although you can exchange money at some hotels and at exchange offices, rates are usually best at banks and at ATMs in the Cirrus and Plus networks. Remember that at banks, you usually need your passport to change money. At ATMs in Italy, you can use only four-digit PIN numbers (so you may need to change your PIN number before departure); note that transaction fees may be higher than at home. Major credit cards are widely accepted. Make sure they have been programmed for use at ATMs if you want to use them to get cash advances.

CHANGING MONEY

Where is . . .	Dov'è . . .	doh-VEH . . .
• the nearest bank?	• la banca più vicina?	• lah BAHN-kah pyoo vee-CEE-nah?
• automatic cash machine?	• un bancomat?	• oon BAHN-koh-maht?
Where can I change . . .	Dove posso cambiare . . .	DOH-veh POHS-soh kam-BYAH-reh . . .
• some dollars?	• dei dollari?	• day DOHL-lah-ree?
• some money?	• dei soldi?	• day SOHL-dee?
• this check?	• questo assegno?	• KWEH-stoh ahs-SEH-nyoh?
Is the bank open?	È aperta la banca?	eh ah-PEHR-tah lah BAHN-kah?
No, it's closed.	No, è chiusa.	noh, eh KYOO-zah
Is there a currency exchange nearby?	C'è un ufficio cambio qui vicino?	cheh oon oof-FEE-choh KAHM-byoh kwee vee-CHEE-noh?
I wish to cash a traveler's check.	Desidero cambiare un travellers cheque.	deh-ZEE-deh-roh kahm-BYAH-reh oon TREH-vehl-lehr check

15

Do you accept . . .	Accettate . . .	ah-cheht-TAH-teh . . .
• personal checks?	• assegni personali?	• ahs-SEH-nyee pehr-soh-NAH-lee?
• a money order?	• un vaglia?	• oon VAH-lyah?
What's the exchange rate?	Qual è il cambio?	kwah-LEH eel KAHM-byoh?
How much is the dollar worth today?	Quanto vale il dollaro oggi?	KWAHN-toh VAH-leh eel DOHL-lah-roh OHD-jee?
Do you need . . .	Ha bisogno . . .	ah bee-ZOH-nyoh . . .
• my identification card?	• della carta d'identità?	• DEHL-lah KAHR-tah dee-dehn-tee-TAH?
• my passport?	• del passaporto?	• dehl pahs-sah-POHR-toh?
• another document?	• di un altro documento?	• dee oon AHL-troh doh-koo-MEHN-toh?
Where do I sign?	Dove firmo?	DOH-veh FEER-moh?
Can you give me . . .	Può darmi . . .	pwoh DAHR-mee . . .
• large bills?	• banconote di grosso taglio?	• bahn-koh-NOH-teh dee GROHS-soh TAH-lyoh?
• small bills?	• banconote di piccolo taglio?	• bahn-koh-NOH-teh dee PEEK-koh-loh TAH-lyoh?
• some change?	• moneta spicciola? (or) spiccioli?	• moh-NEH-tah SPEET-choh-lah? SPEET-choh-lee?
• five ten-thousand lire bills?	• cinque banconote da diecimila?	• CEEN-kweh bahn-koh-NOH-teh dah dyeh-chee-MEE-lah?
I want to send a telex to my bank.	Vorrei mandare un telex alla mia banca.	vohr-RAY mahn-DAH-reh oon TEH-lehks AHL-lah MEE-ah BAHN-kah
Has my money arrived?	È arrivato il mio denaro?	eh ahr-ree-VAH-toh eel MEE-oh deh-NAH-roh?

PAYING THE BILL

How much does it cost?	**Quanto costa?**	KWAHN-toh KOH-stah?
The bill, please.	**Il conto, per favore.**	eel KOHN-toh pehr fah-VOH-reh
How much do I owe you?	**Quanto Le devo?**	KWAHN-toh leh DEH-voh?
Is service included?	**Il servizio è incluso?**	eel sehr-VEE-tsyoh eh een-KLOO-soh?
This is for you.	**Questo è per Lei.**	KWEH-stoh eh pehr lay

TIPPING

Restaurants

If the menu reads *servizio e coperto a parte* (sehr-VEE-tsyoh eh coh-PEHR-toh ah PAHR-teh), or "service not included on the bill," you don't have to leave more than a little small change. In larger cities and at resorts, it's customary to give the waiter a 5 percent tip in addition to the bill.

At a hotel bar, tip about 1,000 lire for drinks, 100 lire or so for drinks standing up at a café or bar, 500 lire or more for table service in a good café. Washroom attendants should be tipped about 200 lire or more, cloakroom attendants and theatre ushers about 500 lire per person.

Train Stations, Airports, Taxis

Railway and airport porters charge a fixed rate per suitcase that is usually posted. Tip an additional 1,000 lire per person if the porter is very helpful. Tip taxi drivers 5–10 percent (remember that cab drivers sometimes add extra charges for luggage and always add a surcharge at night and for pickups).

Hotels

Service charges are generally included in all hotel bills. In general, chambermaids should be given about 1,000 lire per day, 4,000–5,000 a week; bellboys 2,000–4,000 lire for carrying luggage; doormen about 1,000 lire for calling a cab; the

17

concierge gets 5,000–15,000 lire, depending on the service. Tip a minimum of 1,000 lire for room service and valet service.

Barbers and hairdressers should be tipped 3,000–8,000 lire.

TELLING TIME

What time is it?	**Che ora è?**	keh OH-rah eh?
	(or) **Che ore sono?**	keh OH-reh SOH-noh?
It's . . .	**È . . .**	eh . . .
• one o'clock.	• **l'una.**	• LOO-nah
• noon.	• **mezzogiorno.**	• mehd-dzoh-JOHR-noh
• midnight.	• **mezzanotte.**	• mehd-zah-NOHT-teh
It's . . .	**Sono . . .**	SOH-noh . . .
• 2:00.	• **le due.**	• leh DOO-eh
• 2:15.	• **le due e un quarto.**	• leh DOO-eh eh oon KWAHR-toh
• 2:30.	• **le due e mezzo (-a).**	• leh DOO-eh eh MEHD-zoh (-ah)
• 2:45.	• **le due e tre quarti.**	• leh DOO-eh eh treh KWAHR-tee
	(or) **le tre meno un quarto.**	• leh treh MEH-noh oon KWAHR-toh
• 2:50.	• **le tre meno dieci.**	• leh treh MEH-noh DYEH-chee
• 3:10.	• **le tre e dieci.**	• leh treh eh DYEH-chee
• 4:00 sharp.	• **le quattro in punto.**	• leh KWAHT-troh een PUHN-toh
• 5:00 in the morning.	• **le cinque di mattina.**	• leh CHEEN-kweh dee maht-TEE-nah
• 5:00 in the afternoon.	• **le cinque del pomeriggio.**	• leh CHEEN-kweh dehl poh-meh-REED-joh
• 9:00 in the evening.	• **le nove di sera.**	• leh NOH-veh dee SEH-rah
• 1:00 at night.	• **l'una di notte.**	• LOO-nah dee NOHT-teh

18

five minutes ago	**cinque minuti fa**	CHEEN-kweh mee-NOO-tee fah
in a half-hour	**fra mezz'ora**	frah mehdz OH-rah
before 9:00 A.M.	**prima delle nove di mattina**	PREE-mah DEHL-leh NOH-veh dee maht-TEE-nah
after 8:00 P.M.	**dopo le otto di sera**	DOH-poh leh OHT-toh dee SEH-rah
since 3:00 P.M.	**dalle tre del pomeriggio**	DAHL-leh treh dehl poh-meh-REED-joh
When does it begin?	**Quando comincia?**	KWAHN-doh koh-MEEN-chah?
He came . . .	**È arrivato . . .**	eh ahr-ree-VAH-toh . . .
• on time.	• **in orario.**	• een oh-RAH-ryoh
• early.	• **in anticipo.**	• een ahn-TEE-cee-poh
• late.	• **in ritardo.**	• een ree-TAHR-doh

USEFUL EXPRESSIONS

The 24-Hour Clock

In Italy, as in most European countries, the 24-hour system (used by the military in the United States) is generally used for transportation schedules and theatre times. To convert the P.M. hours to the 24-hour system, just add 12 to the regular time. For example, 3 P.M. is 12 plus 3, or 15 hours. The show you are planning to see might start at 7:30 P.M. or 19:30. Midnight, or 24 hours, is also expressed as 00:00, and minutes past midnight are expressed as 00:01, and so forth, until 01:00. The following chart may be used for quick reference:

1 A.M.	01:00	**l'una**	LOO-nah
2 A.M.	02:00	**le due**	leh DOO-eh
3 A.M.	03:00	**le tre**	leh treh
4 A.M.	04:00	**le quattro**	leh KWAHT-troh
5 A.M.	05:00	**le cinque**	leh CHEEN-kweh
6 A.M.	06:00	**le sei**	leh SEH-ee
7 A.M.	07:00	**le sette**	leh SEHT-teh
8 A.M.	08:00	**le otto**	leh OHT-toh
9 A.M.	09:00	**le nove**	leh NOH-veh

10 A.M.	10:00	**le dieci**	leh DYEH-chee
11 A.M.	11:00	**le undici**	leh OON-dee-chee
12 noon	12:00	**le dodici** (mezzogiorno)	leh DOH-dee-choo (mehd-zoh-JOHR-noh)
1 P.M.	13:00	**le tredici**	leh TREH-dee-chee
2 P.M.	14:00	**le quattordici**	leh kwaht-TOHR-dee-chee
3 P.M.	15:00	**le quindici**	leh KWEEN-dee-chee
4 P.M.	16:00	**le sedici**	leh SEH-dee-chee
5 P.M.	17:00	**le diciassette**	leh dee-chahs-SEHT-teh
6 P.M.	18:00	**le diciotto**	leh dee-CHOHT-toh
7 P.M.	19:00	**le diciannove**	leh dee-chahn-NOH-veh
8 P.M.	20:00	**le venti**	leh VEHN-tee
9 P.M.	21:00	**le ventuno**	leh vehn-TOO-noh
10 P.M.	22:00	**le ventidue**	leh vehn-tee-DOO-eh
11 P.M.	23:00	**le ventitre**	leh vehn-tee-TREH
12 midnight	24:00	**le ventiquattro** (mezzanotte)	leh vehn-tee-KWAHT-troh (mehd-zah-NOH-teh)

2/AT THE AIRPORT

Going through customs, *dogana* (doh-GAH-nah), should present no problems for an American, and you should proceed as quickly and smoothly as the number of arriving passengers will allow. Generally, most personal belongings, such as clothing, tobacco products, alcohol, and perfume, are duty free. You may bring in 200 cigarettes or 100 cigarillos or 50 cigars or 250 grams of tobacco; two liters of wine; one bottle of hard liquor; and 50 milliliters of perfume and 250 milliliters of toilet water. When you go through customs, you may find the following phrases in this dialogue quite useful:

DIALOGUE: CUSTOMS AND IMMIGRATION (*CONTROLLO DEI PASSAPORTI*)

Doganiere:	**Buon giorno. Il passaporto, per favore.**	bwohn JOHR-noh, eel pahs-sah-POHR-toh, pehr fah-VOH-reh
Turista:	**Ecco il passaporto.**	EHK-koh eel pahs-sah-POHR-toh
Doganiere:	**È americana?**	eh ah-meh-ree-KAH-nah?
Turista:	**Sì, sono americana.**	see, SOH-noh ah-meh-ree-KAH-nah
Doganiere:	**Quanto tempo si trattiene?**	KWAHN-toh TEHM-poh see traht-TYEH-neh?
Turista:	**Resterò tre settimane.**	reh-steh-ROH treh seht-tee-MAH-neh
Doganiere:	**Buona permanenza!**	BWOH-nah pehr-mah-NEHN-tsah!
Officer:	Good morning. May I see your passport, please?	

21

Tourist:	Here's my passport.	
Officer:	Are you American?	
Tourist:	Yes, I am American.	
Officer:	How long will you stay?	
Tourist:	I'll be here for three weeks.	
Officer:	Have a nice stay!	

CLEARING CUSTOMS

English	Italian	Pronunciation
What is your nationality?	Di che nazionalità è?	dee keh nah-tsyoh-nah-lee-TAH eh?
I am American.	Sono americano (-a).	SOH-noh ah-meh-ree-KAH-noh(-nah)
What's your name?	Come si chiama?	KOH-meh see KYAH-mah?
My name is . . .	Mi chiamo . . .	mee KYAH-moh . . .
Where are you staying?	Dove alloggia?	DOH-veh ahl-LOHD-jah?
I am staying at the . . . Hotel.	Alloggio all'hotel . . .	ahl-LOHD-joh ahl-loh-TEHL . . .
Are you here on vacation?	È qui in vacanza?	eh kwee een vah-KAHN-tsah?
Yes, I am on vacation.	Sì, sono in vacanza.	see, SOH-noh een vah-KAHN-tsah
No, I am passing through.	No, sono di passaggio.	noh, SOH-noh dee pahs-SAHD-joh
I'm here on a business trip.	Sono in viaggio d'affari.	SOH-noh een VYAHD-joh dahf-FAH-ree
I'll be here . . .	Rimarrò . . .	ree-mahr-ROH . . .
• a few days.	• alcuni giorni.	• ahl-KOO-nee JOHR-nee
• a week.	• una settimana.	• OO-nah seht-tee-MAH-nah
• several weeks.	• parecchie settimane.	• pah-REHK-kyeh seht-tee-MAH-neh
• a month.	• un mese.	• oon MEH-zeh
Do you have anything to declare?	Ha qualcosa da dichiarare?	ah kwahl-KOH-zah dah dee-kyah-RAH-reh?

22

I have nothing to declare.	**Non ho niente da dichiarare.**	nohn oh NYEHN-teh dah dee-kyah-RAH-reh
Can you open your bag, please?	**Può aprire la valigia, per cortesia?**	pwoh ah-PREE-reh lah vah-LEE-jah, pehr kohr-teh-ZEE-ah?
Certainly.	**Certamente.**	chehr-tah-MEHN-teh
They are my personal effects.	**Sono effetti personali.**	SOH-noh ehf-FEHT-tee pehr-soh-NAH-lee
They are gifts.	**Sono regali.**	SOH-noh reh-GAH-lee
Do I have to pay duty?	**Devo pagare la dogana?**	DEH-voh pah-GAH-reh lah doh-GAH-nah?
Yes./No.	**Sì./No.**	see/noh
Have a nice stay!	**Buona permanenza!**	BWOH-nah pehr-mah-NEHN-tsah

LUGGAGE AND PORTERS

Porters are usually available at major airports and train stations. Baggage carts may be found at airports. However, they are rare at train stations, so you will have to use a uniformed porter if you are carrying a lot of luggage. Porters charge a standard fee for each piece of baggage.

I need . . .	**Ho bisogno di . . .**	oh bee-ZOH-nyoh dee . . .
• a porter.	• **un portabagali. (or) un facchino.**	• oon pohr-tah-bah-GAH-lyee oon fahk-KEE-noh
• a baggage cart.	• **un carrello.**	• oon kahr-REHL-loh
Here's my luggage.	**Ecco il mio bagaglio.**	EHK-koh eel MEE-oh bah-GAH-lyoh
Take my bags . . .	**Porti le valigie . . .**	POHR-tee leh vah-LEE-jeh . . .
• to the taxi.	• **al taxi.**	• ahl TAHK-see
• to the bus stop.	• **alla fermata dell'autobus.**	• AHL-lah fehr-MAH-tah dehl-OW-toh-boos
• to the luggage checkroom.	• **al deposito bagagli.**	• ahl deh-POH-zee-toh bah-GAH-lyee

to the lockers.	alla custodia automatica.	AHL-lah koo-STOH dyah ow-toh-MAH-tee-kah
Please be careful!	Faccia attenzione, per favore!	FAH-chah aht-tehn-TSYOH-neh, pehr fah-VOH-reh
How much is it?	Quant'è?	kwahn-TEH?

AIRPORT TRANSPORTATION AND SERVICES

Do you know where . . . is?	Sa dov'è . . .	sah doh-VEH . . .
• Alitalia	• l'Alitalia?	• lah-lee-TAH-lyah?
• the information booth	• l'ufficio informazioni?	• luhf-FEE-choh een-fohr-mah-TSYOH-nee?
• the ticket counter	• la biglietteria?	• lah bee-lyeht-teh-REE-ah?
• the luggage check-in	• l'accettazione bagagli?	• lah-cheht-tah-TSY-OH-neh bah-GAH-lyee?
• the duty-free shop	• il negozio duty-free?	• eel neh-GOH-tsyoh duty-free?
• the car rental	• l'autonoleggio?	• low-toh-noh-LEHD-joh?
• the currency exchange	• l'ufficio cambio?	• loof-FEE-choh KAHM-byoh?
• the lost baggage office	• l'ufficio oggetti smarriti?	• loof-FEE-choh ohd-JEHT-tee smahr-REE-tee?
• the taxi stand	• il posteggio dei taxi?	• eel poh-STEHD-joh day TAHK-see?
• the phone	• il telefono?	• eel teh-LEH-foh-noh?
• the travel agency	• l'agenzia viaggi?	• lah-jehn-TSEE-ah VYAHD-jee?
• the booking agency	• l'ufficio prenotazioni?	• luhf-FEE-choh preh-noh-tah-TSYOH-nee?

24

FLIGHT ARRANGEMENTS

English	Italian	Pronunciation
Is there a direct flight to Rome?	C'è un volo diretto per Roma? *(or)* . . . senza scalo . . . ?	cheh oon VOH-loh dee-REHT-toh pehr ROH-mah? . . . SEHN-tsah SKAH-loh . . . ?
What time does it leave?	A che ora parte?	ah keh OH-rah PAHR-teh?
What time does the plane take off?	A che ora decolla l'aereo?	ah keh OH-rah deh-KOHL-lah lah-EH-reh-oh?
What's the flight number?	Qual è il numero del volo?	kwah-LEH eel NOO-meh-roh dehl VOH-loh?
What's the seat number?	Qual è il numero del posto?	kwah-LEH eel NOO-meh-roh dehl POH-stoh?
I would like . . .	Vorrei . . .	vohr-RAY . . .
• a one-way ticket.	• un biglietto di sola andata.	• oon bee-LYEHT-toh dee SOH-lah ahn-DAH-tah
• a round-trip ticket.	• un biglietto di andata e ritorno.	• oon bee-LYEHT-toh dee ahn-DAH-tah eh ree-TOHR-noh
• a first-class ticket.	• di prima classe.	• dee PREE-mah KLAHS-seh
• a seat in tourist class.	• un posto in classe turistica.	• oon POH-stoh een KLAHS-seh too-REE-stee-kah
• a no-smoking section seat.	• un posto nella sezione non fumatori.	• oon POH-stoh NEHL-lah seh-TSYOH-neh nohn foo-mah-TOH-ree
• a window seat.	• un posto vicino al finestrino.	• oon POH-stoh vee-CHEE-noh ahl fee-neh-STREE-noh
• an aisle seat.	• un posto vicino al corridoio.	• oon POH-stoh vee-CHEE-noh ahl kohr-ree-DOH-yoh
• luggage tags.	• dei cartellini.	• day kahr-tehl-LEE-nee

25

English	Italian	Pronunciation
This is my carry-on luggage.	**Questo è il mio bagaglio a mano.**	KWEH-stoh eh eel MEE-oh bah-GAH-lyoh ah MAH-noh
May I have my boarding pass?	**Posso avere la carta d'imbarco?**	POHS-soh ah-VEH-reh lah KAHR-tah deem-BAHR-koh?
What is the arrival time?	**A che ora si arriva?**	ah keh OH-rah see ahr-REE-vah?
What time will we land?	**Quando atterriamo?**	KWAHN-doh aht-tehr-RYAH-moh?
Do I need to change planes?	**Devo cambiare aereo?**	DEH-voh kahm-BYAH-reh ah-EH-reh-oh?
Can I make a connection in . . . for . . . ?	**Posso prendere una coincidenza a . . . per . . . ?**	POHS-soh PREHN-deh-reh OO-nah ko-een-chee-DEHN-tsah ah . . . pehr . . . ?
From what gate does the flight leave?	**Da che uscita parte il volo?**	dah keh oo-SHEE-tah PAHR-teh eel VOH-loh?
I would like to . . . my reservation.	**Vorrei . . . la mia prenotazione.**	vohr-RAY . . . lah MEE-ah preh-noh-tah-TSYOH-neh
• confirm	• **confermare**	• kohn-fehr-MAH-reh
• cancel	• **annullare** (or) **cancellare**	• ahn-nuhl-LAH-reh kahn-chehl-LAH-reh
• change	• **cambiare**	• kahm-BYAH-reh
I missed the plane.	**Ho perso l'aereo.**	oh PEHR-soh lah-EH-reh-oh
Will my ticket be good for the next flight?	**Il biglietto è valido per il prossimo volo?**	eel bee-LYEHT-toh eh VAH-lee-doh pehr eel PROHS-see-moh VOH-loh?

COMMON AIRPORT TERMS AND SIGNS

LINEE NAZIONALI	LEE-neh-eh nah-tsyoh-NAH-lee	NATIONAL AIRLINES
LINEE INTERNAZIONALI	LEE-neh-eh een-tehr-nah-tsyoh-NAH-lee	INTERNATIONAL AIRLINES
VOLI NAZIONALI	VOH-lee nah-tsyoh-NAH-lee	DOMESTIC FLIGHTS

VOLI INTERNAZIONALI	VOH-lee een-tehr-nah-tsyoh-NAH-lee	INTERNATIONAL FLIGHTS
PARTENZE	pahr-TEHN-tseh	DEPARTURES
ARRIVI	ahr-REE-vee	ARRIVALS
USCITA	oo-SHEE-tah	DEPARTURE GATE
TOELETTE	toh-eh-LEHT	RESTROOM(S)
UOMINI/SIGNORI	WOH-mee-nee/see-NYOH-ree	MEN'S RESTROOM
DONNE/SIGNORE	DOHN-neh/see-NYOH-reh	WOMEN'S RESTROOM

Aboard the Aircraft

VIETATO FUMARE	vyeh-TAH-toh foo-MAH-reh	NO SMOKING
ALLACCIARE LE CINTURE DI SICUREZZA	ahl-laht-CHAH-reh leh cheen-TOO-reh dee see-koo-REHTS-sah	FASTEN YOUR SEAT BELTS

DIALOGUE: ON THE STREET (PER LA STRADA)

Turista:	**Scusi, per andare al museo?**	SKOO-see, pehr ahn-DAH-reh ahl moo-ZEH-oh?
Passante:	**Non è lontano da qui. Prosegua per questa strada per altri cento metri e giri a sinistra al primo semaforo.**	nohn eh lohn-TAH-noh dah kwee. proh-SEH-gwah pehr KWEH-stah STRAH-dah pehr AHL-tree chehn-toh MEH-tree eh JEE-ree ah see-NEE-strah ahl PREE-moh seh-MAH-foh-roh
Turista:	**Grazie. Allora posso andarci a piedi. Quanto tempo ci vuole?**	GRAH-tsyeh. ahl-LOH-rah POHS-soh ahn-DAHR-chee ah PYEH-dee. KWAHN-toh TEHM-poh chee VOO-oh-leh?
Passante:	**Ci vorranno cinque, dieci minuti. Però oggi è lunedì e il museo è chiuso.**	chee vohr-RAHN-noh CHEEN-kweh, DYEH-chee mee-NUH-tee. Peh-ROH OHD-jee EH loo-neh-DEE eh eel moo-ZEH-oh EH KYOO-zoh
Turista:	**Peccato. Allora andrò domani. Grazie ancora.**	pehk-KAH-toh. ahl-LOH-rah ahn-DROH doh-MAH-nee. GRAH-tsyeh ahn-KOH-rah

. . . .

Tourist:	Excuse me. How can I get to the museum?
Passerby:	It's not far from here. Continue straight ahead for about a hundred meters, then make a left at the first traffic light.
Tourist:	Thank you. Then, I can walk there. How long will it take?
Passerby:	It will take you five or ten minutes. Anyhow, it's Monday and the museum is closed today.
Tourist:	Too bad. I'll go tomorrow, then. Thanks again.

WALKING AROUND

It is hard to dispute the old saying that the best way to see a city is to explore it on foot. Many guidebooks provide self-guided walking tours of the most interesting landmarks and areas in major cities such as Milan, Venice, Florence, Rome, and Naples. Handy little map guides to the smaller cities can be found at bookstores, newsstands, tobacco stores, train and bus stations, and all tourist offices. When providing street directions, Italians do not tell you how many blocks, *isolati* (ee-zoh-LAH-tee). They are much more likely to refer to the distance in meters, *metri* (MEH-tree) or point out traffic lights, *semafori* (seh-MAH-foh-ree), because the street patterns can be somewhat irregular and unpredictable.

Excuse me, . . .	Scusi, . . .	SKOO-zee . . .
• sir	• **signore**	• see-NYOH-reh
• madam	• **signora**	• see-NYOH-rah
• miss	• **signorina**	• see-nyoh-REE-nah
Where is . . .	Dov'è . . .	doh-VEH . . .
• the train station?	• **la stazione?**	• lah stah-TSYOH-neh?
• the bus stop?	• **la fermata dell'autobus?**	• lah fehr-MAH-tah dehl-OW-toh-boos?
• the subway?	• **la metropolitana?**	• lah meh-troh-poh-lee-TAH-nah?
• the ticket office?	• **la biglietteria?**	• lah bee-lyeht-teh-REE-ah?
Is it far?	**È lontano?**	eh lohn-TAH-noh?
How can I get there?	**Come ci si arriva?**	KOH-meh chee see ahr-REE-vah?
Where can I get a map of the city?	**Dove posso trovare una pianta della città?**	DOH-veh POHS-soh troh-VAH-reh OO-nah PYAHN-tah DEHL-lah cheet-TAH?
Where can I find this address?	**Dov'è questo indirizzo?**	doh-VEH KWEH-stoh een-dee-REET-tsoh?
I think I am lost.	**Penso di essermi smarrito(-a).**	PEHN-soh dee EHS-sehr-mee zmahr-REE-toh(-ah)

Can you show me on my map?	**Può mostrarmelo sulla pianta?**	pwoh moh-STRAHR-meh-loh SUHL-lah PYAHN-tah?

Here are a few possible answers to your questions:

Sempre diritto.	SEHM-preh dee-REET-toh	It's straight ahead.
Giri a destra/a sinistra.	JEE-ree ah DEH-strah/ah see-NEE-strah.	Turn right/left.
È . . .	eh . . .	It's . . .
• **laggiù.**	• lahd-JOOH	• down there.
• **dietro . . .**	• DYEH-troh. . .	• behind . . .
• **davanti a . . .**	• dah-VAHN-tee ah. . .	• in front of . . .
• **accanto a . . .**	• ah-KAHN-toh ah. . .	• next to . . .
• **al di là di . . .**	• ahl dee lah dee . . .	• across . . .
• **dopo . . .**	• DOH-poh. . .	• after . . .
• **vicino a . . .**	• vee-CHEE-noh ah . . .	• near . . .
• **lontano.**	• lohn-TAH-noh	• far.
• **oltre . . .**	• OHL-treh. . .	• beyond . . .
• **all'incrocio.**	• ah-leen-KROH-choh	• at the intersection.
• **all'angolo.**	• ahl-LAHN-goh-loh	• at the corner.
• **dopo il semaforo.**	• DOH-poh eel seh-MAH-foh-roh	• beyond the traffic light.
Ha sbagliato strada.	ah sbah-LYAH-toh STRAH-dah	You're on the wrong road.
Non ci si può andare a piedi.	nohn chee see pwoh ahn-DAH-reh ah PYEH-dee	You can't get there on foot.

TAKING A TAXI

Taxis are generally yellow and have a lighted sign on the roof. Sometimes, they display a logo on the door. Taxis are quite easy to find at airports, railway stations, and taxi stops.

Where is the nearest taxi stand?	**Dov'è il posteggio dei taxi più vicino?**	doh-VEH eel poh-STEHD-joh day TAHK-see pyoo vee-CHEE-noh?

Are there any taxis around here?	Ci sono taxi in questa zona?	chee SOH-noh TAHK-see een KWEH-stah DZOH-nah?
Taxi!	Taxi!	TAHK-see!
Are you free?	È libero?	eh LEE-beh-roh?
Are you taken?	È occupato?	eh ohk-koo-PAH-toh?
Please take me . . .	Per favore, mi porti . . .	pehr fah-VOH-reh mee POHR-tee . . .
• to the airport.	• all'aeroporto.	• ahl-lah-eh-roh-POHR-toh
• to the train station.	• alla stazione.	• AHL-lah stah-TSYOH-neh
• to the bus station.	• alla stazione autolinee.	• AHL-lah stah-TSYOH-neh ow-toh-LEE-neh-eh
• to the center.	• in centro.	• een CHEHN-troh
• to the main square.	• alla piazza principale.	• AHL-lah PYAHT-tsah preen-chee-PAH-leh
• to the hotel.	• all'hotel.	• ahl-loh-TEHL
• to this address.	• a questo indirizzo.	• ah KWEH-stoh een-dee-REET-tsoh
• to this restaurant.	• a questo ristorante.	• ah KWEH-stoh ree-stoh-RAHN-teh
• to this store.	• a questo negozio.	• ah KWEH-stoh neh-GOH-tsyoh
How much is it to . . . ?	Quant'è per . . . ?	kwahn-TEH pehr . . . ?
I'm in a hurry!	Vado di fretta!/Ho fretta!	VAH-doh dee FREHT-tah!/oh FREHT-tah
Stop here, please!	Si fermi qui, per favore!	see FEHR-mee kwee pehr fah-VOH-reh
Wait here for me. I'll be right back.	Mi aspetti qui. Torno subito.	mee ah-SPEHT-tee kwee. TOHR-noh SOO-bee-toh
Please drive more slowly.	Per favore, guidi più adagio.	pehr fah-VOH-reh GWEE-dee pyoo ah-DAH-joh
How much do I owe you?	Quanto Le devo?	KWAHN-toh leh DEH-voh?
Keep the change.	Tenga il resto.	TEHN-gah eel REH-stoh

31

taxi stand	**posteggio taxi**	poh-STEHD-joh TAHK- see
taxi meter	**tassametro**	tahs-SAH-meh-troh
taxi fare	**tariffa**	tah-REEF-fah

ON THE BUS

In Italy, buses are a less expensive way to get around town and to sightsee at the same time. Bus stops are located throughout all Italian cities, according to the urban district lines, and complete itineraries are posted at all bus stops. Tickets must be bought in advance and can be purchased at tobacco stores, newsstands, from automatic ticket machines near main stops, and at ATAF booths. You must cancel your ticket in the small validation machine immediately upon boarding. Two types of tickets are available, both valid for one or more rides on all lines. One costs 1,400 lire and is valid for 60 minutes from the time it is first canceled; the other costs 1,900 lire and is valid for 120 minutes. A multiple ticket—valid for four 60-minute periods—costs 5,400 lire. A 24-hour tourist ticket costs 5,000 lire. Bus entrances are located in the rear and in the front, while the exit is in the middle. A machine stands near the two entrances on the platform. You have to put your ticket into the slot: the date and time will be printed on it, letting you know that your hour ride has begun. You may notice that some passengers do not use the machine. This means that they have a monthly card, *tesserino* (tehs-seh-REE-noh), which does not need to be inserted in the slot. Every so often, an inspector steps in. He shuts the machine down, and gives a fine to those who have not validated their ticket.

| I'm looking for the bus stop. | **Cerco la fermata dell'autobus.** | CHEHR-koh lah fehr-MAH-tah dehl-LOW-toh-boos |
| Where is the nearest bus stop? | **Dovè la fermata dell'autobus più vicina?** | doh-VEH lah fehr-MAH-tah dehl-OW-toh-boos pyoo vee-CHEE-nah? |

English	Italian	Pronunciation
What bus do I take to go to . . . ?	Che autobus devo prendere per andare a . . . ?	keh OW-toh-boos DEH-voh PREHN-deh-reh pehr ahn-DAH-reh ah . . . ?
Does this bus go to . . . ?	Quest'autobus va a . . . ?	kweh-STOW-toh-boos vah ah . . . ?
How many stops until . . . ?	Quante fermate ci sono prima di . . . ?	KWAHN-teh fehr-MAH-teh chee SOH-noh PREE-mah dee . . . ?
Which is the closest stop to . . . ?	Qual è la fermata più vicina a . . . ?	kwah-LEH lah fehr-MAH-tah pyoo vee-CHEE-nah ah . . . ?
How long does it take to get to . . . ?	Quanto ci vuole per arrivare a . . . ?	KWAHN-toh chee voo-OH-leh pehr ahr-ree-VAH-reh ah . . . ?
I want to get off at . . .	Voglio scendere a . . .	VOH-lyoh SHEHN-deh-reh ah . . .
Do I need to change buses?	Devo cambiare autobus?	DEH-voh kahm-BYAH-reh OW-toh-boos?
Where do I take the bus to return?	Dove prendo l'autobus per ritornare?	Doh-veh PREHN-doh LOW-toh-boos pehr ree-tohr-NAH-reh?
When is the next bus?	Quando c'è il prossimo autobus?	KWAHN-doh cheh eel PROHS-see-moh OW-toh-boos?
How often does the bus run?	Ogni quanto passa l'autobus?	OH-nyee KWAHN-toh PAHS-sah LOW-toh-boos?
Where is the bus station?	Dov'è la stazione autolinee?	doh-VEH lah stah-TSYOH-neh ow-toh-LEE-nee-eh?
When does the bus for . . . leave?	Quando parte la corriera per . . . ?	KWAHN-doh PAHR-teh lah kohr-RYEH-rah pehr . . . ?
What is the fare to . . . ?	Quanto costa il biglietto per . . . ?	KWAHN-toh KOH-stah eel bee-LYEHT-toh pehr . . . ?
Should I pay when I get on?	Devo pagare quando salgo?	DEH-voh pah-GAH-reh KWAHN-doh SAHL-goh

I would like . . .	Vorrei . . .	vohr-RAY . . .
• a ticket.	• un biglietto.	• oon bee-LYEHT-toh
• a receipt.	• una ricevuta.	• OO-nah ree-choh-VOO-tah
• a reserved seat.	• un posto numerato.	• oon POH-stoh noo-meh-RAH-toh

USING THE SUBWAY

Only Milan has an efficient and quite extended subway system. In Rome, because the substratum is so rich in archaeological remains, only a few lines could be built.

Where is the nearest subway station?	Dov'è la stazione della metropolitana più vicina?	do-VEH lah stah-TSYOH-neh DEHL-lah meh-troh-poh-lee-TAH-nah pyoo vee-CHEE-nah?
Where can I buy a ticket?	Dove posso comprare un biglietto?	DOH-veh POHS-soh kohm-PRAH-reh oon bee-LYEHT-toh?
How much does it cost?	Quanto costa?	KWAHN-toh KOH-stah?
Is there a map for the metro?	C'è una pianta della metropolitana?	cheh OO-na PYAHN-tah DEHL-lah meh-troh-poh-lee-TAH-nah?
What line goes to . . . ?	Quale linea va a . . . ?	KWAH-leh LEE-neh-ah vah ah . . . ?
Can you tell me when we arrive at . . . ?	Mi può dire quando arriviamo a . . . ?	mee pwoh DEE-reh KWAHN-doh ahr-ree-VYAH-moh ah . . . ?

GOING BY TRAIN

As is the case in most European countries, there is a single state-run system in Italy, which is known as F.S. *(Ferrovie dello Stato).* Traveling by train in Italy is a nice way to see the countryside if you travel by day, and a comfortable way to go overnight on a long stretch, provided that you travel first class and make reservations in advance either at a travel agency or at the railway station.

Types of Trains

E.C.—EUROCITY
(ehoo-roh-SEE-tee)

A luxury, international first- and second-class express train. A fare supplement is required and seat reservations are recommended, at times compulsory.

I.C.—INTERCITY
(een-tehr-SEE-tee)

A luxury express train traveling between major Italian cities; first and second class with fare supplement.

Rapido (RAH-pee-doh)

Express train. Fare supplement and seat reservation compulsory.

Espresso (eh-SPREHS-soh)

A long-distance train with few stops.

Diretto (dee-REHT-toh)

A shorter-distance train making stops at major stations.

Locale/Accelerato
(loh-KAH-leh/aht-cheh-leh-RAH-toh)

A train stopping at almost every station.

Sleeping Arrangements

There are two principal types of sleeping accommodations. Be sure to reserve in advance:

Vagone letto (vah-GOH-neh LEHT-toh)

Sleeping car. First-class private accommodations.

Carrozza cuccette
(kahr-ROHT-tsah koot-CHEHT-teh)

Couchette car. Bunk-style sleeping with blankets and pillows found in second class. Sleeps six per compartment.

Other Cars

Carrozza ristorante
(kahr-ROHT-tsah ree-stoh-RAHN-teh)

Wagon restaurant or dining car. It serves full-course meals. Prices are quite high. Sandwiches, snacks, soft drinks, and coffee may be available from vendors moving on the train from one compartment to another, or from vendors waiting on the station platform and passing by your window.

Bagagliaio
(bah-gah-LYAH-yoh)

Baggage car and guard's van. Only for registered luggage.

Where is . . .	Dov'è . . .	doh-VEH. . .
• the train station?	• la stazione?	• lah stah-TSYOH-neh?
• the ticket window?	• la biglietteria?	• lah bee-lyeht-teh-REE-ah?
• the information office?	• l'ufficio informazioni?	• loof-FEE-choh een-fohr-mah-TSYOH-nee?
• the reservation office?	• l'ufficio prenotazioni?	• loof-FEE-choh preh-noh-tah-TSYOH-nee?
• the waiting room?	• la sala d'aspetto? (or) la sala d'attesa?	• lah SAH-lah dah-SPEHT-toh? . . . lah SAH-lah daht-TEH-zah?
• the first-class compartment?	• lo scompartimento di prima classe?	• loh skohm-pahr-tee-MEHN-toh dee PREE-mah KLAHS-seh?
• the first-class sleeping car?	• il vagone letto?	• eel vah-GOH-neh LEHT-toh?
• the second-class sleeping car?	• le cuccette?	• leh koot-CHEHT-teh?
• the smoking section?	• lo scompartimento fumatori?	• loh skohm-pahr-tee-MEHN-toh foo-mah-TOH-ree?
• the no-smoking section?	• lo scompartimento non fumatori?	• loh skohm-pahr-tee-MEHN-toh nohn foo-mah-TOH-ree?
• the baggage check?	• il deposito bagagli?	• eel deh-POH-zee-toh bah-GAH-lyee?
• the lost and found?	• l'ufficio oggetti smarriti?	• loof-FEE-choh ohd-JEHT-tee smahr-REE-tee?

What train do I take to get to . . . ?	Che treno devo prendere per andare a . . . ?	keh TREH-noh DEH-voh PREHN-deh-reh pehr ahn-DAH-reh ah . . . ?
When does the train leave for . . . ?	Quando parte il treno per . . . ?	KWAHN-doh PAHR-teh eel TREH-noh pehr . . . ?
When does it arrive at . . . ?	Quando arriva a . . . ?	KWAHN-doh ahr-REE-vah ah . . . ?
What kind of train is it?	Che tipo di treno è?	keh TEE-poh dee TREH-noh eh?
Is it an express train?	È un espresso?	eh oon eh-SPREHS-soh?
Is the train . . .	Il treno è . . .	eel TREH-noh eh . . .
• on time?	• in orario?	• een oh-RAH-ryoh?
• late?	• in ritardo?	• een ree-TAHR-doh?
From what platform does the train leave?	Da che binario parte il treno?	dah keh bee-NAH-ryoh PAHR-teh eel TREH-noh?
Is there a change of trains in . . . ?	Devo cambiare treno a . . . ?	DEH-voh kahm-BYAH-reh TREH-noh ah . . . ?
Does the train stop at . . . ?	Questo treno si ferma a . . . ?	KWEH-stoh TREH-noh see FEHR-mah ah . . . ?
I'd like to reserve a bunk . . .	Vorrei prenotare una cuccetta . . .	vohr-RAY preh-noh-TAH-reh OO-nah koot-CHEHT-tah . . .
• on the top.	• in alto.	• een AHL-toh
• in the middle.	• in mezzo.	• een MEHD-zoh
• on the bottom.	• in basso.	• een BAHS-soh
I'd like a bed in the sleeping car.	Vorrei un posto nel vagone letto.	vohr-RAY oon POH-stoh nehl vah-GOH-neh LEHT-toh
I'd like a . . . ticket.	Vorrei un biglietto di . . .	vohr-RAY oon bee-LYEHT-toh dee . . .
• round-trip	• andata e ritorno.	• ahn-DAH-tah eh ree-TOHR-noh
• one-way	• sola andata.	• SOH-lah ahn-DAH-tah
• first-class	• prima classe.	• PREE-mah KLAHS-seh

37

• second-class	• **seconda classe.**	• seh-KOHN-dah KLAHS-seh
I'd like to check my bags.	**Vorrei depositare i miei bagagli.**	vohr-RAY deh-poh-zee-TAH-reh ee mee-AY bah-GAH-lyee
Is this seat taken?	**È occupato questo posto?**	eh ohk-KOO-pah-toh KWEH-stoh POH-stah?
Sorry, this seat is taken.	**Mi dispiace, è occupato.**	mee dee-SPYAH-cheh, eh ohk-KOO-pah-toh
No, it's free. Please make yourself comfortable.	**No, è libero. S'accomodi.**	noh, eh LEE-beh-roh sahk-KOH-moh-dee
Excuse me, may I get by?	**Scusi, mi fa passare?**	SKOO-zee, mee fah pahs-SAH-reh?
Excuse me, this is my seat.	**Scusi, questo è il mio posto.**	SKOO-zee, KWEH-stoh eh eel MEE-oh POH-stoh

TRAVELING BY BOAT

When is the next boat to . . . ?	**A che ora parte il prossimo battello per . . . ?**	ah keh OH-rah PAHR-teh eel PROHS-see-moh baht-TEHL-loh pehr . . . ?
Where does one embark?	**Dove ci si imbarca?**	DOH-veh chee see eem-BAHR-kah?
Where is the port?	**Dov'è il porto?**	doh-VEH eel POHR-toh?
How long is the crossing?	**Quanto dura la traversata?**	KWAHN-toh DOO-rah lah trah-vehr-SAH-tah?
Where does the boat stop?	**Dove si fa scalo?**	DOH-veh see fah SKAH-loh?
How much is a ticket in a single cabin?	**Quanto costa un biglietto in cabina a un letto?**	KWAHN-toh KOH-stah oon bee-LYEHT-toh een kah-BEE-nah ah oon LEHT-toh?

Ship	**La nave**	lah NAH-veh
Boat	**Il battello**	eel baht-TEHL-loh
Ferry	**Il traghetto**	eel trah-GET-toh
Hydrofoil	**L'aliscafo.**	lah-lee-SKAH-foh

COMMON PUBLIC SIGNS

ENTRATA	ehn-TRAH-tah	ENTRANCE
USCITA	oo-SHEE-tah	EXIT
APERTO	ah-PEHR-toh	OPEN
CHIUSO	KYOO-zoh	CLOSED
SPINGERE	SPEEN-jeh-reh	PUSH
TIRARE	tee-RAH-reh	PULL
ALT	ahlt	STOP
PERICOLO	peh-REE-koh-loh	DANGER
VIETATO ENTRARE	vyeh-TAH-toh ehn-TRAH-reh	DO NOT ENTER
GABINETTI	gah-bee-NEHT-tee	TOILETS
UOMINI	WOH-mee-nee	MEN
DONNE	DOHN-neh	WOMEN
LAVABO	lah-VAH-boh	SINK
ACQUA NON POTABILE	AH-kwah nohn poh-TAH-bee-leh	NOT DRINKABLE WATER
RITIRATA	ree-tee-RAH-tah	W.C. (TRAINS)
VIETATO FUMARE	vyeh-TAH-toh foo-MAH-reh	NO SMOKING
USCITA DI EMERGENZA	oo-SHEE-tah dee eh-mehr-JEHN-tsah	EMERGENCY EXIT

4/ACCOMMODATIONS

In most cases, it's best to make hotel reservations and confirm in advance, especially during the high season (April through August). From the very posh to the unpretentious, you will find a variety of accommodations from which to choose.

hotel	oh-TEHL	hotel, one to five stars
albergo	ahl-BEHR-goh	small hotel
motel	moh-TEHL	motel (on main roads, suburban locations, and near airports)
pensione	pehn-SYOH-neh	boarding house offering full board, *pensione completa* (pehn-SYOH-neh kohm-PLEH-tah), or half board, *mezza pensione* (MEHD-zah pehn-SYOH-neh)
appartamento ammobiliato	ahp-pahr-tah-MEHN-toh ahm-moh-bee-LYAH-toh	furnished apartment
residence	REH-see-dehns	temporary furnished apartment or studio
ostello	oh-STEHL-loh	youth hostel

DIALOGUE: AT THE FRONT DESK (*AL BANCO ACCETTAZIONE*)

Turista:	**Buon giorno. Avete una camera per due persone?**	bwohn JOHR-noh. ah-VEH-teh OO-nah KAH-meh-rah pehr DOO-eh pehr-SOH-neh?
Impiegato:	**Per quanto tempo?**	pehr KWAHN-toh TEHM-poh?

Turista:	**Per una settimana.**	pehr OO-nah seht-tee-MAH-nah
Impiegato:	**Un momento . . . Sì, ho una matrimoniale con bagno al terzo piano.***	oon moh-MEHN-toh . . . see, oh OO-nah mah-tree-moh-NYAH-leh kohn BAH-nyoh ahl TEHR-tsoh PYAH-noh
Turista:	**Quanto viene?**	KWAHN-toh VYEH-neh?
Impiegato:	**Centomila lire per notte.**	CHEHN-toh MEE-lah LEE-reh pehr NOHT-teh
Turista:	**Va bene, la prendo. Posso vederla?**	vah BEH-neh, lah PREHN-doh. POHS-soh veh-DEHR-lah?
Impiegato:	**Certamente. Mi segua per favore.**	chehr-tah-MEHN-teh. mee SEH-gwah pehr fah-VOH-reh

. . . .

Tourist:	Hello. Do you have a room for two people?
Clerk:	For how long?
Tourist:	For a week.
Clerk:	One moment. Yes, I have a room with a double bed on the third floor.
Tourist:	How much is it?
Clerk:	One hundred thousand lire per night.
Tourist:	Fine, I'll take it. May I see it?
Clerk:	Certainly. Follow me, please.

*Our first floor is the *pianterreno* (pyahn-tehr-REH-noh), ground floor, in Italy. Thus, their *primo piano* (PREE-moh PYAH-noh), first floor, is our second floor, etc.

HOTEL ARRANGEMENTS AND SERVICES

| I have a reservation. | **Ho fatto la prenotazione.** | oh FAHT-toh lah preh-noh-tah-TSYOH-neh |
| We are going to stay . . . | **Resteremo . . .** | reh-steh-REH-moh . . . |

41

• tonight.	• **stanotte.**	• stah-NOHT-teh
• one night.	• **una notte.**	• OO-nah NOHT-teh
• a few days.	• **alcuni giorni.**	• ahl-KOO-nee JOHR-nee
• a week.	• **una settimana.**	• OO-nah seht-tee-MAH-nah
I'd like a room . . .	**Vorrei una camera . . .**	vohr-RAY OO-nah KAH-meh-rah . . .
• with one bed.	• **singola.**	• SEEN-goh-lah
• with two beds.	• **doppia.**	• DOHP-pyah
• with a double bed.	• **matrimoniale.**	• mah-tree-moh-NYAH-leh
Do you have a room with . . .	**Ha una camera con . . .**	ah OO-nah KAH-meh-rah kohn . . .
• private bathroom?	• **bagno privato?**	• BAH-nyoh pree-VAH-toh?
• a bathtub?	• **vasca da bagno?**	• VAH-skah dah BAH-nyoh?
• a shower?	• **doccia?**	• DOHT-chah?
• hot water?	• **acqua calda?**	• AHK-kwah KAHL-dah?
• air conditioning?	• **aria condizionata?**	• AH-ryah kohn-dee-tsyoh-NAH-tah?
• heat?	• **riscaldamento?**	• ree-skahl-dah-MEHN-toh?
• television?	• **televisore?**	• teh-leh-vee-ZOH-reh?
• radio?	• **radio?**	• RAH-dyoh?
• a balcony?	• **balcone?**	• bahl-KOH-neh?
• a view facing the street?	• **vista sulla strada?**	• VEE-stah SUHL-lah STRAH-dah?
• a view facing the sea?	• **vista sul mare?**	• VEE-stah suhl MAH-reh?
May I see the room?	**Posso vedere la camera?**	POHS-soh veh-DEH-reh lah KAH-meh-rah?
I'll take it.	**La prendo.**	lah PREHN-doh
Do you have a . . . room?	**Avete una camera . . . ?**	ah-VEH-teh OO-nah KAH-meh-rah . . . ?
• quieter	• **più silenziosa?**	• pyoo see-lehn-TSYOH-zah?

English	Italian	Pronunciation
• bigger	• più grande?	• pyoo GRAHN-deh?
• less expensive	• meno cara?	• MEH-noh KAH-rah?
How much is it . . .	Qual è il prezzo . . .	kwah-LEH eel PREHT-soh . . .
• per night?	• per una notte?	• pehr OO-nah NOHT-teh?
• per week?	• per una settimana?	• pehr OO-nah seht-tee-MAH-nah?
• with all meals?	• pasti inclusi?	• PAH-stee een-KLOO-zee?
• with no meals?	• pasti esclusi?	• PAH-stee eh-SKLOO-zee?
• with breakfast?	• con la colazione?	• kohn lah koh-lah-TSYOH-neh?
Does the price include . . .	Il prezzo include . . .	eel PREHT-soh een-KLOO-deh . . .
• service?	• il servizio?	• eel sehr-VEE-tsyoh?
• value-added tax?	• l'I.V.A.?	• LEE-vah?
Does the hotel have . . .	L'hotel ha . . .	loh-TEHL ah . . .
• a restaurant?	• il ristorante?	• eel ree-stoh-RAHN-teh?
• a bar?	• il bar?	• eel bahr?
• a swimming pool?	• la piscina?	• lah pee-SHEE-nah?
• room service?	• il servizio in camera?	• eel sehr-VEE-tsyoh een KAH-meh-rah?
• a garage?	• il garage?	• eel gah-RAHZH?
• a safe-deposit box?	• la cassaforte?	• lah kahs-sah-FOHR-teh?
• laundry service?	• il servizio di lavanderia?	• eel sehr-VEE-tsyoh dee lah-vahn-deh-REE-ah?
What's my room number?	Qual è il numero della mia camera?	kwah-LEH eel NOO-meh-roh DEHL-lah MEE-ah KAH-meh-rah?
Please have my bags sent up to my room.	Può far portare su i bagagli, per favore?	pwoh fahr pohr-TAH-reh soo ee bah-GAH-lyee, pehr fah-VOH-reh?

43

This is for your safe.	Questo è da depositare in cassaforte.	KWHEH-stoh eh dah deh-poh-zee-TAH-reh een kahs-sah-FOHR-teh
I'd like to speak with . . .	Vorrei parlare con . . .	vohr-RAY pahr-LAH-reh kohn . . .
• the manager.	• il direttore.	• eel dee-reht-TOH-reh
• the hall porter.	• il portiere.	• eel pohr-TYEH-reh
• the maid.	• la cameriera.	• lah kah-meh-RYEH-rah
• the bell boy.	• il fattorino.	• eel faht-toh-REE-noh
May I have . . .	Posso avere . . .	POHS-soh ah-VEH-reh
• an extra bed?	• un letto extra?	• oon LEHT-toh EHK-strah?
• a baby crib?	• una culla?	• OO-nah KOOL-lah?
• an ashtray?	• un portacenere?	• oon pohr-tah-CEH-neh-reh?
• another towel?	• un altro asciugamano?	• oo-NAHL-troh ah-shoo-gah-MAH-noh?
• another pillow?	• un altro cuscino?	• oo-NAHL-troh koo-SHEE-noh?
• another blanket?	• un'altra coperta?	• oo-NAHL-trah koh-PEHR-tah?
• some hangers?	• delle grucce?	• DEHL-leh GROOT-cheh?
• some soap?	• del sapone?	• dehl sah-POH-neh?
• some toilet paper?	• della carta igienica?	• DEHL-lah KAHR-tah ee-JEH-nee-kah?
• some stationery?	• della carta da lettere?	• DEHL-lah KAHR-tah dah LEHT-teh-reh?
• some water?	• dell'acqua?	• dehl-LAHK-kwah?
This room is very . . .	Questa camera è molto . . .	KWEH-stah KAH-meh-rah eh MOHL-toh . . .
• small.	• piccola.	• PEEK-koh-lah
• cold.	• fredda.	• FREHD-dah
• hot.	• calda.	• KAHL-dah
• dark.	• buia.	• BOO-yah
• noisy.	• rumorosa.	• roo-moh-ROH-zah

44

The . . . does not work.	Non funziona . . .	nohn foon-TSYOH-nah . . .
• light	• la luce.	• lah LOO-cheh
• lamp	• la lampadina.	• lah lahm-pah-DEE-nah
• heat	• il riscaldamento.	• eel ree-skahl-dah-MEHN-toh
• air-conditioning	• l'aria condizionata.	• LAH-ryah kohn-dee-tsyoh-NAH-tah
• toilet	• il gabinetto.	• eel gah-bee-NEHT-toh
• hot water	• l'acqua calda.	• LAHK-kwah KAHL-dah
• key	• la chiave.	• lah KYAH-veh
• lock	• la serratura.	• lah sehr-rah-TOO-rah
May I change to another room?	E'possibile cambiare camera?	eh pohs-SEE-bee-leh KAHM-byah-reh KAH-meh-rah?
Could you make up the room now?	Può fare la camera adesso?	pwoh FAH-reh lah KAH-meh-rah ah-DEHS-soh?
I'm in room . . .	Sono alla . . .	SOH-noh AHL-lah . . .
I'd like to place an order for room number . . .	Vorrei ordinare qualcosa alla numero . . .	vohr-RAY ohr-dee-NAH-reh kwahl-KOH-zah AHL-lah NOO-meh-roh . . .
I am leaving tomorrow at 10 A.M.	Parto domani mattina alle dieci.	PAHR-toh doh-MAH-nee maht-TEE-nah AHL-leh DYEH-chee
Please prepare the bill.	Per favore, prepari il conto.	pehr fah-VOH-reh, preh-PAH-ree eel KOHN-toh
Could you please call me a cab?	Mi può chiamare un taxi, per cortesia?	mee pwoh kyah-MAH-reh oon TAHK-see, pehr kohr-teh-SEE-ah?
Please have my baggage brought downstairs.	Può far portare giù i bagagli, per favore?	pwoh fahr pohr-TAH-reh joo ee bah-GAH-lyee, pehr fah-VOH-reh?

Meeting people and making new friends are probably among the most memorable and rewarding aspects of an experience abroad.

DIALOGUE: INTRODUCTIONS (*LE PRESENTAZIONI*)

Turista:	**Buon giorno. Mi permetta di presentarmi. Mi chiamo Jim Elliot.**	bwohn JYOHR-noh. mee pehr-MEHT-tah dee preh-zehn-TAHR-mee. mee KYAH-moh Jim Elliot
Sig.ra Rossi:	**Piacere. Io mi chiamo Maria Rossi.**	pyah-CHEH-reh. EE-oh mee KYAH-moh mah-REE-ah ROHS-see
Turista:	**Piacere.**	pyah-CHEH-reh
Sig.ra Rossi:	**È qui in vacanza?**	eh kwee een vah-KAHN-tsah?
Turista:	**Sì, rimarrò due settimane.**	see. ree-mahr-ROH DOO-eh seht-tee-MAH-neh.
Sig.ra Rossi:	**Buona permanenza e si diverta!**	BWOH-nah pehr-mah-NEHN-tsah eh see dee-VEHR-tah!
Turista:	**Grazie. Arrivederci.**	GRAH-tsyeh. ahr-ree-veh-DEHR-chee

. . . .

Tourist:	Hello. Allow me to introduce myself. My name is Jim Elliot.
Mrs. Rossi:	Pleased to meet you. My name is Maria Rossi.
Tourist:	Pleased to meet you.
Mrs. Rossi:	Are you here on vacation?
Tourist:	Yes. I'll be here for two weeks.
Mrs. Rossi:	Have a good stay and enjoy yourself!
Tourist:	Thank you. Good-bye.

INTRODUCTIONS

I'd like to introduce you to . . .	**Vorrei presentarLe . . .**	vohr-RAY preh-zehn-TAHR-leh . . .
• Mr. Rossi.	• **il signor Rossi.**	• eel see-NYOHR ROHS-see
• Mrs. Rossi.	• **la signora Rossi.**	• lah see-NYOH-rah Rohs-see
• Miss/Ms. Rossi.	• **la signorina Rossi.**	• lah see-nyoh-REE-nah Rohs-see
Pleased to meet you.	**Piacere.**	pyah-CHEH-reh
A pleasure.	**Piacere mio.**	pyah-CHEH-reh MEE-oh
Allow me to introduce myself.	**Mi permetta di presentarmi.**	mee pehr-MEHT-tah dee preh-zehn-TAHR-mee
What's your name?	**Come si chiama?**	KOH-meh see KYAH-mah?
My name is . . .	**Mi chiamo . . .**	mee KYAH-moh . . .
I am . . .	**Sono . . .**	SOH-noh . . .
This is . . .	**È . . .**	eh . . .
• my husband.	• **mio marito.**	• MEE-oh mah-REE-toh
• my wife.	• **mia moglie.**	• MEE-ah MOH-lyeh
• my colleague.	• **il mio collega** *(or)* **la mia collega.**	• eel MEE-oh kohl-LEH-gah lah MEE-ah kohl-LEH-gah
• my friend.	• **il mio amico (m.).**	• eel MEE-ah ah-MEE-koh
	la mia amica (f.).	lah MEE-ah ah-MEE-kah
How are you?	**Come sta?**	KOH-meh stah?
Fine, thanks. And you?	**Bene, grazie. E Lei?**	BEH-neh GRAH-tsyeh. eh LEH-ee?
How's it going?	**Come va?**	KOH-meh vah?
It's going well. Thank you.	**Bene, grazie.**	BEH-neh, GRAH-tsyeh

FIRST CONTACT

Where do you live?	**Dove abita?**	DOH-veh AH-bee-tah?
I live in . . .	**Abito . . .**	AH-bee-toh . . .
• the United States.	• **negli Stati Uniti.**	• NEH-lyee STAH-tee oo-NEE-tee
• New York City.	• **a New York.**	• ah noo yohrk
That's in the . . .	**È a . . .**	eh ah . . .
• north.	• **nord.**	• nohrd
• south.	• **sud.**	• sood
• east.	• **est.**	• ehst
• west.	• **ovest.**	• OH-vehst
That's near . . .	**È vicino . . .**	eh vee-CHEE-noh . . .
• the coast.	• **alla costa.**	• AHL-lah KOH-stah
• the border.	• **al confine.**	• ahl kohn-FEE-neh
• the ocean.	• **all'oceano.**	• ahl-loh-CHEH-ah-noh
• the mountains.	• **alle montagne.**	• AHL-leh mohn-TAH-nyeh
I am from San Francisco.	**Sono di San Francisco.**	SOH-noh dee sahn frahn-SEE-skoh
How do you like Italy?	**Le piace l'Italia?**	leh PYAH-cheh lee-TAH-lyah?
I like it very much.	**Mi piace moltissimo.**	mee PYAH-cheh mohl-TEES-see-moh
I'm not sure yet.	**Non sono ancora sicuro(-a).**	nohn SOH-noh ahn-KOH-rah see-KOO-roh(-rah)
I like the people a lot.	**Mi piace molto la gente.***	mee PYAH-cheh MOHL-toh lah JEHN-teh
I like the country.	**Mi piace il paese.***	mee PYAH-cheh eel pah-EH-zeh
Everything is so . . .	**Tutto è così . . .**	TUHT-toh eh koh-ZEE . . .
• interesting.	• **interessante.**	• een-teh-rehs-SAHN-teh

*In Italian, the verb piacere agrees with the object. The literal translation of Mi piace l'Italia is "Italy is pleasing to me." Piace is used when the object is singular, piacciono when the object is plural (see also grammar on p. 206).

- different.
- strange.
- wonderful.

- beautiful.
- nice.
- pretty.

- **differente.**
- **strano.**
- **meraviglioso.**

- **bello.**
- **simpatico.**
- **carino.**

- deef-feh-REHN-teh
- STRAH-noh
- meh-rah-vee-LYOH-zoh

- BEHL-loh
- seem-PAH-tee-koh
- kah-REE-noh

JOBS AND PROFESSIONS

Where do you work?

Dove lavora?

DOH-veh lah-VOH-rah?

What do you do?

Che cosa fa?

keh KOH-zah fah?

What is your profession?*

Che professione esercita?

keh proh-fehs-SYOH-neh eh-SEHR-chee-tah?

What's your field?

In quale campo lavora?

een KWAH-leh KAHM-poh lah-VOH-rah?

I am . . .
- a businessman.

Sono . . .
- **un uomo d'affair.**

SOH-noh . .
- oon WOH-moh dahf-FAH-ree

- a professor.

- **professore (m.).**
professoressa (f.).

- proh-fehs-SOH-reh
proh-fehs-soh-REHS-sah

- a doctor.

- **medico (or)**
dottore (m.).
dottoressa (f.).

- MEH-dee-koh doht-TOH-reh doht-toh-REHS-sah

- a lawyer.

- **avvocato.**

- ahv-voh-KAH-toh

I'm retired.

Sono in pensione (or) pensionato (-a).

SOH-noh een pehn-SYOH-neh
pehn-syoh-NAH-toh (-tah)

I am not working anymore.

Non lavoro più.

nohn lah-VOH-roh pyoo

*For a list of occupations, see p. 182.

MAKING FRIENDS

It's so good to see you.

Che piacere verderLa.

keh pyah-CHEH-reh veh-DEHR-lah

49

SOCIALIZING

It's nice to be here.	È un piacere essere qui.	eh oon pyah-CHEH-reh ehs-SEH-reh kwee
May I buy you a drink?	Posso offrirLe qualcosa da bere?	POHS-soh ohf-FREER-leh kwahl-KOH-sah dah BEH-reh?
Shall we have a drink together?	Beviamo qualcosa insieme?	beh-VYAH-moh kwahl-KOH-zah een-SYEH-meh?
With pleasure.	Con piacere.	kohn pyah-CHEH-reh
Cheers!	Salute!	sah-LOO-teh!
No, thank you.	No, grazie.	noh GRAH-tsyeh
Would you like to go with us to . . .	Vuole venire con noi . . .	voo-OH-leh veh-NEE-reh kohn noy . . .
• a café?	• al bar?	• ahl bahr?
• the theatre?	• a teatro?	• ah teh-AH-troh?
• to the movies?	• al cinema?	• ahl CHEE-neh-mah?
• to a restaurant?	• al ristorante?	• ahl reh-stoh-RAHN-teh?
Gladly.	Volentieri.	voh-lehn-TYEH-ree
May I bring a friend?	Posso portare un amico(-a)?	POHS-soh pohr-TAH-reh oon-ah-MEE-koh(-kah)?
Do you mind if I smoke?	Le dispiace se fumo?	leh dee-SPYAH-cheh seh FOO-moh?
Not at all.	Per niente.	pehr NYEHN-teh
	(or) Affatto.	ahf-FAHT-toh
Yes, it bothers me.	Sì, mi dà fastidio.	see, mee dah fah-STEE-dyoh
May I telephone you?	Posso telefonarLe?	POHS-soh teh-leh-foh-NAHR-leh?
What's your number?	Qual è il Suo numero di telefono?	kwah-LEH eel SOO-oh NOO-meh-roh dee teh-LEH-foh-noh?
What's your address?	Qual è il Suo indirizzo?	kwah-LEH eel SOO-oh een-dee-REET-soh?
Are you married?	È sposato (-a)?	eh spoh-ZAH-toh (-tah)?
No, I'm . . .	No, sono . . .	noh, SOH-noh . . .
• single (m.).	• celibe	• CHEH-lee-beh
	(or) scapolo.	SKAH-poh-loh

• single (f.).	• **nubile.**	• NOO-bee-leh
I have . . .	**Ho . . .**	oh . . .
• a boyfriend.	• **il ragazzo.**	• eel rah-GAHT-soh
• a girlfriend.	• **la ragazza.**	• lah rah-GAHT-sah
• a fiancé.	• **il fidanzato.**	• eel fee-dahn-TSAH-toh
• a fiancée.	• **la fidanzata.**	• lah fee-dahn-TSAH-tah
I'm divorced.	**Sono divorziato (-a).**	SOH-noh dee-vohr-TSYAH-toh(-tah)
I'm separated.	**Sono separato(-a).**	SOH-noh seh-pah-RAH-toh(-tah)
I am a widow(er).	**Sono vedova(-o).**	SOH-noh VEH-doh-vah(-voh)
I'm alone.	**Sono solo(-a).**	SOH-noh SOH-loh(-lah)
I'm traveling with a friend.	**Viaggio con un amico(-a).**	VYAHD-joh kohn oon-ah-MEE-koh(-kah)
You should come visit us (at our house).	**Perché non ci viene a trovare?**	pehr-KEH nohn cee VYEH-neh ah troh-VAH-reh?
You're so kind!	**Molto gentile!**	MOHL-toh jehn-TEE-leh!
Are you free . . .	**È libero(-a) . . .**	eh LEE-beh-roh (-rah) . . .
• this evening?	• **stasera?**	• stah-SEH-rah?
• tomorrow?	• **domani?**	• doh-MAH-nee?
I'll wait for you here.	**L'aspetto qui.**	lah-SPEHT-toh kwee
I'll pick you up at the hotel.	**La vengo a prendere in albergo.**	lah VEHN-goh ah PREHN-deh-reh een ahl-BEHR-goh
It's getting late.	**Si sta facendo tardi.**	see stah fah-CHEHN-doh TAHR-dee
It's time to go back.	**È ora di rientrare.**	eh OH-rah dee ryehn-TRAH-reh
We are leaving tomorrow.	**Partiamo domani.**	pahr-TYAH-moh doh-MAH-nee
Thanks for everything.	**Grazie di tutto.**	GRAH-tsyeh dee TOOT-toh

I had a very good time.	Mi sono divertito (-a) molto.	mee SOH-noh dee-vehr-TEE-toh(-tah) MOHL-toh
We are going to miss you.	Ci mancherà.	chee mahn-keh-RAH
It was nice to have met you.	È stato un piacere aver fatto la Sua conoscenza.	eh STAH-toh oon pyah-CHEH-reh ah-VEHR FAHT-toh lah SOO-ah koh-noh-SHEHN-tsah
Give my best to . . .	Mi saluti . . .	mee sah-LOO-tee . . .
Can I give you a ride?	Posso darLe un passaggio?	POHS-soh DAHR-leh oon pahs-SAHD-joh?
Don't bother, thank you.	Non si disturbi, grazie.	nohn see dee-STOOR-bee, GRAH-tsyeh
I can take a taxi.	Posso prendere un taxi.	POHS-soh PREHN-deh-reh oon TAHK-see
Bye.	Arrivederci.	ahr-ree-veh-DEHR-chee

THE FAMILY

I have a . . . family.	Ho una famiglia . . .	oh OO-nah fah-MEE-lyah . . .
• big	• numerosa.	• noo-meh-ROH-zah
• small	• piccola.	• PEEK-koh-lah
Here is . . .	Ecco . . .	EHK-koh . . .
• my husband.	• mio marito.	• MEE-oh mah-REE-toh
• my wife.	• mia moglie.	• MEE-ah MOH-lyeh
• my son.	• mio figlio.	• MEE-oh FEE-lyoh
• my daughter.	• mia figlia.	• MEE-ah FEE-lyah
I have . . .	Ho . . .	oh . . .
• two sons.	• due maschi.	• DOO-eh MAH-skee
• two daughters.	• due femmine.	• DOO-eh FEHM-mee-neh
• three small children.	• tre bambini.	• treh bahm-BEE-nee
• three children.	• tre figli.	• treh FEE-lyee

SOCIALIZING

52

Here are my parents!	Ecco i miei genitori!	EHK-koh ee mee-AY jeh-nee-TOH-ree!
Here is . . .	Ecco . . .	EHK-koh . . . .
• my father.	• mio padre.	• MEE-oh PAH-dreh
• my mother.	• mia madre.	• MEE-ah MAH-dreh
I have many relatives.	Ho molti parenti.	oh MOHL-tee pah-REHN-tee
I have . . .	Ho . . .	oh . . .
• a brother.	• un fratello.	• oon frah-TEHL-loh
• a sister.	• una sorella.	• OO-nah soh-REHL-lah
• a grandfather.	• un nonno.	• oon NOHN-noh
• a grandmother.	• una nonna.	• OO-nah NOHN-nah
• a grandson/ nephew.	• un nipote.	• oon nee-POH-teh
• a granddaughter/ niece.	• una nipote.	• OO-nah nee-POH-teh
• a cousin (m.).	• un cugino.	• oon koo-JEE-noh
• a cousin (f.).	• una cugina.	• OO-nah koo-JEE-nah
• an aunt.	• una zia.	• OO-nah TSEE-ah
• an uncle.	• uno zio.	• OO-noh TSEE-oh
• in-laws.	• dei suoceri.	• day SWOH-cheh-ree
• a brother-in-law.	• un cognato.	• oon koh-NYAH-toh
• a sister-in-law.	• una cognata.	• OO-nah koh-NYAH-tah
• a father-in-law.	• un suocero.	• oon SWOH-cheh-roh
• a mother-in-law.	• una suocera.	• OO-nah SWOH-cheh-rah
my eldest son	mio figlio maggiore	MEE-oh FEE-lyoh mahd-JOH-reh
my youngest daughter	mia figlia minore	MEE-ah FEE-lyah mee-NOH-reh

TALKING ABOUT LANGUAGE

Do you speak . . .*	Parla . . .	PAHR-lah . . .
• English?	• inglese?	• een-GLEH-zeh?
• French?	• francese?	• frahn-CHEH-zeh?

• Spanish?	• spagnolo?	• spah-NYOH-loh?
I only speak English.	Parlo solamente inglese.	PAHR-loh soh-lah-MEHN-teh een-GLEH-zeh
I don't speak Italian.	Non parlo italiano.	nohn PAHR-loh ee-tah-LYAH-noh
I speak very little.	Parlo poco.	PAHR-loh POH-koh
I speak a little Italian.	Parlo un po' d'italiano.	PAHR-loh oon poh dee-tah-LYAH-noh
I want to learn Italian.	Voglio imparare l'italiano.	VOH-lyoh eem-pah-RAH-reh lee-tah-LYAH-noh
I understand.	Capisco.	kah-PEE-skoh
I don't understand.	Non capisco.	nohn kah-PEE-skoh
Can you understand me?	Mi capisce?	mee kah-PEE-sheh?
Please speak more slowly.	Per favore, parli più adagio.	pehr fah-VOH-reh, PAHR-lee pyoo ah-DAH-joh
Please repeat that.	Può ripetere per favore?	pwoh ree-PEH-teh-reh pehr fah-VOH-reh?
How do you write that?	Come si scrive?	KOH-meh see SCREE-veh?
How do you say "spoon" in Italian?	Come si dice "spoon" in italiano?	KOH-meh see DEE-cheh "spoon" een ee-tah-LYAH-noh?
Is there anyone here who speaks English?	C'è qualcuno qui che parla inglese?	cheh kwahl-KOO-noh kwee keh PAHR-lah een-GLEH-zeh?
Could you translate this for me?	Mi può tradurre questo?	mee pwoh trah-DOOR-reh KWEH-stoh?

*For a more complete list of languages, see pp. 181–182.

IN THE HOME

Make yourself at home.	Faccia come a casa Sua.	FAHT-chah KOH-meh ah KAH-zah SOO-ah
You may sit here.	Prego, s'accomodi qui.	PREH-goh sahk-KOH-moh-dee kwee

SOCIALIZING

English	Italian	Pronunciation
What a pretty house!	Che bella casa!	keh BEHL-lah KAH-zah!
I really like this neighborhood.	Mi piace molto questa zona.	mee PYAH-cheh MOHL-toh KWEH-stah ZOH-nah
Here is . . .	Ecco . . .	EHK-koh . . .
• the kitchen.	• la cucina.	• lah koo-CHEE-nah
• the living room.	• il salotto.	• eel sah-LOHT-toh
• the dining room.	• la sala da pranzo.	• lah SAH-lah dah PRAHN-dzoh
• the bedroom.	• la camera da letto.	• lah KAH-meh-rah dah LEHT-toh
• the bathroom.	• il bagno.	• eel BAH-nyoh
• the closets.	• gli armadi.	• lyee ahr-MAH-dee
• the couch.	• il divano.	• eel dee-VAH-noh
• the armchair.	• la poltrona.	• lah pohl-TROH-nah
• the table.	• la tavola.	• lah TAH-voh-lah
• the chairs.	• le sedie.	• leh SEH-dyeh
• the lamp.	• la lampada.	• lah LAHM-pah-dah
• the door.	• la porta.	• lah POHR-tah
• the window.	• la finestra.	• lah fee-NEH-strah
• the ceiling.	• il soffitto.	• eel sohf-FEET-toh
• the floor.	• il pavimento.	• eel pah-vee-MEHN-toh
It's . . .	È . . .	eh . . .
• a house.	• una casa.	• OO-nah KAH-zah
• an apartment.	• un appartamento.	• oon-ahp-pahr-tah-MEHN-toh
• a mansion.	• una casa signorile.	• OO-nah KAH-zah see-nyoh-REE-leh
• a villa.	• una villa.	• OO-nah VEEL-lah
• a condominium.	• un condominio.	• oon kohn-doh-MEE-nyoh
• a country house.	• una casa di campagna.	• OO-nah KAH-zah dee kahm-PAH-nyah
Thanks for the invitation.	Grazie dell'invito.	GRAH-tsyeh dehl-leen-VEE-toh.
You must come and visit us sometime.	Ci venga a trovare qualche volta.	chee VEHN-gah ah troh-VAH-reh KWAHL-keh VOHL-tah

55

6/DINING OUT

Even though to many visitors Italy means pasta, you will be amazed at the variety and originality of cooking, which includes rice, meat, fish, poultry, shellfish, cheeses, mouth-watering cakes, and ice creams. Prices vary according to the type of restaurant.

autogrill
(ow-toh-GREEL)

Restaurant located on an express high-way; bar and snack services are also available.

bar/caffè
(bahr/kahf-FEH)

The quintessential Italian institution. Life without it would be inconceivable for an Italian. There, the rite of the morning *espresso* begins, and it is repeated numerous times throughout the day. These establishments serve coffee, tea, soft drinks, beer, liquor, and snacks such as toasts, sandwiches, and pastries. It's the perfect place to hang out, relax, refresh yourself, read, write, talk, watch, and be watched.

gelateria
(jeh-lah-teh-REE-ah)

Ice cream parlor that serves *gelato* (jeh-LAH-toh), rich, tasty ice cream.

locanda
(loh-KAHN-dah)

Restaurant usually located outside the city serving simple, local food. Originally an inn with bed and board.

osteria
(oh-steh-REE-ah)

An informal, rustic place, serving simple but very good food at moderate prices.

paninoteca
(pah-nee-noh-TEH-kah)

Sandwich bar, where you can sample a great variety of hot and cold sandwiches, *panini* (pah-NEE-nee).

pizzeria
(peet-tseh-REE-ah)

Pizza parlor. Pizzas galore. Many different styles for every taste. Other food is often served.

ristorante (ree-stoh-RAHN-teh)	The range of style, ambiance, and price category is impressive. Make sure, when possible, you check the menu in the window, when displayed, to get an idea of the prices before you decide to go in.
rosticceria (roh-steet-cheh-REE-ah)	A place specializing mainly in grilled chicken to take out. Today, thanks to the addition of tables and chairs, you can also eat on the premises.
sala da tè (SAH-lah dah teh)	"Tea room," where pastries and other desserts are served along with tea, coffee, and hot chocolate. Light meals may be offered in some salons.
snack-bar	Place often found near bus and train stations: just what it sounds like.
taverna (tah-VEHR-nah)	Eatery that lacks the refined atmosphere of a restaurant or even a trattoria. However, the food is tasty, well prepared, and inexpensive.
tavola calda/fredda (TAH-voh-lah KAHL-dah/ FREHD-dah)	Hot/cold table. Restaurant resembling a cafeteria. You may buy hot and cold dishes, moderately priced.
trattoria (traht-toh-REE-ah)	Medium-priced restaurant, often family-run, where one can find home cooking, *cucina casalinga* (koo-CHEE-nah kah-sah-LEEN-gah). The food is excellent.

MEALS AND MEALTIMES

Breakfast, *la colazione* or *la prima colazione* (lah koh-lah-TSYOH-neh/lah PREE-mah koh-lah-TSYOH-neh), is a very light meal and is commonly served between 7:00 A.M. and 10:00 A.M. at hotels.* If breakfast is included in the price of your room, it

*In some areas, especially in large towns, the name of a meal can be misleading. Sometimes lunch, *il pranzo*, can be referred to as *la colazione*, or breakfast. Make sure you ask in advance so you won't show up for the wrong meal.

usually consists of coffee, tea, or hot chocolate, and fresh bread, butter, and jam. Warm milk is always served on the side so that you can blend equal parts of coffee and milk and make your own *caffè latte* (kahf-feh LAHT-teh), or just add a few drops to your coffee for a *caffè macchiato* (kahf-FEH mahk-KYAH-toh). If breakfast is not included with your hotel room, you will probably find that it is less expensive and more fun at the corner bar, mingling with the Italians. Italians usually have *espresso* (eh-SPREHS-soh) or *cappuccino* (kahp-poot-CHEE-noh), steamy, frothy milk added to espresso, and a brioche for breakfast, and that's it.

Lunch, *la colazione* or *il pranzo* (lah koh-lah TSYOH-neh/eel PRAHN-dzoh) is traditionally the big meal of the day. In recent years, shorter midday breaks have led to quicker lunches for many working people. In general, lunch is served between 12:30 P.M. and 2:30 to 3:00 P.M. Many businesses and most public services close at lunchtime: stores are closed between 12:30 or 1:00 P.M. and 3:30 or 4:00 P.M., depending on the city. At this time you may find that eateries fill up quite quickly. Those who have the time prefer to have a quiet, relaxed lunch at home.

Dinner, *la cena* (lah CHEH-nah), begins later in Italy than in the United States. Restaurants begin serving around 7:30 or 8:00 P.M. Evening dining is a leisurely affair, with people lingering over their food and drinks. The Italian dinner provides a very relaxed opportunity to spend some time with your family and friends, and discuss things over a sumptuous meal.

DIALOGUE: AT THE RESTAURANT (*AL RISTORANTE*)

Cameriere:	**Desidera?**	deh-ZEE-deh-rah?
Cliente:	**Non so. Qual è la specialità della casa?**	nohn soh. kwah-LEH lah speh-chah-lee-TAH DEHL-lah KAH-zah?
Cameriere:	**Oggi Le consiglio le tagliatelle alla bolognese.**	OHD-jee leh kohn-SEE-lyoh leh tah-lyah-TEHL-leh AHL-lah boh-loh-NYEH-zeh

Cliente:	**Bene. Proviamole!**	BEH-neh. proh-VYAH-moh-leh!
Cameriere:	**Desidera qualcosa da bere?**	deh-ZEE-deh-rah kwahl-KOH-zah dah BEH-reh?
Cliente:	**Sì. Una mezza bottiglia di vino bianco e una minerale, per favore.**	see. OO-nah MEHD-zah boh-TEE-lyah dee VEE-noh BYAHN-koh eh OO-nah mee-neh-RAH-leh, pehr fah-VOH-reh
Cameriere:	**Naturale o gassata?**	nah-too-RAH-leh oh gahs-SAH-tah?
Cliente:	**Naturale, grazie.**	nah-too-RAH-leh, GRAH-tsyeh

. . . .

Waiter:	What would you like to order?
Customer:	I don't know. What's the specialty of the house?
Waiter:	Today I would recommend noodles with meat sauce.
Customer:	Fine. I'll try it!
Waiter:	Something to drink?
Customer:	Yes. Half a bottle of white wine and a bottle of mineral water, please.
Waiter:	Natural or carbonated?
Customer:	Natural, thank you.

EATING OUT

Can you recommend a good restaurant?	**Può consigliarmi un buon ristorante?**	pwoh kohn-see-LYAHR-mee oon bwon ree-stoh-RAHN-teh?
Do you know any good restaurants nearby?	**Conosce un buon ristorante nei dintorni?**	koh-NOH-sheh oon bwon ree-stoh-RAHN-teh nay deen-TOHR-nee?
There are several.	**Ce ne sono parecchi.**	cheh neh SOH-noh pah-REHK-kee

I want a . . . restaurant.	**Voglio un ristorante . . .**	VOH-lyoh oon ree-stoh-RAHN-teh . . .
• typical	• **típico.**	• TEE-pee-koh
• very good	• **molto buono.**	• MOHL-toh BWOH-noh
Is it expensive?	**È caro?**	eh KAH-roh?
No, it's inexpensive.	**No, è economico.**	noh, eh eh-koh-NOH-mee-koh
What's the name of the restaurant?	**Come si chiama il ristorante?**	KOH-meh see KYAH-mah eel ree-stoh-RAHN-teh?
It's called . . .	**Si chiama . . .**	see KYAH-mah . . .
Where is it located?	**Dove si trova?**	DOH-veh see TROH-vah?
Do you need to make reservations?	**Si deve prenotare?**	see DEH-veh preh-noh-TAH-reh?
I'd like to reserve a table . . .	**Vorrei prenotare un tavolo . . .**	vohr-RAY preh-noh-TAH-reh oon TAH-voh-loh . . .
• for two people.	• **per due (persone).**	• pehr DOO-eh (pehr-SOH-neh)
• for this evening.	• **per questa sera.**	• pehr KWEH-stah SEH-rah
• for tomorrow evening.	• **per domani sera.**	• pehr doh-MAH-nee SEH-rah
• for nine P.M.	• **per le ventuno.**	• pehr leh vehn-TOO-noh
• on the terrace.	• **sul terrazzo.**	• suhl tehr-RAHT-tsoh
• by the window.	• **vicino alla finestra.**	• vee-CHEE-noh AHL-lah fee-NEH-strah
• outside.	• **all'aperto.** *(or)* **fuori.**	• ahl-lah-PEHR-toh FWOH-ree
• inside.	• **dentro.**	• DEHN-troh

RESTAURANT ITEMS

| Waiter/Waitress! | **Cameriere(-a)!** | kah-meh-RYEH-reh (-rah)! |
| The menu, please. | **Il menu, per favore.** | eel meh-NOO, pehr fah-VOH-reh |

The wine list, please.	La lista dei vini, per piacere.	lah LEE-stah day VEE-nee, pehr pyah-CHEH-reh
Do you have any special local dishes?	Avete piatti locali tipici?	ah-VEH-teh PYAHT-tee loh-KAH-lee TEE-pee-chee?
I'd like . . .	Vorrei . . .	vohr-RAY . . .
• something light.	• qualcosa di leggero.	• kwahl-KOH-zah dee lehd-JEH-roh
• a full meal.	• un pasto completo.	• oon PAH-stoh kohm-PLEH-toh
• the dish of the day.	• il piatto del giorno.	• eel PYAHT-toh dehl JOHR-noh
Do you have children's portions?	Avete mezze porzioni per bambini?	ah-VEH-teh MEHD-zeh pohr-TSYOH-nee pehr bahm-BEE-nee?
I'm ready to order.	Sono pronto(-a) per ordinare.	SOH-noh PROHN-toh (-tah) pehr ohr-dee-NAH-reh
To begin, I would like . . .	Per cominciare vorrei . . .	pehr koh-meen-CHAH-reh vohr-RAY . . .
Next . . .	Poi . . .	poy . . .
Finally . . .	Per finire . . .	pehr fee-NEE-reh . . .
That's all.	È tutto.	eh TOOT-toh
Have you finished?	Ha finito?	ah fee-NEE-toh?
Could we have . . .	Potremmo avere . . .	poh-TREHM-moh ah-VEH-reh . . .
• tap water?	• dell'acqua?	• dehl-LAHK-wah?
• silverware?	• delle posate?	• DEHL-leh poh-ZAH-teh?
• a napkin?	• un tovagliolo?	• oon toh-vah-LYOH-loh?
• a fork?	• una forchetta?	• OO-nah fohr-KEHT-tah?
• a knife?	• un coltello?	• oon kohl-TEHL-loh?
• a spoon?	• un cucchiaio?	• oon kook-KYAH-yoh?
• a plate?	• un piatto?	• oon PYAHT-toh?
• a bowl?	• una scodella?	• OO-nah skoh-DEHL-lah?

61

• a glass?	• **un bicchiere?**	• oon beek-KYEH-reh?
• a cup?	• **una tazza?**	• OO-nah TAHT-tsah?
• a demitasse?	• **una tazzina?**	• OO-nah tah-TSEE-nah?
• a saucer?	• **un piattino?**	• oon pyaht-TEE-noh?
• a teaspoon?	• **un cucchiaino?**	• oon kook-kyah-EE-noh?
• some bread?	• **del pane?**	• dehl PAH-neh?
• some butter?	• **del burro?**	• dehl BOOR-roh?
• some salt?	• **del sale?**	• dehl SAH-leh?
• some pepper?	• **del pepe?**	• dehl PEH-peh?
• some mustard?	• **della senape?**	• DEHL-lah SEH-nah-peh?
• some ketchup?	• **del ketchup?**	• dehl KEHCH-ahp?
• some mayonnaise?	• **della maionese?**	• DEHL-lah mah-yoh-NEH-zeh?
• some lemon?	• **del limone?**	• dehl lee-MOH-neh?
• some sugar?	• **dello zucchero?**	• DEHL-loh TSOOK-keh-roh?
• some saccarine?	• **della saccarina?**	• DEHL-lah sahk-kah-REE-nah?
• a toothpick?	• **uno stuzzicadenti?**	• OO-noh stoot-tsee-kah-DEHN-tee?
• an ashtray?	• **un portacenere?**	• oon pohr-tah-CHEH-neh-reh?
• a little more . . . ?	• **ancora un po' di . . . ?**	• ahn-KOH-rah oon poh dee . . . ?

APPETIZERS (*ANTIPASTI*)

Appetizers may be hot or cold. However, in Italian cuisine, because of the importance of the pasta course, appetizers are not very common. They may be more popular during the summer, when people eat a little less pasta. Here is a sampler of some types of the most common *antipasti* (ahn-tee-PAH-stee).

affettato misto
(ahf-feht-TAH-toh MEE-stoh)

mixed cold cuts: ham, salami, mortadella, etc., garnished with mixed pickled vegetables

antipasto misto
(ahn-tee-PAH-stoh MEE-stoh)

mixed antipasto: anchovies, artichoke hearts, olives, pickles, sliced eggs, salami, etc.

caprese
(kah-PREH-zeh)

slices of mozzarella cheese with tomatoes, basil, and olive oil

caviale
(kah-VYAH-leh)

caviar

cocktail di gamberi
(KOHK-tehl dee GAHM-beh-ree)

shrimp cocktail

insalata di frutti di mare
(een-sah-LAH-tah dee FROOT-tee dee MAH-reh)

seafood salad made with clams, mussels, squid, prawns, and cuttlefish, seasoned with lemon

prosciutto e melone o fichi
(proh-SHOOT-toh eh meh-LOH-neh oh FEE-kee)

prosciutto ham and slices of melon or figs; very delicious and very refreshing—a typical and popular summer antipasto

PIZZA

Pizza is probably the most popular Italian contribution to fast food, and Italians often make a whole meal out of it. The Italian pizza is usually a single, round-shaped serving, as wide as the whole platter on which it's served. Pizza parlors, *pizzerie* (peet-tseh-REE-eh), offer a great variety of *pizze* (PEET-tseh) and topping combinations. Here are the most popular variations:

calzone
(kahl-TSOH-neh)

pastry pouch filled with mozzarella, ham, sausage, and mushrooms

capricciosa
(kah-preet-CHOH-zah)

with tomato, mozzarella, ham, mushrooms, and artichoke hearts

margherita
(mahr-geh-REE-tah)

with tomato, mozzarella, and basil

marinara
(mah-ree-NAH-rah)

with tomato, oregano, and garlic

napoletana (nah-poh-leh-TAH-nah)	with tomato, mozzarella, anchovies, and oregano
quattro stagioni (KWAHT-troh stah-JOH-nee)	with tomato, mozzarella, ham, sausage, mushrooms, and artichoke hearts, and divided into four quadrants (the "four seasons")
romana (roh-MAH-nah)	with tomato, mozzarella, anchovies, capers, and oregano
siciliana (see-chee-LYAH-nah)	with tomato, anchovies, and pecorino cheese

SOUPS *(MINISTRE IN BRODO)*

brodo . . .	BROH-doh . . .	. . . broth
• di cappone	• dee kahp-POH-neh	• capon
• di manzo	• dee MAHN-dzoh	• beef
• di pollo	• dee POHL-loh	• chicken
cacciucco	kaht-CHOOK-koh	spicy seafood chowder
crema . . .	KREH-mah . . .	cream . . . soup
• di asparagi	• dee ah-SPAH-rah-jee	• of asparagus
• di funghi	• dee FOON-ghee	• of mushrooms
• di pomodoro	• dee poh-moh-DOH-roh	• of tomato
minestrone	mee-neh-STROH-neh	vegetable soup
passatelli	pahs-sah-TEHL-lee	spatzos (broth with small dumplings)
passato di piselli	pahs-SAH-toh dee pee-ZEHL-lee	cream of pea soup
passato di verdura	pahs-SAH-toh dee vehr-DOO-rah	cream of vegetable soup
pasta e fagioli	PAH-stah eh fah-JOH-lee	pasta and beans
pastina in brodo	pah-STEE-nah een BROH-doh	broth and tiny pasta disks
stracciatella	straht-chah-TEHL-lah	egg-drop soup
zuppa di pesce	TSOOP-pah dee PEH-sheh	seafood stew

PASTA

Pastasciutta (pah-stah-SHOOT-tah), or pasta with sauce, is the traditional Italian first course, a national treasure, a gastronomic religion. In many parts of Italy, no meal would be conceivable without it.

Pasta comes in different kinds, shapes, and has many names—*spaghetti, maccheroni, bucatini, fettuccine, tagliatelle, vermicelli, ziti, linguine,* among others. It's usually served with the classic tomato sauce, with meat sauce, or with other tasty sauces for which Italy is famous.

Typical First Courses *(Primi tipici)*

agnolotti (ah-nyoh-LOHT-tee)	tiny ravioli stuffed with meat and cabbage, spinach, or pumpkin
cannelloni (kahn-nehl-LOH-nee)	large noodles filled with ground meat or ricotta and spinach, topped with white sauce, and browned in the oven
cappelletti (kahp-pehl-LEHT-tee)	round-shaped "little hats" filled with chopped chicken breasts, ham, cheese, and eggs
fettuccine (feht-toot-CHEE-neh)	noodles in the form of narrow ribbons, served with a variety of sauces
gnocchi (NYOHK-kee)	potato or semolina dumplings, at times also made with spinach
lasagne verdi (lah-ZAH-nyeh VEHR-dee)	baked layers of thin, square spinach noodles, bechamel, meat sauce, and parmesan cheese
ravioli (rah-VYOH-lee)	freshly prepared thin pasta squares filled with chopped chicken, spinach, ricotta, or ground meat
rigatoni (ree-gah-TOH-nee)	macaroni made in large, short, furrowed tubes
spaghetti (spah-GEHT-tee)	semolina pasta made in thin, solid strings

tagliatelle (tah-lyah-TEHL-leh)	flat, narrow strips of pasta usually served with bolognese meat sauce and parmesan cheese
tortellini (tohr-tehl-LEE-nee)	pasta rings stuffed with ground turkey or chicken breast, ham, mortadella, parmesan cheese, nutmeg, and served in broth, with meat sauce, or with cream and grated cheese
tortelloni (tohr-tehl-LOH-nee)	larger pasta rings, usually stuffed with ricotta and spinach

RICE (*RISO*)

Rice is more popular in northern Italy than it is in the south, and it often replaces pasta. It may be served with a sauce or with a variety of ingredients such as beans, herbs and spices, mushrooms, and seafood. Here are some of the most popular:

risi e bisi (REE-zee eh BEE-zee)	rice with green peas and bacon
riso in bianco (REE-zoh een BYAHN-koh)	rice with butter and grated cheese
riso al pomodoro (REE-zoh ahl poh-moh-DOH-roh)	rice with tomato sauce and herbs
risotto (ree-ZOHT-toh)	rice boiled in broth
• **alla marinara** (AHL-lah mah-ree-NAH-rah)	• with seafood
• **alla milanese** (AHL-lah mee-lah-NEH-zeh)	• with saffron and bone marrow

SAUCES (*SALSE E SUGHI*)

Pasta would not be pasta without a sauce to make it so tasty. Italy has a wide range of sauces:

aglio, olio, e peperoncino (AH-lyoh, OH-lyoh, eh peh-peh-rohn-CHEE-noh)
garlic, olive oil, and dried red pepper

all'amatriciana (ahl-lah-mah-tree-CHAH-nah)
with tomatoes, bacon, garlic, red peppers, and onions

alla bolognese/al ragù (AHL-lah boh-loh-NYEH-zeh/ahl rah-GOO)
with tomato paste and small chopped onion, simmered with carrot and celery stick, and combined with minced meat, some white or red wine, and a dash of milk or cream

alla carbonara (AHL-lah kahr-boh-NAH-rah)
with eggs, ham or bacon, and cheese

alla carrettiera (AHL-lah kahr-reht-TYEH-rah)
with tomato paste, tuna, and mushrooms

alla marinara (AHL-lah mah-ree-NAH-rah)
with tomatoes, onions, garlic, and oregano, and with olives, mussels, and clams, if desired

al pesto (ahl PEH-stoh)
with a pestled mixture of cheese, garlic, basil, pine kernels, and olive oil

al pomodoro (ahl poh-moh-DOH-roh)
with crushed tomatoes and tomato puree, basil, garlic, and oil

alla pizzaiola (AHL-lah peet-tsah-YOH-lah)
with fresh tomatoes, garlic, olive oil, and herbs

alla puttanesca (AHL-lah poot-tah-NEH-skah)
with olives, garlic, capers, dried red pepper, and oil

alle vongole (AHL-leh VOHN-goh-leh)
with clams, tomatoes, parsley, garlic, and olive oil

besciamella (beh-shah-MEHL-lah)
white sauce made with melted butter, flour, cream, and milk

67

FISH AND SEAFOOD (PESCE E FRUTTI DI MARE)

I'd like some fish.	**Vorrei del pesce.**	vohr-RAY dehl PEH-sheh
What kind of seafood do you have?	**Che tipo di frutti di mare avete?**	keh TEE-poh dee FROOT-tee dee MAH-reh ah-VEH-teh?
acciughe	aht-CHOO-geh	anchovies
anguilla	ahn-GWEEL-lah	eel
aragosta	ah-rah-GOH-stah	lobster
aringa	ah-REEN-gah	herring
arselle	ahr-SEHL-leh	scallops
baccalà	bahk-kah-LAH	salt-dried cod
branzino	brahn-DZEE-noh	bass
calamari	kah-lah-MAH-ree	squid
carpa	KAHR-pah	carp
cozze	KOHT-tseh	mussels
dentice	DEHN-tee-cheh	bream
gamberi	GAHM-beh-ree	shrimps
granchi	GRAHN-kee	crabs
luccio	LOOT-choh	pike
lumache di mare	loo-MAH-keh dee MAH-reh	sea snails
merluzzo	mehr-LOOT-tsoh	cod
orata	oh-RAH-tah	sea bream
ostriche	OH-stree-keh	oysters
pesce spada	PEH-sheh SPAH-dah	swordfish
polipo	POH-lee-poh	octopus
ricci	REET-chee	sea urchins
rombo	ROHM-boh	turbot
salmone	sahl-MOH-neh	salmon
sardine	sahr-DEE-neh	sardines
scampi	SKAHM-pee	prawns
seppia	SEHP-pyah	cuttlefish
sgombro	SGOHM-broh	mackerel
sogliola	SOH-lyoh-lah	sole
spigola	SPEE-goh-lah	sea bass
storione	stoh-RYOH-neh	sturgeon
tonno	TOHN-noh	tuna
triglia	TREE-lyah	red mullet

trota	TROH-tah	trout
vongole	VOHN-goh-leh	clams

Preparation Methods for Fish

affogato	ahf-foh-GAH-toh	poached
al cartoccio	ahl kahr-TOHT-choh	sealed in parchment
al forno	ahl FOHR-noh	baked
alla graticola	AHL-lah grah-TEE-koh-lah	broiled
alla griglia	AHL-lah GREE-lyah	grilled
al vapore	ahl vah-POH-reh	steamed
fritto	FREET-toh	fried
in umido	een OO-mee-doh	stewed
lesso	LEHS-soh	boiled
marinato	mah-ree-NAH-toh	marinated

MEAT (*CARNE*)

A slice of meat, *una fettina* (unah feht-TEE-nah), usually follows pasta, and is ordered with a side dish, *un contorno* (oon kohn-TOHR-noh), the most common being a mixed green salad.

I'd like . . .	**Vorrei . . .**	voh-RAY . . .
• some beef.	• **del manzo.**	• dehl MAHN-dzoh
• some lamb.	• **dell'agnello.**	• dehl-lah-NYEHL-loh
• some pork.	• **del maiale.**	• dehl mah-YAH-leh
• some veal.	• **del vitello.**	• dehl vee-TEHL-loh
abbacchio	ahb-BAHK-kyoh	baby lamb
animelle	ah-nee-MEHL-leh	sweetbreads
arrosto	ahr-ROH-stoh	roast
bistecca	bee-STEHK-kah	steak
braciola	brah-CHOH-lah	chop
cervello	cher-VEHL-loh	brain
coppa	KOHP-pah	neck
costoletta	koh-stoh-LEHT-tah	rib
cotoletta	koh-toh-LEHT-tah	cutlet
fegato	FEH-gah-toh	liver
fesa	FEH-zah	round cut
filetto	fee-LEHT-toh	fillet
lingua	LEEN-gwah	tongue
lombata	lohm-BAH-tah	loin

medaglioni	meh-dah-LYOH-nee	round tenderloin
midollo	mee-DOHL-loh	marrow
mortadella	mohr-tah-DEHL-lah	Bologna
nodini	noh-DEE-nee	veal chops
pancetta affumicata	pahn-CHEHT-tah ahf-foo-mee-KAH-tah	smoked bacon
polpette	pohl-PEHT-teh	meat balls
polpettone	pohl-peht-TOH-neh	meat loaf
porchetta	pohr-KEHT-tah	suckling pig
prosciutto	proh-SHOOT-toh	Parma ham
rognoni	roh-NYOH-nee	kidneys
rosbif	ROHZ-beef	roast beef
salame	sah-LAH-meh	salami
salsiccia	sahl-SEET-chah	sausage
scaloppine	skah-lohp-PEE-neh	escalope, thin slice of meat

Methods of Meat Preparation

ai ferri	ahy FEHR-ree	barbecued
al forno	ahl FOHR-noh	baked
alla griglia	AHL-lah GREE-lyah	grilled
allo spiedo	AHL-loh SPYEH-doh	broiled on a spit
arrosto	ahr-ROHS-stoh	roasted
brasato	brah-ZAH-toh	braised
farcito	fahr-CHEE-toh	stuffed
fritto	FREET-toh	fried
in umido	een OO-mee-doh	stewed
lesso	LEHS-soh	boiled
saltato	sahl-TAH-toh	sauteed
How do you like your meat?	**Come desidera la carne?**	KOH-meh deh-ZEE-deh-rah lah KAHR-neh?
I like it . . .	**La preferisco . . .**	lah preh-feh-REE-skoh . . .
• rare.	• **al sangue.**	• ahl SAHN-gweh
• medium.	• **poco cotta.**	• POH-koh KOHT-tah
	(or) **cottura media.**	koht-TOO-rah MEH-dyah
• well-done.	• **ben cotta.**	• behn KOHT-tah

Typical Meat Dishes *(Piatti di carne tipici)*

abbacchio alla romana (ahb-BAHK-kyoh AHL-lah roh-MAH-nah)

a typical Easter dish: spring lamb flavored with garlic and rosemary and roasted with thin wedges of potatoes

fiorentina (fyoh-rehn-TEE-nah)

thick, juicy steak broiled under a flame and flavored with olive oil, salt, pepper, and lemon juice

carpaccio (kahr-PAHT-choh)

thinly sliced beef with oil and lemon, covered with flakes of parmesan cheese

cima alla genovese (CHEE-mah AHL-lah jeh-noh-VEH-zeh)

breast of veal stuffed with hard-boiled eggs, minced shoulder of pork, shelled peas, and marjoram

ossobuco alla milanese (ohs-soh-BOO-koh AHL-lah mee-lah-NEH-zeh)

shin of veal braised in broth with chopped onions, carrots, and tomatoes

saltimbocca alla romana (sahl-teem-BOHK-kah AHL-lah roh-MAH-nah)

veal cutlet rolled up with prosciutto and sage, secured with a toothpick, sauteed in butter, and simmered in wine

vitello tonnato (vee-TEHL-loh tohn-NAH-toh)

slices of cold veal covered with a sauce made of tuna, mayonnaise, lemon juice, anchovies, and capers

POULTRY AND GAME *(POLLAME E CACCIAGIONE)*

I would like some game.	**Vorrei della cacciagione.**	vohr-RAY DEHL-lah kaht-chah-JOH-neh
What kind of poultry do you have?	**Che tipo di pollame avete?**	keh TEE poh dee pohl-LAH-meh ah-VEH-teh?

allodola	ahl-LOH-doh-lah	lark
anatra	AH-nah-trah	duck
beccaccia	behk-KAH-chah	woodcock
cappone	kahp-POH-neh	capon
capretto	kah-PREHT-toh	kid goat
capriolo	kah-pree-OH-loh	roebuck
cervo	CHEHR-voh	deer
cinghiale	cheen-GYAH-leh	wild boar
coniglio	koh-NEE-lyoh	rabbit
fagiana	fah-JAH-noh	pheasant
faraona	fah-rah-OH-nah	guinea fowl
gallina	gahl-LEE-nah	stewing chicken
lepre	LEH-preh	hare
oca	OH-kah	goose
pernice	pehr-NEE-cheh	partridge
piccione	peet-CHOH-neh	pigeon
pollo	POHL-loh	chicken
pollo novello	POHL-loh noh-VEHL-loh	spring chicken
quaglia	KWAH-lyah	quail
selvaggina	sehl-vahd-JEE-nah	venison
tacchino	tahk-KEE-noh	turkey
tordo	TOHR-doh	mockingbird

VEGETABLES (VERDURA)

asparagi	ah-SPAH-rah-jee	asparagus
barbabietola	bahr-bah-BYEH-toh-lah	beet
broccoli	BROHK-koh-lee	broccoli
carciofi	kahr-CHOH-fee	artichokes
cardo	KAHR-doh	cardoon
carote	kah-ROH-teh	carrots
cavolfiore	kah-vohl-FYOH-reh	cauliflower
cavolini di Bruxelles	kah-voh-LEE-nee dee Broos-SEHL	brussels sprout
cavolo	KAH-voh-lah	cabbage
ceci	CHEH-chee	chick peas
cetrioli	cheh-tree-OH-lee	cucumbers
cicoria	chee-KOH-ryah	chicory
cipolle	chee-POHL-leh	onions

fagioli	fah-JOH-lee	beans
fagiolini	fah-joh-LEE-nee	string beans
fave	FAH-veh	broad beans
finocchio	fee-NOHK-kyoh	fennel
funghi	FOON-gee	mushrooms
granoturco	grah-noh-TOOR-koh	corn
indivia	een-DEE-vyah	endive
insalata	een-sah-LAH-tah	salad/lettuce
lattuga	laht-TOO-gah	lettuce
lenticchie	lehn-TEEK-kyeh	lentils
mais	MAH-ees	corn
melanzana	meh-lahn-TSAH-nah	eggplant
patate	pah-TAH-teh	potatoes
peperoni	peh-peh-ROH-nee	peppers
piselli	pee-ZEHL-lee	peas
pomodori	poh-moh-DOH-ree	tomatoes
porcini	pohr-CHEE-nee	*boletus edulis* mushroom
porro	POHR-roh	leek
radicchio	rah-DEEK-kyoh	radicchio
ravanelli	rah-vah-NEHL-lee	radishes
sedano	SEH-dah-nah	celery
spinaci	spee-NAH-chee	spinach
tartufi	tahr-TOO-fee	truffles
verza	VEHR-dzah	savoy cabbage
zucca	TSOOK-kah	pumpkin
zucchini	tsook-KEE-nee	green summer squash

HERBS AND SPICES (ODORI E SPEZIE)

aglio	AH-lyoh	garlic
alloro	ahl-LOH-roh	bay leaves
aneto	ah-NEH-toh	dill
basilico	bah-ZEE-lee-koh	basil
cannella	kahn-NEHL-lah	cinnamon
capperi	KAHP-peh-ree	capers
chiodi di garofano	KYOH-dee dee gah-ROH-fah-noh	cloves
cipollotti	chee-pohl-LOHT-tee	chives
maggiorana	mahd-joh-RAH-nah	marjoram
menta	MEHN-tah	mint

noce moscata	NOH-cheh moh-SKAH-tah	nutmeg
origano	oh-REE-gah-noh	oregano
prezzemolo	preht-TSEH-moh-loh	parsley
rosmarino	roh-smah-REE-noh	rosemary
salvia	SAHL-vyah	sage
timo	TEE-moh	thyme
zafferano	dzahf-feh-RAH-noh	saffron
zenzero	DZEHN-dzeh-roh	ginger

POTATOES (PATATE)

I'd like some . . .	Vorrei delle patate . . .	vohr-RAY-DEHL-leh pah-TAH-teh . . .
• potatoes cooked with butter and parsley.	• al burro.	• ahl BOOR-roh
• potatoes baked with oil and rosemary.	• arrosto.	• ahr-ROH-stoh
• fried potatoes.	• fritte.	• FREET-teh
• boiled potatoes.	• lesse.	• LEHS-seh
• mashed potatoes.	• purè.	• poo-REH

SALADS (INSALATE)

I'd like . . .	Vorrei un'insalata . . .	vohr-RAY oon-een-sah-LAH-tah . . .
• a tomato salad.	• di pomodori.	• dee poh-moh-DOH-ree
• a radicchio salad.	• di radicchi.	• dee rah-DEEK-kee
• a mixed salad.	• mista.	• MEE-stah
• diced cooked vegetables with mayonnaise.	• russa.	• ROOS-sah
• a green salad.	• verde.	• VEHR-deh

CHEESE (*FORMAGGI*)

Cheese is used extensively in Italian cooking. Here's a list of the most renowned Italian cheeses:

asiago
(ah-ZYAH-goh)
soft, pale yellow cheese, a little sharp and with little holes; a winter cheese

Bel Paese
(behl pah-EH-zeh)
mild, soft, pale yellow cheese, creamy and quite delicate

caciocavallo
(kah-choh-kah-VAHL-loh)
pear-shaped, yellow, hard-textured cheese with a tangy flavor; may be consumed fresh or seasoned for grating

carnia (KAHR-nyah)
soft, yellow cheese with sharp taste

fontina
(fohn-TEE-nah)
creamy, soft, yellow cheese, with a mild flavor if consumed within eight months; aged for sharper taste

gorgonzola
(gohr-gohn-DZOH-lah)
flavored, pungent, creamy, white cheese with green mold; like blue cheese, but creamier and softer

grana padano (GRAH-nah pah-DAH-noh)
also known as *parmigiano-reggiano*; yellow, hard cheese, dry and grainy; at its best when seasoned between 24 and 36 months, this is Italy's complement to pasta

mascarpone
(mah-skahr-POH-neh)
very soft, creamy, sweet white cheese that looks like whipped cream; made with heavy cream; to be eaten within ten days

mozzarella
(moht-tsah-REHL-lah)
moist, soft, white, unsalted cheese made with buffalo's milk

pecorino
(peh-koh-REE-noh)
sharp, off-white cheese, made with sheep's milk

provolone
(proh-voh-LOH-neh)
hard-textured, sharp, light yellow cheese, at times made with the addition of sheep's milk

ricotta (ree-KOHT-tah)	white, creamy cottage cheese, made only with sheep's milk; can be sweet or strong and salty	
robbiola (rohb-BYOH-lah)	moist, off-white, soft cheese with a Brie-like crust, made with cow and sheep's milk	
stracchino (strahk-KEE-noh)	soft, creamy, off-white cheese, excellent with fried polenta	

FRUIT (*FRUTTA*)

Served after the cheese, fruit may also be a dessert.

I would like . . .	Vorrei . . .	vohr-RAY . . .
• some fresh fruit	• della frutta fresca	• DEHL-lah FROOT-tah FREH-skah
• a fruit cocktail	• una macedonia	• OO-nah mah-cheh-DOH-nyah
• an apricot	• un'albicocca	• oo-nahl-bee-KOHK-kah
• some pineapple	• dell'ananas	• dehl-LAH-nah-nahs
• some watermelon	• dell'anguria	• dehl-lahn-GOO-ryah
• an orange	• un'arancia	• oo-nah-RAHN-chah
• a persimmon	• un caco	• oon KAH-koh
• some lime	• del cedro	• dehl CHEH-droh
• some cherries	• delle ciliegie	• DEHL-leh chee-LYEH-jeh
• some watermelon	• del cocomero	• dehl koh-KOH-meh-roh
• some dates	• dei datteri	• day DAHT-teh-ree
• some figs	• dei fichi	• day FEE-kee
• some strawberries	• delle fragole	• DEHL-leh FRAH-goh-leh
• some raspberries	• dei lamponi	• day lahm-POH-nee
• some lemon	• del limone	• dehl lee-MOH-neh
• a tangerine	• un mandarino	• oon mahn-dah-REE-noh
• an apple	• una mela	• OO-nah MEH-lah
• some melon	• del melone	• dehl meh-LOH-neh
• some blueberries	• dei mirtilli	• day meer-TEEL-lee

• some blackberries	• **delle more**	• DEHL-leh MOH-reh
• a pear	• **una pera**	• OO-nah PEH-rah
• a peach	• **una pesca**	• OO-nah PEH-skah
• a grapefruit	• **un pompelmo**	• oon pohm-PEHL-moh
• a Sicilian orange	• **un tarocco**	• oon tah-ROHK-koh
• some white grapes	• **dell'uva bianca**	• dehl-LOO-vah BYAHN-kah
• some gooseberries	• **dell'uva spina**	• dehl-LOO-vah SPEE-nah

NUTS AND DRIED FRUIT (*NOCI E FRUTTA SECCA*)

peanuts	**noccioline**	noht-choh-LEE-neh
chestnuts	**castagne**	kah-STAH-nyeh
coconut	**cocco**	KOHK-koh
dried figs	**fichi secchi**	FEE-kee SEHK-kee
almonds	**mandorle**	MAHN-dohr-leh
hazelnuts	**nocciole**	noht-CHOH-leh
walnuts	**noci**	NOH-chee
pine kernels	**pignoli**	pee-NYOH-lee
dried plums	**prugne secche**	PROO-nyeh SEHK-keh
raisins	**uva passa/uvetta**	OO-vah PAHS-sah/oo-VEHT-tah

DESSERTS (*DOLCI*)

To finish your meal, choose from a variety of the tasty cakes and luscious ice-creams for which Italy is famous. Here's a list of the most tempting desserts.

millefoglie (meel-leh-FOH-lyeh)	"a thousand leaves" or layers of crisp, light, buttery pastry dough
tiramisù (tee-rah-mee-SOO)	cake made with sweet, creamy mascarpone cheese and sprinkled with cocoa powder
zabaglione (dzah-bah-LYOH-neh)	egg yolks, sugar, and Marsala; may be served right away or chilled
zuccotto (tsook-KOHT-toh)	round sponge cake with chocolate, cream, and candied fruit; best if chilled

I'd like some dessert.	**Vorrei del dolce.**	vohr-RAY dehl DOHL-cheh.
I'd like a slice of cake with whipped cream.	**Vorrei una fetta di torta con panna montata.**	vohr-RAY OO-nah FEHT-tah dee TOHR-tah kohn PAHN-nah mohn-TAH-tah
Waiter, bring me . . .	**Cameriere, mi porti . . .**	kah-meh-RYEH-reh, mee POHR-tee . . .
• almond macaroons.	• **amaretti.**	• ah-mah-REHT-tee
• pudding.	• **budino.**	• boo-DEE-noh
• cannolo.	• **cannolo.**	• kahn-NOH-loh
• spumoni.	• **cassata.**	• kahs-SAH-tah
• pound cake.	• **ciambella.**	• chahm-BEHL-lah
• custard preserve.	• **crostata.**	• kroh-STAH-tah
• . . . ice cream.	• **gelato . . .**	• jeh-LAH-toh . . .
chocolate	**al cioccolato.**	ahl chohk-koh-LAH-toh
strawberry	**alla fragola.**	AHL-lah FRAH-goh-lah
lemon	**al limone.**	ahl lee-MOH-neh
vanilla	**alla vaniglia.**	AHL-lah vah-NEE-lyah
mixed	**misto.**	MEE-stoh
• some shaved ice . . .	• **granita . . .**	• grah-NEE-tah . . .
with coffee.	**al caffè.**	ahl kahf-FEH
with mint syrup.	**alla menta.**	AHL-lah MEHN-tah
with tamarind syrup.	**al tamarindo.**	ahl tah-mah-REEN-doh
• sponge cake.	• **pan di Spagna.**	• pahn dee SPAH-nyah
• apple strudel.	• **strudel.**	• STROO-dehl
• chocolate truffle.	• **tartufo.**	• tahr-TOO-foh
• . . . cake.	• **torta . . .**	• TOHR-tah . . .
chocolate	**al cioccolato.**	al chohk-koh-LAH-toh

NONALCOHOLIC BEVERAGES *(BEVANDE ANALCOLICHE)*

The most popular nonalcoholic drink in Italy is *caffè espresso* (kahf-FEH eh-SPREHS-soh), which comes in different varieties:

caffè con panna (kahf-FEH kohn PAHN-nah) — coffee with whipped cream

caffè corretto (kahf-FEH kohr-REHT-toh) — coffee with a dash of liquor such as sambuca or grappa

caffè lungo (kahf-FEH LOON-goh) — larger cup of weaker coffee; synonym for American coffee

caffè ristretto (kahf-FEH ree-STREHT-toh) — the one and only espresso, thick and condensed

caffellatte (kahf-fehl-LAHT-teh) — coffee with milk

cappuccino (kahp-poot-CHEE-noh) — coffee with steamed, frothy milk

Waiter, please bring me . . .	Cameriere, per favore mi porti . . .	kah-meh-RYEH-reh, pehr fah-VOH-reh mee POHR-tee . . .
• some . . . water.	• dell'acqua . . .	• dehl-LAHK-kwah . . .
light tonic	brillante.	breel-LAHN-teh
cold	fresca.	FREH-skah
ice	con ghiaccio.	kohn GYAHT-choh
carbonated mineral	minerale gassata.	mee-neh-RAH-leh gahs-SAH-tah
noncarbonated mineral	minerale naturale.	mee-neh-RAH-leh nah-too-RAH-leh
tonic	tonica.	TOH-nee-kah
• an orange soda	• un'aranciata.	• oo-nah-rahn-CHAH-tah
• a soda	• una bevanda gassata.	• OO-nah beh-VAHN-dah gahs-SAH-tah
• a bitter	• un bitter.	• oon BEET-tehr
• a . . . coffee. decaffeinated	• un caffè . . . decaffeinato.	• oon kahf-FEH . . . deh-kahf-fay-NAH-toh
• a lemonade.	• una limonata.	• OO-nah lee-moh-NAH-tah
• a . . . juice.	• un succo . . .	• oon SOOK-koh . . .

79

orange	d'arancia.	dah-RAHN-chah
fruit	di frutta.	dee FROOT-tah
• a cup of tea . . .	• un tè . . .	• oon teh
with milk.	con latte.	kohn LAHT-teh
with lemon.	con limone.	kohn lee-MOH-neh
• an iced tea.	• un tè freddo.	• oon teh FREHD-doh

ALCOHOLIC BEVERAGES (BEVANDE ALCOLICHE)

Aperitifs (Aperitivi)

The *aperitivo* (ah-peh-ree-TEE-voh) is taken leisurely before dinner as an appetite stimulant. Italians do not usually have cocktails before their meals as most Americans do. The aperitifs may be either sweet, like vermouth, or bitter, made from a combination of herbs, spirits, and sometimes quinine. Here are the most common:

americano (ah-meh-ree-KAH-noh)	a combination of sweet vermouth, brandy, bitters, and lemon peel
Bellini (behl-LEE-nee)	chilled dry, white wine or champagne, and peach juice
Punt e Mes (poont eh mehs)	red-brown bitters with quinine, served with soda and a twist of orange
vermut (VEHR-moot)	the most famous Italian aperitif, a blend of wine, fortified and distilled with an array of herbs; it may be either white, *bianco* (BYAHN-koh), or red, *rosso* (ROHS-soh), either dry, *secco* (SEHK-koh), or sweet, *dolce* (DOHL-cheh)

Phrases for Ordering Drinks

straight	liscio	LEE-shoh
on the rocks	con ghiaccio	kohn GYAHT-choh
with seltzer/soda	con seltz/soda	kohn sehltz/SOH-dah
with water	con acqua	kohn AHK-kwah

80

Beer *(Birra)*

Beer is getting more and more popular among young Italians, especially accompanying a sandwich, a pizza, or a light meal.

I'd like a . . . beer.	**Vorrei una birra . . .**	vohr-RAY OO-nah BEER-rah . . .
• bottled	• **in bottiglia.**	• een boht-TEE-lyah
• can of	• **in lattina.**	• een laht-TEE-nah
• dark	• **scura.**	• SKOO-rah
• draft	• **alla spina.**	• AHL-lah SPEE-nah
• foreign	• **estera.**	• EH-steh-rah
• light	• **bionda.**	• BYOHN-dah
• local	• **nazionale.**	• nah-tsyoh-NAH-leh
Bring me a beer, please.	**Mi porti una birra, per favore.**	mee POHR-tee OO-nah BEER-rah, pehr fah-VOH-reh

Wine *(Vino)*

Italy is one of the great wine-producing countries of the world, with vineyards all over the peninsula and the islands. Every region of the country, due to its favorable climate and soil conditions, produces notable wine. The vineyards of greatest renown are in Piedmont, Veneto, Tuscany, and Sicily. Here's a list of the most renowned wines and the region where they are produced:

Dry White Wine	Sweet White Wine	Red Wine
Albana (Emilia-Romagna)	**Aleatico** (Isle of Elba)	**Barbera** (Piedmont)
Est Est Est (Latium)	**Malvasia** (Sicily)	**Bardolino** (Veneto)
Frascati (Latium)	**Marsala** (Sicily)	**Barolo** (Piedmont)
Orvieto (Umbria)	**Verduzzo** (Trentino)	**Brunello di Montalcino** (Tuscany)
Pinot (Veneto)	**Vin Santo** (Tuscany)	
Soave (Veneto)	**Lacrima Christi** (Campania)	**Chianti** (Tuscany)
Verdicchio (Marches)		**Corvo** (Sicily)

81

Vernaccia (Tuscany)

Lambrusco (Emilia-Romagna)
Valpolicella
(Veneto)

Sparkling Wines

Asti Spumante Brut

Berlucchi Brut

Ferrari Brut

Ordering Wine

What wine do you recommend?	**Che vino consiglia?**	keh VEE-noh kohn-SEE-lyah?
Where does this wine come from?	**Di dov'è questo vino?**	dee doh-VEH KWEH-stoh VEE-noh?
I'd like . . .	**Vorrei . . .**	vohr-RAY . . .
• a bottle of . . .	• **una bottiglia di . . .**	• OO-nah boht-TEE-lyah dee . . .
red wine.	**vino rosso.**	VEE-noh ROHS-soh
rosé.	**vino rosé.**	VEE-noh roh-ZEH
white wine.	**vino bianco.**	VEE-noh BYAHN-koh
dry wine.	**vino secco.**	VEE-noh SEHK-koh
light wine.	**vino leggero.**	VEE-noh lehd-JEH-roh
sweet wine.	**vino dolce.**	VEE-noh DOHL-cheh
full-bodied wine.	**vino corposo.**	VEE-noh kohr-POH-zoh
sparkling wine.	**spumante.**	spoo-MAHN-teh
champagne.	**champagne.**	shahm-PAHN
• a carafe.	• **una caraffa.**	• OO-nah kah-RAHF-fah
• a glass.	• **un bicchiere.**	• oon beek-KYEH-reh
• a half-bottle.	• **una mezza bottiglia.**	• OO-nah MEHD-dzah boht-TEE-lyah
• another bottle.	• **un'altra bottiglia.**	• oo-NAHL-trah boht-TEE-lyah
• a liter.	• **un litro.**	• oon LEE-troh
• a local wine.	• **del vino locale.**	• dehl VEE-noh loh-KAH-leh
• to taste some . . .	• **assaggiare un po' di . . .**	• ahs-sahd-JAH-reh oon poh dee . . .

| • to see the wine list. | • vedere la lista dei vini. | • veh-DEH-reh lah LEE-stah day VEE-nee |
| To your health/Cheers! | Salute! (or) Cin cin! | sah-LOO-teh cheen cheen |

After-Dinner Drinks *(Liquori e digestivi)*

Here is a list of some of the more prominent after-dinner drinks.

bitters	un amaro	oo-nah-MAH-roh
brandy	un brandy	oon BREHN-dee
cognac	un cognac	oon KOH-nyahk
grappa	una grappa	OO-nah GRAHP-pah
sambuca	una sambuca	OO-nah sahm-BOO-kah

Among the most popular Italian brandies is Vecchia Romagna Etichetta Nera. The bitter Fernet Branca, Branca Menta, China Martini, and Amaro Averna are well-known digestive drinks. You may also want to try the strong northern Italian aquavit, grappa, or, on the sweeter side, the anise-flavored *sambuca* or the almond-flavored *amaretto*.

SPECIAL DIETS

I am on a diet.	Sono a dieta.	SON-noh ah DYEH-tah
I am on a special diet.	Seguo una dieta speciale.	SEH-gwoh OO-nah DYEH-tah speh-CHAH-leh
Do you have vegetarian dishes?	Servite piatti vegetariani?	sehr-VEE-teh PYAHT-tee veh-jeh-tah-RYAH-nee?
I am a vegetarian.	Sono vegetartiano (-a).	SOH-noh veh-jeh-tah-RYAH-noh (-nah)
I am allergic to . . .	Sono allergico(-a) a . . .	SOH-noh ahl-LEHR-jee-koh(-kah) ah . . .
I can't eat . . .	Devo evitare . . .	DEH-voh eh-vee-TAH-reh . . .
• salt.	• il sale.	• eel SAH-leh

83

• fat.	• **i grassi.**	• ee GRAHS-see
• sugar,	• **lo zucchero**	• loh TSOOK-keh-roh
• flour.	• **la farina.**	• lah tah-REE-nah
I am diabetic.	**Soffro di diabete.**	SOHF-froh dee dyah-BEH-teh
I don't eat pork.	**Non mangio carne di maiale.**	nohn MAHN-joh KAHR-neh dee mah-YAH-leh
I want to lose/gain weight.	**Voglio dimagrire/ ingrassare.**	VOH-lyoh dee-mah-GREE-reh/ een-grahs-SAH-reh

COMPLAINTS

I didn't order this.	**Non è quello che avevo ordinato.**	nohn eh KWEHL-loh keh ah-VEH-voh ohr-dee-NAH-toh
May I change this?	**Posso cambiare questo?**	POHS-soh kahm-BYAH-reh KWEH-stoh?
This is too . . .	**È troppo . . .**	eh TROHP-poh . . .
• rare.	• **al sangue.**	• ahl SAHN-gweh
• well done.	• **cotto.**	• KOHT-toh
• tough.	• **duro.**	• DOO-roh
• salty.	• **salato.**	• sah-LAH-toh
• bitter.	• **amaro.**	• ah-MAH-roh
• sweet.	• **dolce.**	• DOHL-cheh
I don't like it.	**Non mi piace.**	nohn mee PYAH-cheh
This is not clean.	**Non è pulito.**	nohn eh poo-LEE-toh
This is cold.	**È freddo.**	eh FREHD-doh
It isn't fresh.	**Non è fresco.**	nohn eh FREH-skoh
This wine tastes of cork.	**Il vino sa di tappo.**	eel VEE-noh sah dee TAHP-poh
There's a knife missing.	**Manca un coltello.**	MAHN-kah oon kohl-TEHL-loh

THE BILL (*IL CONTO*)

Waiter!/Miss! The check, please.	**Cameriere(-a)! Il conto, per favore.**	kah-meh-RYEH-reh (-rah)! eel KOHN-toh, pehr fah-VOH-reh

84

Only one check, please.	**Faccia un conto unico, per favore.**	FAHT-chah oon KOHN-toh oo-NEE-koh, pehr fah-VOH-reh
Please, give us separate checks.	**Conti separati, per cortesia.**	KOHN-tee seh-pah-RAH-tee pehr kohr-teh-ZEE-ah
We are going Dutch (literally, Roman).	**Facciamo alla romana.**	faht-CHAH-moh AHL-lah roh-MAH-nah
Is service included?	**Il servizio è compreso?**	eel sehr-VEE-tsyoh eh kohm-PREH-zoh?
What's this amount for?	**Per che cos'è quest'importo?**	pehr keh koh-ZEH kweh-steem-POHR-toh?
I think there's a mistake.	**Penso che ci sia un errore.**	PEHN-soh keh chee SEE-ah oon ehr-ROH-reh
The meal was excellent.	**È stato un pasto delizioso.**	eh STAH-toh oon PAH-stoh deh-lee-TSYOH-soh
The service was very good.	**Il servizio è stato ottimo.**	eel sehr-VEE-tsyoh eh STAH-toh OHT-tee-moh

7/PERSONAL CARE

DIALOGUE: GETTING A HAIRCUT *(IL TAGLIO DEI CAPELLI)*

Parrucchiere:	**A chi tocca?**	ah kee TOHK-kah?
Signora:	**Tocca a me. Vorrei tagliarmi i capelli.**	TOHK-kah ah meh, vohr-RAY tah-LYAHR-mee ee kah-PEHL-lee
Parrucchiere:	**Certamente, signora. Come vuole i capelli?**	chehr-tah-MEHN-teh, see-NYOH-rah. KOH-meh voo-OH-leh ee kah-PEHL-lee?
Signora:	**Li lasci lunghi davanti e ai lati e me li accorci di un paio di centimetri di dietro.**	lee LAH-shee LOON-ghee dah-VAHN tee eh ahy LAH-tee eh meh lee ahk-KOHR-chee dee oon PAH-yoh dee chehn-TEE-meh-tree dee DYEH-troh
Parrucchiere:	**Bene. Allora prima glieli lavo con un ottimo shampoo alle erbe, e poi, il taglio.**	BEH-neh. ahl-LOH-rah PREE-mah LYEH-lee LAH-voh kohn oon OHT-tee-moh SHAHM-poo AHL-leh EHR-beh, eh poy eel TAH-lyoh
Signora:	**D'accordo. Faccia pure.**	dahk-KOHR-doh. FAH-chah POO-reh

. . . .

Hairdresser:	Who's next?
Customer:	I am. I'd like a haircut.
Hairdresser:	Certainly, madam. How would you like it?
Customer:	Long in the front and on the sides, and about an inch shorter in the back.
Hairdresser:	Well, first I'll wash it with an excellent herbal shampoo, and then, I'll cut it.
Customer:	All right. Go ahead.

AT THE BARBERSHOP

Is there a . . . nearby?	C'è un . . . qui vicino?	cheh oon . . . kwee vee-CHEE-noh?
• barbershop	• barbiere	• bahr-BYEH-reh
• hairdresser	• parrucchiere per uomo	• pahr-rook-KYEH-reh pehr WOH-moh
I'd like . . .	Vorrei . . .	vohr-RAY . . .
• a haircut.	• tagliarmi i capelli.	• tah-LYAHR-mee ee kah-PEHL-lee
• a razor cut.	• un taglio scolpito al rasoio.	• oon TAH-lyoh skohl-PEE-toh ahl rah-ZOH-yoh
• a shampoo.	• uno shampoo.	• OO-noh SHAHM-poh
• a shave.	• farmi la barba.	• FAHR-mee lah BAHR-bah
Cut it a bit more . . .	Me li tagli un po' di più . . .	meh lee TAH-lyee oon poh dee pyoo . . .
• right here.	• qui.	• kwee
• in the front.	• davanti.	• dah-VAHN-tee
• on the sides.	• ai lati.	• ahy LAH-tee
• on the neck.	• sul collo.	• suhl KOHL-loh
• in the back.	• dietro.	• DYEH-troh
• on the top.	• in cima.	• een CHEE-mah
Leave it a little longer right here.	Li lasci un po' più lunghi qui.	lee LAH-shee oon poh pyoo LOON-ghee kwee
Cut it short.	Li accorci.	lee ahk-KOHR-chee
Cut it a little shorter.	Un po' più corti.	oon poh pyoo KOHR-tee
Not too short!	Non troppo corti!	nohn TROHP-poh KOHR-tee!
I'd like the part . . .	Vorrei la riga . . .	vohr-RAY lah REE-gah . . .
• on the right.	• a destra.	• ah DEH-strah
• on the left.	• a sinistra.	• ah see-NEE-strah
• down the middle.	• in mezzo.	• een MEHD-dzoh
Also trim my . . .	Può spuntarmi anche . . .	pwoh spoon-TAHR-mee AHN-keh . . .
• beard.	• la barba?	• lah BAHR-bah?
• mustache.	• i baffi?	• ee BAHF-fee?

87

| • sideburns. | • le basette? | • leh bah-ZEHT-teh? |
| It's fine like that. | Va bene così. | vah BEH-neh koh-ZEE |

AT THE BEAUTY PARLOR

I need to go to a hairdresser.	Devo andare dal parrucchiere.	DEH-voh ahn-DAH-reh dahl pahr-rook-KYEH-reh
Is there a beauty parlor in this area?	C'è un istituto di bellezza in questa zona?	cheh oon ee-stee-TOO-toh dee behl-LEHT-tsah een KWEH-stah DZOH-nah?
Do I need an appointment?	Devo prendere l'appuntamento?	DEH-voh prehn-DEH-reh lahp-poon-tah-MEHN-toh?
Is there a long wait?	C'è molto da aspettare?	cheh MOHL-toh dah ah-speht-TAH-reh?
Can I make an appointment for . . .	Posso prendere l'appuntamento per . . .	POHS-soh PREHN-deh-reh lahp-poon-tah-MEHN-toh pehr . . .
• later?	• più tardi?	• pyoo TAHR-dee?
• this afternoon?	• questo pomeriggio?	• KWEH-stoh poh-meh-REED-joh?
• three o'clock?	• le quindici?	• leh KWEEN-dee-chee?
• tomorrow?	• domani?	• doh-MAH-nee?
I'd like a . . .	Vorrei fare . . .	vohr-RAY FAH-reh . . .
• shampoo.	• lo shampoo.	• loh SHAHM-poh
• blowdry.	• l'asciugatura col phon.	• lah-shoo-gah-TOO-rah kohl fohn
• set.	• la messinpiega.	• lah mehs-seen-PYEH-gah
• permanent.	• la permanente.	• lah pehr-mah-NEHN-teh
• color rinse.	• un cachet.	• oon kah-SHEH
• dye.	• la tinta.	• lah TEEN-tah
• bleach.	• la decolorazione.	• lah deh-koh-loh-rah-TSYOH-neh
• facial.	• una maschera.	• OO-nah MAH-skeh-rah

• manicure.	• il manicure. *(or)* le mani.	• eel mah-nee-KOOR leh MAH-nee
• pedicure.	• il pedicure. *(or)* i piedi.	• eel peh-dee-KOOR ee PYEH-dee
• haircut.	• un taglio.	• oon TAH-lyoh
Could I see a color chart?	Mi fa vedere la tabella dei colori?	mee fah veh-DEH-reh lah tah-BEHL-lah day koh-LOH-ree?
I prefer . . .	Preferisco . . .	preh-feh-REE-skoh . . .
• a lighter shade.	• una tinta più chiara.	• OO-nah TEEN-tah pyoo KYAH-rah
• a darker shade.	• una tinta più scura.	• OO-nah TEEN-tah pyoo SKOO-rah
No hairspray, please.	Niente lacca, per favore.	NYEHN-teh LAHK-kah, pehr fah-VOH-reh
A little gel, please.	Un po' di gel, per piacere. *(or)* . . . di gommina . . .	oon poh dee jehl, pehr pyah-CHEH-reh . . . dee gohm-MEE-nah . . .
That's perfect!	Perfetto!	pehr-FEHT-toh!

LAUNDRY AND DRY CLEANING

I'm looking for . . .	Cerco . . .	CHEHR-koh . . .
• a laundry.	• una lavanderia.	• OO-nah lah-vahn-deh-REE-ah
• a dry cleaner.	• una tintoria.	• OO-nah teen-toh-REE-ah
• a laundromat.	• una lavanderia automatica. *(or)* a gettone.	• OO-nah lah-vahn-deh-REE-ah ow-toh-MAH-tee-kah ah jeht-TOH-neh
I have some clothes to be . . .	Ho della roba da far . . .	oh DEHL-lah ROH-bah dah fahr . . .
• washed.	• lavare.	• lah-VAH-reh
• dry cleaned.	• lavare a secco.	• lah-VAH-reh ah SEHK-koh
• ironed.	• stirare.	• stee-RAH-reh
• mended.	• rammendare.	• rahm-mehn-DAH-reh
• stitched.	• cucire.	• koo-CHEE-reh

89

English	Italian	Pronunciation
These clothes are dirty	**Questi vestiti sono sporchi.**	KWEH-stee veh-STEE-tee SOH-noh SPOHR-kee
Can they be cleaned today?	**Può lavarli oggi?**	pwoh lah-VAHR-lee OHD-jee?
When will they be ready?	**Quando sono pronti?**	KWAHN-doh SOH-noh PROHN-tee?
I need them . . .	**Ne ho bisogno . . .**	neh oh bee-ZOH-nyoh . . .
• tomorrow.	• **domani.**	• doh-MAH-nee
• as soon as possible.	• **il più presto possible.**	• eel pyoo PREH-stoh pohs-SEE-bee-leh
	(or) **al più presto.**	ahl pyoo PREH-stoh
I'm leaving tomorrow.	**Parto domani.**	PAHR-toh doh-MAH-nee
This isn't mine.	**Questo non è mio.**	KWEH-stoh nohn eh MEE-oh
There's an item missing.	**Manca un capo.**	MAHN-kah oon KAH-poh
	(or) **un indumento.**	oon een-doo-MEHN-toh . . .
Can you get this stain out?	**Può togliere questa macchia?**	pwoh TOH-lyeh-reh KWEH-stah MAHK-kyah?
Can you sew on this button?	**Può attaccare questo bottone?**	pwoh aht-tahk-KAH-reh KWEH-stoh boht-TOH-neh?
Here's my list:	**Ecco la lista:**	EHK-koh lah LEE-stah
• two shirts	• **due camicie**	• DOO-eh kah-MEE-cheh
• a suit	• **un abito**	• oon AH-bee-toh
• eight pairs of socks	• **otto paia di calzini**	• OHT-toh PAH-yah dee kahl-TSEE-nee

8/HEALTH CARE

It's a good idea to check with your health insurance company to find out what accident and illness expenses overseas are covered by your policy. Many doctors in Italy speak English, especially in the large cities. The American embassies or consulates are often helpful in locating English-speaking doctors.

You should carry basic medicine such as aspirin and any prescription drugs you are currently using. If you are traveling with prescribed medications be sure to keep the prescription or label handy, so that you can show it to the druggist, or the customs authorities to avoid any problems. Druggists are generally helpful and will suggest over-the-counter remedies for minor ailments. They will also take your blood pressure. Shots are not required. Tap water, although generally safe to drink, except for some areas in the south, can often taste of chlorine.

DIALOGUE: FINDING A DOCTOR (ALLA RICERCA DI UN MEDICO)

Turista:	**Non mi sento bene.**	nohn mee SEHN-toh BEH-neh
Farmacista:	**Ha bisogno di un medico?**	ah bee-ZOH-nyoh dee oon MEH-dee-koh?
Turista:	**Credo di sì. Me ne può raccomandare-uno?**	KREH-doh dee see. meh neh pwoh rahk-koh-mahn-DAH-reh OO-noh?
Farmacista:	**Sì. Ce ne è uno che presta servizio proprio all'ambulatorio qui vicino.**	see. cheh neh eh OO-noh keh PREH-stah sehr-VEE-tsyoh PROH-pryoh ahl-lahm-boo-lah-TOH-ryoh kwee vee-CHEE-noh.
Turista:	**Parla inglese?**	PAHR-lah een-GLEH-zeh?
Farmacista:	**Lui no, ma la sua infermiera sì: è americana.**	LOO-ee noh, mah lah SOO-ah een-fehr-MYEH-rah see: eh ah-meh-ree-KAH-nah

Tourist:	I don't feel well.
Pharmacist:	Do you need a doctor?
Tourist:	I think so. Can you recommend one?
Pharmacist:	Yes. There is one on duty right at the medical center near here.
Tourist:	Does he speak English?
Pharmacist:	No, but his nurse does: she is an American.

FINDING A DOCTOR

Is there a doctor here?	**C'è un dottore qui?**	cheh oon doht-TOH-reh kwee?
Could you call me a doctor?	**Può chiamarmi un dottore?**	pwoh kyah-MAHR-mee oon doht-TOH-reh?
Where is the doctor's office/outpatient clinic?	**Dov'è l'ambulatorio?**	doh-VEH lahm-boo-lah-TOH-ryoh?
I need a doctor who speaks English.	**Ho bisogno di un dottore che parli inglese.**	oh bee-ZOH-nyoh dee oon doht-TOH-reh keh PAHR-lee een-GLEH-zeh
When can I see the doctor?	**Quando posso vedere il dottore?**	KWAHN-doh POHS-soh veh-DEH-reh eel doht-TOH-reh?
Can the doctor see me now?	**Mi può visitare ora?**	mee pwoh vee-zee-TAH-reh OH-rah?
It's an emergency.	**È un'emergenza.**	eh oo-neh-mehr-JEHN-tsah
Do I need an appointment?	**Devo prendere l'appunta-mento?**	DEH-voh PREHN-deh-reh lahp-poon-tah-MEHN-toh?
Can I have an appointment . . .	**Può fissarmi un appuntamento . . .**	pwoh fees-SAHR-mee oon ahp-poon-tah-MEHN-toh . . .

• as soon as possible?	• quanto prima?	• QWAHN-toh PREE-mah?
• today?	• oggi?	• OHD-jee?
• for 2 o'clock?	• per le quattordici?	• pehr leh kwaht-TOHR-dee-chee?
What are the doctor's visiting hours?	A che ora visita il dottore?	ah keh OH-rah vee-ZEE-tah eel doht-TOH-reh?
I need . . .	Ho bisogno di . . .	oh bee-ZOH-nyoh dee . . .
• a general practitioner.	• un medico generico.	• oon MEH-dee-koh jeh-NEH-ree-koh
• a pediatrician.	• un pediatra.	• oon peh-DYAH-trah
• a gynecologist.	• un ginecologo.	• oon jee-neh-KOH-loh-goh
• an eye doctor.	• un oculista.	• oon oh-koo-LEE-stah
• a dentist.	• un dentista.	• oon dehn-TEE-stah

TALKING TO THE DOCTOR

I don't feel well.	Non mi sento bene.	nohn mee SEHN-toh BEH-neh
I'm sick.	Sono ammalato (-a).	SOH-noh ahm-mah-LAH-toh(-tah)
I don't know what I have.	Non so cosa ho.	nohn soh KOH-zah oh
I feel weak.	Mi sento debole.	mee SEHN-toh DEH-boh-leh
I'm feeling dizzy.	Mi gira la testa.	mee JEE-rah lah TEH-stah
I have a fever.	Ho la febbre.	oh lah FEHB-breh
I don't have a temperature.	Non ho la febbre.	nohn oh lah FEHB-breh
I'm nauseated.	Ho la nausea.	oh lah NOW-zeh-ah
I can't sleep.	Non riesco a dormire.	nohn RYEH-skoh ah dohr-MEE-reh
I threw up.	Ho vomitato.	oh voh-mee-TAH-toh
I'm constipated.	Sono stitico(-a).	SOH-noh STEE-tee-koh (-kah)
I have . . .	Ho . . .	oh . . .
• asthma.	• l'asma.	• LAH-smah

93

• a bite.	• preso un morso.	• PREH-zoh oon MOHR-soh
• bruises.	• delle contusioni. (or) degli ematomi.	• DEHL-leh kohn-too-ZYOH-nee DEH-lyee eh-mah-TOH-mee
• a bump.	• un bernoccolo.	• oon behr-NOHK-koh-loh
• a burn.	• una bruciatura. (or) una scottatura.	• OO-nah broo-chah-TOO-rah OO-nah skoht-tah-TOO-rah
• something in my eye.	• qualcosa in un occhio.	• kwahl-KOH-zah een oon OHK-kyoh
• a cold.	• il raffreddore.	• eel rahf-frehd-DOH-reh
• a cough.	• la tosse.	• lah TOHS-seh
• cramps.	• i crampi.	• ee KRAHM-pee
• a cut.	• una ferita.	• OO-nah feh-REE-tah
• the flu.	• l'influenza.	• leen-floo-EHN-tsah
• diarrhea.	• la diarrea.	• lah dyahr-REH-ah
• a headache.	• mal di testa.	• mahl dee TEH-stah
• a lump.	• un nodulo.	• oon NOH-doo-loh
• a rash.	• un'irritazione.	• oo-neer-ree-tah-TSYOH-neh
• rheumatism.	• i reumatismi.	• ee reh-oo-mah-TEE-zmee
• a sore throat.	• mal di gola.	• mahl dee GOH-lah
• a sting.	• una puntura d'insetto. (or) sono stato(-a) punto(-a).	• OO-nah poon-TOO-rah deen-SEHT-toh SOH-noh STAH-toh (-tah) POON-toh (-tah)
• a stomach ache.	• mal di stomaco.	• mahl dee STOH-mah-koh
• a sunstroke.	• preso un'insolazione.	• PREH-zoh oo-neen-soh-lah-TSYOH-neh
• a swelling.	• un gonfiore.	• oon gohn-FYOH-reh
• an upset stomach.	• imbarazzo di stomaco.	• eem-bah-RAHT-tsoh dee STOH-mah-koh
My . . . hurt(s).	Ho male . . .	oh MAH-leh . . .

94

head	alla testa.	AHL-lah TEH-stah
stomach	allo stomaco.	AHL-loh STOH-mah-koh
neck	al collo.	ahl KOHL-loh
feet	ai piedi.	ahy PYEH-dee
I am allergic to . . .	Sono allergico (-a) . . .	SOH-noh ahl-LEHR-jee-koh(-kah) . . .
penicillin.	alla penicillina.	AHL-lah peh-nee-cheel-LEE-nah
sulfa.	ai sulfamidici.	ahy sool-fah-MEE-dee-chee
certain medicines.	a certe medicine.	ah CHER-teh meh-dee-CHEE-neh
Here's the medicine I take.	Questa è la medicina che prendo.	KWEH-stah eh lah meh-dee-CHEE-nah keh PREHN-doh
I've had this pain for two days.	Sono due giorni che avverto questo disturbo.	SOH-noh DOO-eh JOHR-nee keh ahv-VEHR-toh KWEH-stoh dee-STOOR-boh
I had a heart attack four years ago.	Ho avuto un infarto quattro anni fa.	oh ah-VOO-toh oon een-FAHR-toh KWAHT-troh AHN-nee fah
I am three months pregnant.	Sono incinta di tre mesi.	SOH-noh een-CHEEN-tah dee treh MEH-zee
I have menstrual cramps.	Ho dolori mestruali.	oh doh-LOH-ree meh-stroo-AH-lee

Parts of the Body

ankle (left/right)	la caviglia (sinistra/destra)	lah kah-VEE-lyah (see-NEE-strah/DEH-strah)
appendix	l'appendice	lahp-PEHN-dee-cheh
arm	il braccio	eel BRAHT-choh
artery	l'arteria	lahr-TEH-ryah
back	la schiena	lah SKYEH-nah
bladder	la vescica	lah veh-SHEE-kah

95

bones	le ossa	leh OHS-sah
bowels	l'intestino	leen teh-STFF-noh
breast	il seno	eel SEH-noh
buttocks	le natiche	leh NAH-tee-keh
calf	il polpaccio	eel pohl-PAHT-choh
chest	il petto	eel PEHT-toh
	(or) il torace	eel toh-RAH-cheh
ear	l'orecchio	loh-REHK-kyoh
an eye	un occhio	oon OHK-kyoh
eyes	gli occhi	lyee OHK-kee
face	la faccia	lah FAHT-chah
finger	il dito	eel DEE-toh
foot	il piede	eel PYEH-deh
forehead	la fronte	lah FROHN-teh
glands	le glandole	leh GLAHN-doh-leh
hair	i capelli	ee kah-PEHL-lee
hair (body)	i peli	ee PEH-lee
hand	la mano	lah MAH-noh
head	la testa	lah TEH-stah
heart	il cuore	eel KWOH-reh
hip	l'anca	LAHN-kah
jaw	la mascella	lah mah-SHEHL-lah
joint	l'articolazione	lahr-tee-koh-lah-TSYOH-neh
kidneys	i reni	ee REH-nee
knee	il ginocchio	eel jee-NOHK-kyoh
leg	la gamba	lah GAHM-bah
lip	il labbro	eel LAHB-broh
liver	il fegato	eel FEH-gah-toh
lungs	i polmoni	ee POHL-moh-nee
mouth	la bocca	lah BOHK-kah
muscle	il muscolo	eel MOO-skoh-loh
nail	l'unghia	LOON-gyah
neck	il collo	eel KOHL-loh
nose	il naso	eel NAH-zoh
penis	il pene	eel PEH-neh
ribs	le costole	leh KOH-stoh-leh
shoulder	la spalla	lah SPAHL-lah
skin	la pelle	lah PEHL-leh
spine	la colonna vertebrale	lah koh-LOHN-nah vehr-teh-BRAH-leh

stomach	**lo stomaco**	loh STOH-mah-koh
teeth	**i denti**	ee DEHN-tee
thigh	**la coscia**	lah KOH-shah
throat	**la gola**	lah GOH-lah
thumb	**il pollice**	eel POHL-lee-cheh
toe	**il dito del piede**	eel DEE-toh dehl PYEH-deh
tongue	**la lingua**	lah LEEN-gwah
tonsils	**le tonsille**	leh tohn-SEEL-leh
torso	**il torso**	eel TOHR-soh
vagina	**la vagina**	lah vah-GEE-nah
vein	**la vena**	lah VEH-nah
wrist	**il polso**	eel POHL-soh

What the Doctor Says

Che sintomi ha?	keh SEEN-toh-mee ah?	What symptoms do you have?
Si spogli.	see SPOH-lyee	Get undressed.
Si spogli fino alla cintola	see SPOH-lyee FEE-noh AHL-lah CHEEN-toh-lah	Undress to the waist.
(or) . . . **vita.**	. . . VEE-tah	
Si stenda qui.	see STEHN-dah kwee	Lie down here.
Apra la bocca.	AH-prah lah BOHK-kah	Open your mouth.
Tossisca.	tohs-SEE-skah	Cough.
Respiri profondamente.	reh-SPEE-ree proh-fohn-dah-MEHN-teh	Take a deep breath.
Mi dica dove Le fa male.	mee DEE-kah DOH-veh leh fah MAH-leh	Show me where it hurts.
Faccia vedere la lingua.	FAHT-chah veh-DEH-reh lah LEEN-gwah	Stick out your tongue.
Si vesta.	see VEH-stah	Get dressed.
Da quanto tempo soffre di questi disturbi?	dah KWAHN-toh TEHM-poh SOHF-freh dee KWEH-stee dee-STOOR-bee?	How long have you had these pains?
Le misuro . . .	leh mee-ZOO-roh . . .	I'm going to take . . .
• **la febbre.**	• lah FEHB-breh	• your temperature.

97

• la pressione.	• lah prehs-SYOH-neh	• your blood pressure.
Ho bisogno di un campione di . . .	oh bee-ZOH-nyoh dee oon kahm-PYOH-neh dee . . .	I need a sample of your . . .
• sangue.	• SAHN-gweh	• blood.
• feci.	• FEH-chee	• stools.
• urina.	• oo-REE-nah	• urine.
Le do un . . .	leh doh oon . . .	I'm going to give you . . .
• analgesico.	• ah-nahl-JEH-zee-koh	• a pain killer.
• un calmante.	• oon kahl-MAHN-teh	• a sedative.
(or) un sedativo.	oon seh-dah-TEE-voh	
Deve . . .	DEH-veh . . .	You need . . .
• fare una radiografia.	• FAH-reh OO-nah rah-dyoh-grah-FEE-ah	• an X ray.
• fare un'iniezione.	• FAH-reh oo-nee-nyeh-TSYOH-neh	• an injection.
• andare all'ospedale.	• ahn-DAH-reh ahl-loh-speh-DAH-leh	• to go to the hospital.
• consultare uno specialista.	• kohn-sool-TAH-reh OO-noh speh-chah-LEE-stah	• to see a specialist.
È grave.	eh GRAH-veh	It's grave.
Non è grave.	nohn eh GRAH-veh	It's not serious.
È . . .	eh . . .	It's . . .
• slogato.	• zloh-GAH-toh	• dislocated.
• rotto.	• ROHT-toh	• broken.
• lussato.	• loos-SAH-toh	• sprained.
• infetto.	• een-FEHT-toh	• infected.
Ha . . .	ah . . .	You have . . .
• l'appendicite.	• lahp-pehn-dee-CHEE-teh	• appendicitis.
• una cistite.	• OO-nah chee-STEE-teh	• cystitis.
• una frattura.	• OO-nah fraht-TOO-rah	• a fracture.
• la gastrite.	• lah gah-STREE-teh	• gastritis.
• l'influenza.	• leen-floo-EHN-tsah	• the flu.

• un' intossicazione da cibo.	• oo-neen-tohs-see-kah-TSYOH-neh dah CHEE-boh	• food poisoning.
• il morbillo.	• eel mohr-BEEL-loh	• measels.
• un osso rotto.	• oon OHS-soh ROHT-toh	• a broken bone.
• la polmonite.	• lah pohl-moh-NEE-teh	• pneumonia.
• la scarlattina.	• lah skahr-laht-TEE-nah	• scarlet fever.
• la dissenteria.	• lah dees-sehn-teh-REE-ah	• dysentery.
• una malattia venerea.	• OO-nah mah-laht-TEE-ah veh-NEH-reh-ah	• a venereal disease.

Patient's Questions

Is it serious?	È grave?	eh GRAH-veh?
Is it contagious?	È contagioso?	eh kohn-tah-JOH-zoh?
How long should I stay in bed?	Quanto tempo devo rimanere a letto?	KWAHN-toh TEHM-poh DEH-voh ree-mah-NEH-reh ah LEHT-toh?
What exactly is wrong with me?	Cosa ho esattamente?	KOH-sah oh eh-zaht-tah-MEHN-teh?
How frequently should I take the medication?	Ogni quante ore devo prendere la medicina?	OH-nyee KWAHN-teh OH-reh DEH-voh PREHN-deh-reh lah meh-dee-CHEE-nah?
How many times a day?	Quante volte al giorno?	KWAHN-teh VOHL-teh ahl JOHR-noh?
Do I need to see you again?	Devo ritornare?	DEH-voh ree-TOHR-nah-reh?
Do I need a prescription?	Ho bisogno di una ricetta?	oh bee-ZOH-nyoh dee OO-nah ree-CHEHT-tah?
When can I start traveling again?	Quando posso riprendere il viaggio?	KWAHN-doh POHS-soh ree-PREHN-deh-reh eel VYAHD-joh?

Can you give me a prescription for . . .	Può farmi una ricetta per . . .	pwoh FAHR-mee OO-nah ree-CHEHT-tah pehr . . .
• a painkiller?	• un analgesico?	• oon ah-nahl-JEH-zee-koh?
• • a tranquilizer?	• un tranquillante?	• oon trahn-kweel-LAHN-teh?
Can I have a bill for my insurance?	Mi può fare una ricevuta per la mia assicurazione?	mee pwoh FAH-reh OO-nah ree-cheh-VOO-tah pehr lah MEE-ah ahs-see-koo-rah-TSYOH-neh?
Could you fill out this medical form?	Può compilare questo modulo?	pwoh kohm-pee-LAH-reh KWEH-stoh MOH-doo-loh?

AT THE HOSPITAL

Where is the nearest hospital?	Dov'è l'ospedale più vicino?	doh-VEH loh-speh-DAH-leh pyoo vee-CHEE-noh?
Call an ambulance!	Chiami un'ambulanza!	KYAH-mee oo-nahm-boo-LAHN-tsah!
Help me, please.	Mi aiuti, per favore.	mee ah-YOO-tee pehr fah-VOH-reh
Get me to a hospital!	Mi porti all'ospedale!	mee POHR-tee ahl-loh-speh-DAH-leh!
I need first aid fast!	Ho bisogno del pronto soccorso. È urgente!	oh bee-ZOH-nyoh dehl PROHN-toh sohk-KOHR-soh, eh oor-JEHN-tehl
I was in an accident.	Ho avuto un incidente.	oh ah-VOO-toh oo-neen-chee-DEHN-teh
I cut . . .	Mi sono tagliato (-a) . . .	mee SOH-noh tah-LYAH-toh(-tah) . . .
• my hand.	• la mano.	• lah MAH-noh
• my leg.	• la gamba.	• lah GAHM-bah
• my face.	• la faccia.	• lah FAHT-chah
• my finger.	• il dito.	• eel DEE-toh

100

English	Italian	Pronunciation
• my neck.	• il collo.	• eel KOHL-loh
I can't move.	Non riesco a muovermi.	nohn RYEH-skoh ah MWOH-vehr-mee
He/she hurt his/her head.	Si è fatto(-a) male alla testa.	see eh FAHT-toh(-tah) MAH-leh AHL-lah TEH-stah
His/her ankle is . . .	Ha la caviglia . . .	ah lah kah-VEE-lyah . . .
• broken.	• rotta.	• ROHT-tah
• swollen.	• gonfia.	• GOHN-fyah
• twisted.	• storta.	• STOHR-tah
• dislocated.	• slogata.	• zloh-GAH-tah
He/she is bleeding heavily.	Perde molto sangue.	PEHR-deh MOHL-toh SAHN-gweh
She/he is unconscious.	È priva(-o) di conoscenza.	eh PREE-vah(-voh) dee koh-noh-SHEHN-tsah
He/she has fainted.	È svenuto(-a).	eh zveh-NOO-toh (-tah)
He/she burned himself/herself.	Si è bruciato(-a).	see eh broo-CHAH-toh(-tah)
I got food poisoning.	Ho un'intossi-cazione da cibo.	oh oo-neen-tohs-see-kah-TSYOH-neh dah CHEE-boh
When can I leave?	Quando sarò dimesso?	KWAHN-doh sah-ROH dee-MEHS-soh?
When will the doctor come?	Quando viene il dottore?	KWAHN-doh VYEH-neh eel doht-TOH-reh?
Where's the nurse?	Dov'è l'infermiera?	doh-VEH leen-fehr-MYEH-rah?
What are the visiting hours?	Qual è l'orario di visita?	kwah-LEH loh-RAH-ryoh dee VEE-zee-tah?

THE DENTIST

English	Italian	Pronunciation
I need to see a dentist.	Devo andare dal dentista.	DEH-voh ahn-DAH-reh dahl dehn-TEE-stah
I have a toothache.	Ho mal di denti.	oh mahl dee DEHN-tee

101

It's an emergency.	È un'emergenza.	eh oo-neh-mehr-JEHN-tsah
I'm in a lot of pain.	Mi fa molto male.	mee fah MOHL-toh MAH-leh
My gums are bleeding.	Mi sanguinano le gengive.	mee sahn-GWEE-nah-noh leh jehn-JEE-veh
I've lost a filling.	Mi è venuta via un'otturazione.	mee eh veh-NOO-tah VEE-ah oo-noht-too-rah-TSYOH-neh
I broke a tooth.	Mi si è rotto un dente.	mee see eh ROHT-toh oon DEHN-teh
This tooth hurts.	Mi duole questo dente.	mee DWOH-leh KWEH-stoh DEHN-teh
I don't want to have it extracted.	Non lo voglio togliere.	nohn loh VOH-lyoh TOH-lyeh-reh
Can you fill it . . .	Lo può otturare . . .	loh pwoh oht-too-RAH-reh . . .
• with gold?	• con dell'oro?	• kohn dehl-LOH-roh?
• with silver?	• con dell'argento?	• kohn dehl-lahr-JEHN-toh?
• temporarily?	• provvisoriamente?	• prohv-vee-zoh-ryah-MEHN-teh?
I want a local anesthetic.	Vorrei l'anestesia locale.	vohr-RAY lah-neh-steh-ZEE-ah loh-KAH-leh
My . . . is broken.	Mi si è rotta . . .	mee see eh ROHT-tah
• denture	• la dentiera.	• lah dehn-TYEH-rah
• crown	• la corona.	• lah koh-ROH-nah
My bridge is broken.	Mi si è rotto il ponte.	mee see eh ROHT-toh eel POHN-teh
Can you fix it?	Lo/la può riparare?	loh/lah pwoh ree-pah-RAH-reh?

What the Dentist Says

Ha . . .	ah . . .	You have . . .
• un'infezione.	• oo-neen-feh-TSYOH-neh	• an infection.
• una carie.	• OO-nah KAH-ryeh	• a cavity.
• un ascesso.	• oo-nah-SHEHS-soh	• an abscess.

Le fa male?	leh fah MAH-leh?	Does it hurt?
Bisogna togliere questo dente.	bee-ZOH-nyah TOH-lyeh-reh KWEH-stoh DEHN-teh	This tooth must come out.
Posso ripararLe . . .	POHS-soh ree-pah-RAHR-leh . . .	I can fix . . . for you.
• il ponte.	• eel POHN-teh	• this bridge
• la capsula.	• lah KAHP-soo-lah	• this cap
Ritorni . . .	ree-TOHR-nee . . .	Come back . . .
• domani.	• doh-MAH-nee	• tomorrow.
• fra qualche giorno.	• frah KWAHL-keh JOHR-noh	• in a few days.

THE OPTICIAN

If you wear prescription glasses or contact lenses, it's a good idea to take along both an extra pair and a copy of your prescription in case of loss.

I broke . . .	Ho rotto . . .	oh ROHT-toh . . .
• a lens.	• una lente.	• OO-nah LEHN-teh
• the frame.	• la montatura.	• lah mohn-tah-TOO-rah
I have lost my . . .	Ho perso . . .	oh PEHR-soh . . .
• glasses.	• gli occhiali.	• lyee ohk-KYAH-lee
• a contact lens.	• una lente a contatto.	• OO-nah LEHN-teh ah kohn-TAHT-toh
Can you replace them right away?	È possibile sostituirli subito?	eh pohs-SEE-bee-leh soh-stee-too-EER-lee SOO-bee-toh?
I'd like soft contact lenses.	Vorrei delle lenti a contatto morbide.	vohr-RAY DEHL-leh LEHN-tee ah kohn-TAHT-toh MOHR-bee-deh
Here's the prescription.	Ecco la ricetta.	EHK-koh lah ree-CHEHT-tah
When can I pick them up?	Quando posso venire a ritirarli?	KWAHN-doh POHS-soh veh-NEE-reh ah ree tee-RAHR-lee?
Do you have sunglasses?	Avete occhiali da sole?	ah-VEH-teh ohk-KYAH-lee dah SOH-leh?

103

AT THE PHARMACY

The typical Italian pharmacy is more specialized than its counterpart in the United States, dealing primarily with prescriptions and over-the-counter drugs and other health products. You'll find household goods and toilet articles at the *drogheria* (droh-geh-REE-ah) or the *supermercato* (soo-perhr-mehr-KAH-toh).

Is there . . . near here?	**C'è . . . qui vicino?**	cheh . . . kwee vee-CHEE-noh?
• a pharmacy	• **una farmacia**	• OO-nah fahr-mah-CHEE-ah
• an all-night pharmacy	• **una farmacia di turno**	• OO-nah fahr-mah-CHEE-ah dee TOOR-noh
When does the pharmacy open?	**Quando apre la farmacia?**	KWAHN-doh AH-preh lah fahr-mah-CHEE-ah?
I need something for . . .	**Ho bisogno di qualcosa contro . . .**	oh bee-ZOH-nyoh dee kwahl-KOH-zah KOHN-troh . . .
• an allergy.	• **l'allergia.**	• lahl-lehr-JEE-ah
• a cold.	• **il raffreddore.**	• eel rahf-frehd-DOH-reh
• constipation.	• **la stitichezza.**	• lah stee-tee-KEHT-tsah
• a cough.	• **la tosse.**	• lah TOHS-seh
• diarrhea.	• **la diarrea.**	• lah dyahr-REH-ah
• fever.	• **la febbre.**	• lah FEHB-breh
• hay fever.	• **la febbre da fieno.**	• lah FEHB-breh dah FYEH-noh
• a headache.	• **l'emicrania.**	• leh-mee-KRAH-nyah
• an insect bite.	• **una puntura d'insetto.**	• OO-nah poon-TOO-rah deen-SEHT-toh
• sunburn.	• **una scottatura.**	• OO-nah skoht-tah-TOO-rah
• a burn.	• **una bruciatura.**	• OO-nah broo-chah-TOO-rah
• car sickness.	• **il mal d'auto.**	• eel mahl DOW-toh
• sea sickness.	• **il mal di mare.**	• eel mahl dee MAH-reh
• an upset stomach.	• **il mal di stomaco.**	• eel mahl dee STOH-mah-koh

• indigestion.	• l'indigestione.	• leen-dee-jeh-STYOH-neh
I'd like . . .	Vorrei . . .	vohr-RAY . . .
• an antiseptic.	• un antisettico.	• oo-nahn-tee-SEHT-tee-koh
• some aspirin.	• dell'aspirina.	• dehl-lah-spee-REE-nah
• some band-aids.	• dei cerotti.	• day cheh-ROHT-tee
• some condoms.	• dei preservativi. (or) dei profilattici.	• day preh-zehr-vah-TEE-vee day proh-fee-LAHT-tee-chee
• some contact lens cleaner.	• del detergente per lenti a contatto.	• dehl deh-tehr-JEHN-teh pehr LEHN-tee ah kohn-TAHT-toh
• some solution.	• della soluzione.	• DEHL-la soh-loo-TSYOH-neh
• some contraceptives.	• degli anticoncezionali.	• DEH-lyee ahn-tee-kohn-cheh-tsyoh-NAH-lee
• some cotton.	• del cotone idrofilo.	• dehl koh-TOH-neh ee-DROH-fee-loh
• some cough drops.	• delle pastiglie per la tosse.	• DEHL-leh pah-STEE-lyeh pehr lah TOHS-seh
• a laxative.	• un lassativo.	• oon lahs-sah-TEE-voh
• some mouthwash.	• del collutorio.	• dehl kohl-loo-TOH-ryoh
• some nose drops.	• delle gocce per il naso.	• DEHL-leh GOHT-cheh pehr eel NAH-zoh
• some sanitary napkins.	• degli assorbenti igienici.	• DEH-lyee ahs-sohr-BEHN-tee ee-JEH-nee-chee
• some tampons.	• dei tamponi.	• day tahm-POH-nee.
• a thermometer.	• un termometro.	• oon tehr-MOH-meh-troh
• some vitamins.	• delle vitamine.	• DEHL-leh vee-tah-MEE-neh

105

9/ON THE ROAD

CAR RENTALS

Italy has an excellent, widespread highway system linking all major Italian cities. The most famous is the *Autostrada del Sole* (ow-toh-STRAH-deh dehl SOH-leh), running along the spine of Italy from north to south. Some roadside stops are veritable resort areas, offering restaurants, supermarkets, motels, and cafés.

You may use your valid American driver's license to rent a car in Italy. It's not a bad idea to get an international driver's license, available at a nominal charge from the American Automobile Association in the United States. If you wish to have a car upon arrival, it is best to make arrangements with one of the major car-rental agencies before departing, even though many of the major automobile rental companies have branches in Italy.

Always check the advertised daily rate and type of cars offered and also see if taxes and insurance are included. Also, remember that in Europe, manual transmissions are standard and air-conditioning is rare; rentals with automatic transmissions cost more. Your hotel can also help you rent a car after your arrival, but keep in mind that making arrangements from the United States is usually much cheaper.

DIALOGUE: AT THE CAR-RENTAL AGENCY (*ALL'AUTONOLEGGIO*)

Turista:	**Buon giorno. Vorrei noleggiare una macchina.**	bwohn JOHR-noh. vohr-RAY noh-lehd-JAH-reh OO-nah MAHK-kee-nah
Impiegato:	**L'ha prenotata?**	lah preh-noh-TAH-tah?
Turista:	**Purtroppo no. Comunque, non ne ha una disponibile?**	poor-TROHP-poh noh. koh-MOON-kweh, nohn neh ah OO-nah dee-spoh-NEE-bee-leh?

Impiegato:	**Sì. Ho una FIAT Uno con cambio automatico. Quanto tempo la vuole tenere?**	see. oh OO-nah FEE-aht OO-noh kohn KAHM-byoh ow-toh-MAH-tee-koh. KWAHN-toh TEHM-poh lah voo-OH-leh teh-NEH-reh?
Turista:	**Una settimana.**	OO-nah seht-tee-MAH-nah
Impiegato:	**Benissimo. E il chilometraggio illimitato è incluso nel prezzo.**	beh-NEES-see-moh, eh eel kee-loh-meh-TRAHD-joh eel-lee-mee-TAH-toh eh een-KLOO-zoh nehl PREHT-tsoh
Turista:	**D'accordo. La prendo.**	dahk-KOHR-doh. lah PREHN-doh
Impiegato:	**Bene. Il passaporto e la patente per favore.**	BEH-neh. eel pahs-sah-POHR-toh eh lah pah-TEHN-teh pehr fah-VOH-reh

Tourist:	Hello. I'd like to rent a car.
Clerk:	Do you have a reservation?
Tourist:	Unfortunately I don't. However, do you have one available?
Clerk:	Yes. I have a FIAT Uno with automatic transmission. How long do you want it for?
Tourist:	For a week.
Clerk:	Very well. And unlimited mileage is included in the price.
Tourist:	Perfect. I'll take it.
Clerk:	Very good. Passport and driver's license, please.

Is there a car rental agency nearby?	**C'è un autonoleggio qui vicino?**	cheh oon ow-toh-noh-LEHD-joh kwee vee-CHEE-noh?
I'd like to rent . . .	**Vorrei noleggiare . . .**	vohr-RAY noh-lehd-JAH-reh . . .
• a car.	• **una macchina.**	• OO-nah MAHK-kee-nah

English	Italian	Pronunciation
• a compact car.	• un'utilitaria.	• oo-noo-tee-lee-TAH-ryah
• a midsize car.	• una vettura di media cilindrata.	• OO-nah veht-TOO-rah dee MEH-dyah chee-leen-DRAH-tah
• a sports car.	• una macchina sportiva.	• OO-nah MAHK-kee-nah spohr-TEE-vah
• a car with automatic transmission.	• una macchina col cambio automatico.	• OO-nah MAHK-kee-nah kohl KAHM-byoh ow-toh-MAH-tee-koh
• a station wagon.	• una familiare.	• OO-nah fah-mee-LYAH-reh
• the least expensive car.	• la meno cara.	• lah MEH-noh KAH-rah
Do you have un-limited mileage?	Il chilometraggio è illimitato?	eel kee-loh-meh-TRAHD-joh eh eel-lee-mee-TAH-toh?
I'd like full insurance coverage.	Vorrei fare l'assicurazione contro ogni rischio.	vohr-RAY FAH-reh lahs-see-koo-rah-TSYOH-neh KOHN-troh OH-nyee REE-skyoh
How much is the rate . . .	Qual è la tariffa . . .	kwah-LEH lah tah-REEF-fah . . .
• per day?	• giornaliera?	• johr-nah-LYEH-rah?
• per week?	• settimanale?	• seht-tee-mah-NAH-leh?
• per month?	• mensile?	• mehn-SEE-leh?
• per kilometer?	• per chilometro?	• pehr kee-LOH-meh-troh?
Do you need a deposit?	Devo lasciare un deposito?	DEH-voh lah-SHAH-reh oon deh-POH-zee-toh?
Do you need my driver's license?	Ha bisogno della patente?	ah bee-ZOH-nyoh DEH-lah pah-TEHN-teh?
Can I leave the car in another city?	Posso lasciare la macchina in un'altra città?	POHS-soh lah-SHAH-reh lah MAHK-kee-nah een oo-NAHL-trah cheet-TAH?

THE SERVICE STATION

Where is the nearest service station?	**Dov'è il benzinaio più vicino?**	doh-VEH eel behn-dzee-NAH-yoh pyoo vee-CHEE-noh?
Fill it, please!	**Il pieno, per favore!**	eel PYEH-noh, pehr fah-VOH-reh
Give me twenty liters of . . . gasoline.	**Mi dia venti litri di benzina . . .**	mee DEE-ah VEHN-tee LEE-tree dee behn-DZEE-nah . . .
• regular	• **normale.**	• nohr-MAH-leh
• super	• **super.**	SOO-pehr
• unleaded	• **senza piombo.**	• SEHN-tsah PYOHM-boh
Fill it with . . .	**Metta . . .**	MEHT-tah . . .
• diesel.	• **del gasolio.**	• dehl gah-ZOH-lyoh
• gas/oil mixture. (for mopeds and scooters)	• **della miscela.**	• DEHL-lah mee-SHEH-lah
Give me 50.000 lire of super.	**Metta cinquantamila di super.**	MEHT-tah cheen-kwahn-tah-MEE-lah dee SOO-pehr
Please check . . .	**Per favore, controlli . . .**	pehr fah-VOH-reh, kohn-TROHL-lee . . .
• the battery.	• **la batteria.**	• lah baht-teh-REE-ah
• the brake fluid.	• **l'olio dei freni.**	• LOH-lyoh day FREH-nee
• the carburetor.	• **il carburatore.**	• eel kahr-boo-rah-TOH-reh
• the oil.	• **l'olio.**	• LOH-lyoh
• the spark plugs.	• **le candele.**	• leh kahn-DEH-leh
• the spare tire.	• **la ruota di scorta.**	• lah RWOH-tah dee SKOHR-tah
• the tire pressure.	• **le gomme.**	• leh GOHM-meh
• the water.	• **l'acqua.**	• LAHK-kwah
Change the oil.	**Cambi l'olio.**	KAHM-bee LOH-lyoh

DISTANCES AND LIQUID MEASURES

Distances in Italy, as in most European countries, are expressed in kilometers, *chilometri* (kee-LOH mch tree), and liquid measures (for gas and oil) in liters, *litri* (LEE-tree). Unless you are a whiz at mental calculating, converting one system to another can be hard to get used to. The following conversion formulas and charts should help.

Distance Conversions

1 kilometer (km.) = .62 miles 1 mile = 1.61 km.	
Kilometers	**Miles**
1	0.62
5	3.1
8	5.0
10	6.2
15	9.3
20	12.4
50	31.0
75	46.6
100	62.1

Liquid Measure Conversions

1 liter (l) = .26 gallon 1 gallon = 3.78 liters	
Liters	**Gallons**
10	2.6
15	4.0
20	5.3
30	7.9
40	10.6
50	13.2
60	15.8
70	18.5

DRIVING

Get a map before your departure and prepare your itinerary in advance, allowing for plenty of time to sightsee along the way. Any major tourist office in Italy can provide excellent road maps and may be helpful in advising you on car travel.

The highways have different names, such as *superstrada* (soo-pehr-STRAH-dah) and *autostrada* (ow-toh-STRAH-dah), that appear on the road maps. Your map will also show the local roads. Highways are subject to a toll based on distance traveled and on the type of vehicle. Toll payment is made upon exit: you must present the ticket you picked up when you first got on the highway. It is advisable to carry change to save time. On most highways, a special credit card, VIACARD, may be used, and it may be obtained for amounts up to 50.000 and 90.000 lire at ACI *(Automobile Club Italiano)* and TCI *(Touring Club Italiano)* offices, at main service areas called *Autogrill,* at the administrative offices of *Autostrade,* and at some tobacconist's shops.

Besides carrying the required driving documents, observe the following traffic regulations: (1) always carry a triangular reflector, *triangolo* (tree-AHN-goh-loh), to warn others of danger in case you should stop for some reason; (2) no hitchhiking is allowed on highways; (3) the speed limit is 50 km per hour in town (unless otherwise indicated), 90 km per hour on roads, and from 110 to 130 km per hour on highways.

Remember that Italian traffic sometimes appears to be a chaotic merry-go-round. Not all drivers pay attention to speed limits and infractions are quite common. This is not to say that there is no highway enforcement. Speed is monitored and you can get a ticket, *multa* (MOOL-tah), if you exceed the speed limit or if you run a red light. If you park in a no-parking zone, your car may be towed away, especially if it obstructs traffic. Like every country, Italy has parking problems, and finding a space is quite difficult during certain hours. All major cities have outdoor parking lots *parcheggi* (pahr-KEHD-jee), watched by attendants. They can be easily identified because they are marked by blue signs that have a *P.* The rate depends on how long you park. Aside from these parking lots and meters, *parchimetri* (pahr-KEE-meh-tree), you can park anywhere it's allowed, at no expense, by simply posting a parking disk, *disco orario* (DEE-skoh oh-RAH-ryoh), in your windshield, set to show your arrival time. This time cannot exceed one and a half hours. These disks may be obtained at garages, gas stations, tourist offices, etc. If you do not find your car where you left it, you should call the city police, *Vigili Urbani* (VEE-jee-lee oor-BAH-nee).

Your best bet, to avoid all trouble, would be to leave your car outside the city perimeters and proceed by bus or public transportation. You can always buy tickets in advance at local transportation ticket offices, authorized offices, and tobacco stores.

Excuse me, how do I get to . . . ?	Scusi, come si va a . . . ?	SKOO-zee, KOH-meh see vah ah . . . ?
Is this the road to . . . ?	È questa la strada per . . . ?	eh KWEH-stah lah STRAH-dah pehr . . . ?
How far is it to . . . from here?	Quanto dista . . . da qui?	KWAHN-toh DEE-stah . . . dah kwee?
Is there a . . . road?	C'è una strada . . .	cheh OO-nah STRAH-dah . . .
• better	• migliore?	• mee-LYOH-reh?
• less congested?	• con meno traffico?	• kohn MEH-noh TRAHF-fee-koh?
Is there a shortcut?	C'è una scorciatoia?	cheh OO-nah skohr-chah-TOH-yah?
Where can I get a road map?	Dove posso avere una carta stradale?	DOH-veh POHS-soh ah-VEH-reh OO-nah KAHR-tah strah-DAH-leh?
I think I'm lost.	Penso di essermi perso.	PEHN-soh dee EHS-sehr-mee PEHR-soh.
I think I'm . . .	Credo di aver sbagliato . . .	KREH-doh dee ah-VEHR zbah-LYAH-toh . . .
• on the wrong road.	• strada.	• STRAH-dah
• in the wrong lane.	• corsia.	• kohr-SEE-ah
• at the wrong exit.	• uscita.	• oo-SHEE-tah
We are . . .	Siamo . . .	SYAH-moh . . .
• in the center of town.	• in centro.	• een CHEHN-troh
• in the outskirts.	• in periferia.	• een peh-ree-feh-REE-ah
Are we on the right road?	Siamo sulla strada giusta?	SYAH-moh SOOL-lah STRAH-dah JOO-stah?
How far is . . .	Quanto dista . . .	KWAHN-toh DEE-stah . . .
• the next village?	• il prossimo paese?	• eel PROHS-see-moh pah-EH-zeh?
• the highway?	• l'autostrada?	• low-toh-STRAH-dah?

• the center of town?	• il centro?	• eel CHEHN-troh?
How long does it take by car?	Quanto ci vuole in macchina?	KWAHN-toh chee VOO-oh-leh een MAHK-kee-nah?
Do I go . . .	Devo andare . . .	DEH-voh ahn-DAH-reh . . .
• straight ahead?	• diritto?	• dee-REET-toh?
• to the right?	• a destra?	• ah DEH-strah?
• to the left?	• a sinistra?	• ah see-NEE-strah?
• to the traffic light?	• al semaforo?	• ahl seh-MAH-foh-roh?
• to the next corner?	• al prossimo angolo?	• ahl PROHS-see-moh AHN-goh-loh?
Do I make a U-turn here?	Devo fare inversione di marcia qui?	DEH-voh FAH-reh een-vehr-SYOH-neh dee MAHR-chah kwee?
I want to get to . . .	Voglio andare a . . .	VOH-lyoh ahn-DAH-reh ah . . .
What do I do at the next intersection?	Cosa faccio al prossimo incrocio?	KOH-sah FAHT-choh ahl PROHS-see-moh een-KROH-choh?
Where can I park?	Dove posso parcheggiare?	DOH-veh POHS-soh pahr-kehd-JAH-reh?
Can I park here?	Posso parcheggiare qui?	POHS-soh pahr-kehd-JAH-reh kwee?
Is there a parking lot nearby?	C'è un parcheggio in zona?	cheh oon pahr-KEHD-joh een DZOH-nah?

EMERGENCIES AND CAR PROBLEMS

In case of emergency, the *ACI* (Italian Automobile Club) provides assistance throughout Italy both on highways and roads. If you have car problems while driving on the highway, you can dial 116 on the SOS telephones on yellow poles set at a distance of 2 km apart. If you are not close to one of these phones, wait for the road police.

113

My car won't start.	La macchina non si mette in moto. *(or)* . . . non parte.	lah MAHK-kee-nah nohn see MEHT-teh een MOH-toh . . . nohn PAHR-teh
Something must be wrong.	C'è qualcosa che non funziona/va.	cheh kwahl-KOH-zah keh nohn foon-TSYOH-nah/vah.
I have a flat tire.	Ho una gomma a terra.	oh OO-nah GOHM-mah ah TEHR-rah
I'm out of gas.	Sono senza benzina.	SOH-noh SEHN-tsah behn-DZEE-nah
The battery is dead.	La batteria è scarica.	lah baht-teh-REE-ah eh SKAH-ree-kah
It's overheating.	È surriscaldata.	eh soor-ree-skahl-DAH-tah
I left the keys inside the car.	Ho lasciato le chiavi in macchina.	oh lah-SHAH-toh leh KYAH-vee een MAHK-kee-nah
Can you open the . . .	Può aprire . . .	pwoh ah-PREE-reh . . .
• hood?	• il cofano?	• eel KOH-fah-noh?
• trunk?	• il portabagagli?	• eel pohr-tah-bah-GAH-lyee?
• gas tank?	• il serbatoio?	• eel sehr-bah-TOH-yoh?
Can you change . . .	Può cambiare . . .	pwoh kahm-BYAH-reh . . .
• my battery?	• la batteria?	• lah baht-teh-REE-ah?
• the tire?	• la gomma?	• lah GOHM-mah?
Can you tow the car to a nearby garage?	Può rimorchiare la macchina al garage più vicino?	pwoh ree-mohr-KYAH-reh lah MAHK-kee-nah ahl gah-RAHZH pyoo vee-CHEE-noh?

Car Repairs

| My car has broken down. | Ho la macchina in panne. | oh lah MAHK-kee-nah een PAHN-neh |

114

Can you repair it?	La può riparare?	lah pwoh ree-pah-RAH-reh?
Do you have the part?	Ha il pezzo di ricambio?	ah eel PEHT-tsoh dee ree-KAHM-byoh?
There is something wrong with the . . .	C'è qualcosa che non funziona/va . . .	cheh kwahl-KOH-zah keh nohn foon-TSYOH-nah/vah . . .
• brakes.	• nei freni.	• nay FREH-nee
• clutch.	• nella frizione.	• NEHL-lah free-TSYOH-neh
• motor.	• nel motore.	• nehl moh-TOH-reh
• fuel pump.	• nella pompa di alimentazione.	• NEHL-lah POHM-pah dee ah-lee-mehn-tah-TSYOH-neh
• water pump.	• nella pompa dell'acqua.	• NEHL-lah POHM-pah dehl-LAHK-kwah
I have a problem with the . . .	Ho problemi con . . .	oh proh-BLEH-mee kohn . . .
• directional lights.	• le frecce.	• leh FREHT-cheh
• fan belt.	• la cinghia del ventilatore.	• lah CHEEN-gyah dehl vehn-tee-lah-TOH-reh
• gearshift.	• il cambio.	• eel KAHM-byoh
• headlights/taillights.	• i fari anteriori/posteriori.	• ee FAH-ree ahn-teh-RYOH-ree/poh-steh-RYOH-ree
• high beams.	• gli abbaglianti.	• lyee ahb-bah-LYAHN-tee
• side lights.	• le luci di posizione.	• leh LOO-chee dee poh-zee-TSYOH-neh
• ignition.	• l'accensione.	• laht-chehn-SYOH-neh
• radiator.	• il radiatore.	• eel rah-dyah-TOH-reh
• spark plugs.	• le candele.	• leh kahn-DEH-leh
• starter.	• lo starter.	• loh STAHR-ter
• stop lights.	• le luci di arresto.	• leh LOO-chee dee ahr-REH-stoh

115

• transmission.	• **l'albero di trasmissione.**	• LAHL-beh-roh dee trah-smees-SYOH-neh
• windshield wipers.	• **il tergicristallo.**	• eel tehr-jee-kree-STAHL-loh
Can you repair . . .	**Può riparare . . .**	pwah ree-pah-RAH-reh . . .
• the horn?	• **il clacson?**	• eel KLAHK-sohn?
• the radio?	• **la radio?**	• lah RAH-dyoh?
• the steering wheel?	• **il volante?**	• eel voh-LAHN-teh?
• the door handle?	• **la maniglia?**	• lah mah-NEE-lyah?
• the speedometer?	• **il tachimetro?**	• eel tah-KEE-meh-troh?
How long will it take?	**Quanto ci vorrà?**	KWAHN-toh chee vohr-RAH?
How much will it cost?	**Quanto verrà a costare?**	KWAHN-toh vehr-RAH ah koh-STAH-reh?
I need it today.	**Ne ho bisogno oggi.**	neh oh bee-ZOH-nyoh OHD-jee

ROAD SIGNS

SENSO UNICO	SEHN-soh OO-nee-koh	ONE WAY
STRADA PRINCIPALE	STRAH-dah preen-chee-PAH-leh	MAIN ROAD
PARCHEGGIO	pahr-KEHD-joh	PARKING
SUPERSTRADA	soo-pehr-STRAH-dah	SUPERHIGHWAY
AUTOSTRADA	ow-toh-STRAH-dah	HIGHWAY
DARE LA PRECEDENZA	DAH-reh lah preh-cheh-DEHN-tsah	YIELD
RIFORNIMENTO	ree-fohr-nee-MEHN-toh	GAS STATION
PERICOLO	peh-REE-koh-loh	DANGER AHEAD
DISCESA PERICOLOSA	dee-SHEH-zah peh-ree-koh-LOH-zah	DANGEROUS DESCENT
CUNETTA	koo-NEHT-tah	BUMPS
(OR) DOSSO	DOHS-soh	
STRETTOIA	streht-TOH-yah	ROAD NARROWS
PASSAGGIO A LIVELLO	pahs-SAHD-joh ah lee-VEHL-loh	RAILROAD CROSSING

ZONA DI CIRCOLAZIONE A DOPPIO SENSO SU UNA CARREGGIATA A SENSO UNICO	DZOH-nah dee cheer-coh-lah-TSYOH-neh ah DOHP-pyoh SEHN-soh soo OO-nah kahr-rehd-JAH-tah ah SEHN-soh OO-nee-koh	TWO-WAY TRAFFIC
STRADA SDRUCCIOLEVOLE	STRAH-dah zdroot-choh-LEH-voh-leh	SLIPPERY ROAD
CURVE PERICOLOSE	KOOR-veh peh-ree-koh-LOH-zeh	SHARP CURVES
PASSAGGIO PEDONALE	pahs-SAHD-joh peh-doh-NAH-leh	PEDESTRIAN CROSSING
TRANSITO VIETATO AGLI AUTOVEICOLI	TRAHN-zee-toh vieh-TAH-toh AH-lyee ow-toh-veh-EE-koh-lee	NO ENTRY FOR MOTOR VEHICLES
INCROCIO	een-KROH-choh	DANGEROUS INTERSECTION
STOP	stohp	STOP
(OR) ALT	ahlt	
DIVIETO DI ACCESSO	dee-VYEH-toh dee aht-CHEHS-soh	NO ENTRY
LIMITE MINIMO DI VELOCITÀ	LEE-mee-teh MEE-nee-moh dee veh-loh-chee-TAH	MINIMUM SPEED
LIMITE DI VELOCITÀ	LEE-mee-teh dee veh-loh-chee-TAH	SPEED LIMIT
DIREZIONE OBBLIGATORIA	dee-reh-TSYOH-neh ohb-blee-gah-TOH-ryah	DIRECTION TO BE FOLLOWED
TRAFFICO VIETATO AI VEICOLI DI ALTEZZA SUPERIORE AI M. 3.50	TRAHF-fee-koh vyeh-TAH-toh ahy veh-EE-koh-lee dee ahl-TEHT-tsah soo-peh-RYOH-reh ah MEH-tree treh eh cheen-KWAHN-tah	OVERHEAD CLEARANCE 3.50 M.
ROTATORIA	roh-tah-TOH-ryah	ROTARY
DIVIETO DI SORPASSO	dee-VYEH-toh dee sohr-PAHS-soh	NO PASSING

ONE WAY

MAIN ROAD

PARKING

SUPERHIGHWAY

YIELD

GAS
(10 km ahead)

**DANGER
AHEAD**

**DANGEROUS
DESCENT**

BUMPS

**ROAD
NARROWS**

**LEVEL
(RAILROAD)
CROSSING**

**TWO-WAY
TRAFFIC**

**SLIPPERY
ROAD**

**CAUTION—SHARP
CURVES**

**PEDESTRIAN
CROSSING**

118

NO ENTRY FOR MOTOR VEHICLES

DANGEROUS INTERSECTION AHEAD

STOP

NO ENTRY

MINIMUM SPEED (km/hr)

SPEED LIMIT (km/hr)

DIRECTION TO BE FOLLOWED

OVERHEAD CLEARANCE (meters)

ROTARY

NO PASSING

END OF NO PASSING ZONE

END OF RESTRICTION

NO LEFT TURN

NO U-TURN

NO PARKING

FINE DIVIETO DI SORPASSO	FEE-neh dee-VYEH-toh dee sohr-PAHS-soh	END OF NO PASSING ZONE
FINE DIVIETO	FEE-neh dee-VYEH toh	END OF RESTRICTION
DIVIETO DI SVOLTA A SINISTRA	dee-VYEH-toh dee ZVOHL-tah ah see-NEE-strah	NO LEFT TURN
DIVIETO DI INVERSIONE AD "U"	dee-VYEH-toh dee een-vehr-ZYOH-neh ahd oo	NO U-TURN
SOSTA VIETATA	SOH-stah vyeh-TAH-tah	NO PARKING

Other Signs

PEDAGGIO	peh-DAHD-joh	TOLL
CASELLO	kah-ZEHL-loh	TOLL BOOTH
CORSIA	kohr-SEE-ah	LANE
CORSIA DESTRA	kohr-SEE-ah DEH-strah	RIGHT LANE
CORSIA SINISTRA	kohr-SEE-ah see-NEE-strah	LEFT LANE
LIMITARE LA VELOCITÀ	lee-mee-TAH-reh lah veh-loh-chee-TAH	REDUCE SPEED
USCITA	oo-SHEE-tah	EXIT
LAVORI IN CORSO	lah-VOH-ree een KOHR-soh	ROAD CONSTRUCTION
DIVIETO DI TRANSITO	dee-VYEH-toh dee TRAHN-zee-toh	NO THOROUGHFARE
SOSTA A GIORNI ALTERNI	SOH-stah ah JOHR-nee ahl-TEHR-nee	PARKING PERMITTED ALTERNATE DAYS
VICOLO CIECO	VEE-koh-loh CHEH-koh	NO THROUGH WAY
DIVIETO DI SEGNALAZIONI ACUSTICHE	dee-VYEH-toh dee seh-nyah-lah-TSYOH-nee ah-KOO-stee-keh	NO HONKING

120

10/COMMUNICATIONS

DIALOGUE: ON THE TELEPHONE (*AL TELEFONO*)

Sig.ra Rossi:	**Pronto?**	PROHN-toh?
Marco:	**Pronto. Sono Marco. Vorrei parlare con Angela, per favore.**	PROHN-toh. SOH-noh MAHR-koh. vohr-RAY pahr-LAH-reh kohn AHN-jeh-lah, pehr fah-VOH-reh
Sig.ra Rossi:	**Rimanga in linea . . . Mi dispiace ma è uscita.**	ree-MAHN-gah een LEE-neh-ah . . . mee dee-SPYAH-cheh mah eh oo-SHEE-tah
Marco:	**Sa quando rientra?**	sah KWAHN-doh ree-EHN-trah?
Sig.ra Rossi:	**Questa sera, verso le otto.**	KWEH-stah SEH-rah, VEHR-soh leh OHT-toh
Marco:	**Posso lasciare un messaggio?**	POHS-soh lah-SHAH-reh oon mehs-SAHD-joh?
Sig.ra Rossi:	**Certo, mi dica.**	CHER-toh, mee DEE-kah
Marco:	**Può dirle di richiamarmi appena rientra. È urgente.**	pwoh DEER-leh dee ree-kyah-MAHR-mee ahp-PEH-nah ree-EHN-trah. eh oor-JEHN-teh
Sig.ra Rossi.	**Sicuramente, riferirò.**	see-koo-rah-MEHN-teh. ree-feh-ree-ROH
Marco:	**Grazie. ArrivederLa.**	GRAH-tsyeh. ahr-ree-veh-DEHR-lah

. . . .

Mrs. Rossi:	Hello?
Marco:	Hello. This is Marco. I would like to speak with Angela, please.

Mrs. Rossi:	Hold the line . . . I'm sorry, but she went out.
Marco:	Do you know when she'll be back?
Mrs. Rossi:	This evening around eight o'clock.
Marco:	Can I leave a message?
Mrs. Rossi:	Certainly.
Marco:	Please tell her to call me as soon as she comes back. It's urgent.
Mrs. Rossi:	Very well. I'll give her the message.
Marco:	Thank you. Good-bye.

TELEPHONES

Pay phones are found in most public places. To make a call you need either a token, *un gettone* (oon jeht-TOH-neh), or 100 and 200 lire coins. You may purchase tokens at tobacco stores. Recently the phone company, especially in the larger cities, has added new units with which, instead of using tokens or coins, you insert a plastic card, *la carta telefonica* (lah KAHR-tah teh-leh-FOH-nee-kah) or *tessera S.I.P.* (TEHS-seh-rah seep), to place a call. You can buy these cards either at the *S.I.P. (Società Italiana per l'Esercizio delle Telecommunicazioni)*, the Italian telephone company, or at tobacco stores or other points of sale. After inserting the card, a digital readout tells you how many lire are left on your card to be used to place more calls. The value of these cards is 5.000 or 10.000 lire.

You can use public phones for local and long-distance calls, but for international calls you need to go to a special telephone company location, *i telefoni di stato* (ee teh-LEH-foh-nee dee STAH-toh). It makes sense to call collect or to use a telephone credit card for international calls, if possible. Remember that hotels usually add a surcharge to these calls. To place a direct call to the United States or Canada, dial 001 + area code + number. If you are calling collect, dial 170 and ask for an operator to assist you. For general information in English, dial 176.

Is there a . . .	C'è . . .	cheh . . .
• public telephone?	• un telefono pubblico?	• oon teh-LEH-foh-noh POOB-blee-koh?

122

English	Italian	Pronunciation
• telephone booth?	• una cabina telefonica?	• OO-nah kah-BEE-nah teh-leh-FOH-nee-kah?
Are tokens needed?	C'è bisogno di gettoni?	cheh bee-ZOH-nyoh dee jeht-TOH-nee?
I would like some tokens.	Vorrei dei gettoni.	vohr-RAY day jeht-TOH-nee
Do you have a phone directory?	Ha un elenco telefonico?	ah oo-neh-LEHN-koh teh-leh-FOH-nee-koh?
Operator . . .	Centralinista . . .	chen-trah-lee-NEE-stah . . .
I'd like to call . . .	Vorrei chiamare . . .	vohr-RAY kyah-MAH-reh . . .
• this number.	• questo numero.	• KWEH-stoh NOO-meh-roh
• information.	• il servizio informazioni.	• eel sehr-VEE-tsyoh een-fohr-mah-TSYOH-nee
• the international operator.	• l'operatore internazionale.	• loh peh-rah-TOH-reh een-tehr-nah-tsyoh-NAH-leh
I'd like to use my credit card.	Vorrei usare la mia carta di credito.	vohr-RAY oo-ZAH-reh lah MEE-ah KAHR-tah dee KREH-dee-toh
I'd like to make . . .	Vorrei fare una telefonata . . .	vohr-RAY FAH-reh OO-nah teh-leh-foh-NAH-tah . . .
• a collect call.	• a carico del destinatario.	• ah KAH-ree-koh dehl deh-stee-nah-TAH-ryoh
• a local call.	• urbana.	• oor-BAH-nah
• a long-distance call.	• interurbana.	• een-teh-roor-BAH-nah
• an overseas call.	• internazionale.	• een-tehr-nah-tsyoh-NAH-leh
• a person-to-person call.	• con preavviso.	• kohn preh-ahv-VEE-zoh
What is the area code for . . . ?	Qual è il prefisso per . . . ?	kwah-LEH eel preh-FEES-soh pehr . . . ?

123

What the Caller Says

Hello!	**Pronto!**	PROHN-toh!
This is . . .	**Sono . . .**	SOH-noh . . .
• Mr. . . .	• **il signor . . .**	• eel see-NYOHR . . .
• Mrs. . . .	• **la signora . . .**	• lah see-NYOH-rah . . .
• Miss/Ms. . . .	• **la signorina . . .**	• lah see-nyoh-REE-nah . . .
To whom am I speaking?	**Con chi parlo?**	kohn kee PAHR-loh?
May I speak to . . . ?	**Posso parlare con . . . ?**	POHS-soh pahr-LAH-reh kohn . . . ?
Speak more slowly, please.	**Parli più adagio, per favore.**	PAHR-lee pyoo ah-DAH-joh, pehr fah-VOH-reh
Can you repeat?	**Può ripetere?**	pwoh ree-PEH-teh-reh?
I can't hear very well.	**Non La sento bene.**	nohn lah SEHN-toh BEH-neh
Speak louder, please.	**Parli più forte, per favore.**	PAHR-lee pyoo FOHR-teh, pehr fah-VOH-reh
It's a bad connection.	**La linea è disturbata.**	lah LEE-neh-ah eh dee-stoor-BAH-tah
I was cut off.	**È caduta la linea.**	eh kah-DOO-tah lah LEE-neh-ah
I'd like to leave a message.	**Vorrei lasciare un messaggio.**	vohr-RAY lah-SHAH-reh oon mehs-SAHD-joh
Please tell him/her to call me back at this number . . .	**Per favore, gli/le dica di richiamarmi a questo numero . . .**	pehr fah-VOH-reh, lyee/leh DEE-kah dee ree-kyah-MAHR-mee ah KWEH-stoh NOO-meh-roh . . .

What the Operator Says

Chi parla?	kee PAHR-lah?	Who's calling?
Rimanga in linea.	ree-MAHN-gah een LEE-neh-ah	Hold the line.

124

Non risponde nessuno.	nohn ree-SPOHN-deh nehs-SOO-noh	They don't answer.
La linea è occupata.	lah LEE-neh-ah eh ohk-koo-PAH-tah	The line is busy.
Ha sbagliato numero.	ah zbah-LYAH-toh NOO-meh-roh	You got a wrong number.
Desidera lasciare un messaggio?	deh-ZEE-deh-rah lah-SHAH-reh oon mehs-SAHD-joh?	Do you wish to leave a message?
Ripeta, per favore.	ree-PEH-tah, pehr fah-VOH-reh	Please repeat.
Può chiamare più tardi?	pwoh kyah-MAH-reh pyoo TAHR-dee?	Can you call later?
Con chi desidera parlare?	kohn kee deh-ZEE-deh-rah pahr-LAH-reh?	Who do you want to speak with?
Un momento, per favore.	oon moh-MEHN-toh, pehr fah-VOH-reh	One moment, please.
Non riattacchi.	nohn ryaht-TAHK-kee	Don't hang up.
La vogliono al telefono.	lah VOH-lyoh-noh ahl teh-LEH-foh-noh	You have a call.
C'è una chiamata per Lei.	cheh OO-nah kyah-MAH-tah pehr lay	There is a telephone call for you.
Si è interrotta la comunicazione.	see eh een-tehr-ROHT-tah lah koh-moo-nee-kah-TSYOH-neh	Your call was disconnected.
Desidera che continui a provare?	deh-ZEE-deh-rah keh kohn-TEE-nwee ah proh-VAH-reh?	Do you want me to keep trying?
Il telefono non funziona.	eel teh-LEH-foh-noh nohn foon-TSYOH-nah	The telephone is out of order.

THE POST OFFICE

Mail from Italy to the United States may take one to two weeks. Stamps may be purchased at post offices or tobacco stores, *dal tabaccaio* (dahl tah-bahk-KAH-yoh). Post offices bear the *PT* sign and are usually open 8:00 A.M. to 2:00 P.M. Monday through

125

Friday, 8:30 A.M. until noon on Saturday. The main post office operates 8:00 A.M. to 8:00 or 9:00 P.M. Mailboxes can also be found outside tobacco stores and are painted in red.

I'm looking for the post office.	**Cerco un ufficio postale.**	CHER-koh oon oof-FEE-choh poh-STAH-leh
I'd like to mail . . .	**Vorrei spedire . . .**	vohr-RAY speh-DEE-reh . . .
• a letter	• **una lettera.**	• OO-nah LEHT-teh-rah
• a postcard.	• **una cartolina.**	• OO-nah kahr-toh-LEE-nah
• a registered letter.	• **una raccomandata.**	• OO-nah rahk-koh-mahn-DAH-tah
• a special delivery letter.	• **una lettera espresso.**	• OO-nah LEHT-teh-rah eh-SPREHS-soh
• a certified letter.	• **una raccomandata A.R. (con avviso di ricevuta).**	• OO-nah rahk-koh-mahn-DAH-tah ah EHR-reh (kohn ahv-VEE-zoh dee ree-cheh-VOO-tah)
• a package.	• **un pacco.**	• oon PAHK-koh
How many stamps do I need for . . .	**Quanti francobolli occorrono per . . .**	KWAHN-tee frahn-koh-BOHL-lee ohk-KOHR-roh-noh pehr . . .
• surface mail?	• **posta normale?**	• POH-stah nohr-MAH-leh?
• airmail?	• **posta aerea?**	• POH-stah ah-EH-reh-ah?
• a letter to the United States?	• **una lettera per gli Stati Uniti?**	• OO-nah LEHT-teh-rah pehr lyee STAH-tee oo-NEE-tee?
• a postcard?	• **una cartolina?**	• OO-nah kahr-toh-LEE-nah . . . ?
• five postcards?	• **cinque cartoline?**	• CHEEN-kweh kahr-toh-LEE-neh?
Which window is it for . . .	**Dov'è lo sportello . . .**	doh-VEH loh spohr-TEHL-loh . . .
• general delivery?	• **del fermo posta?**	• dehl FEHR-moh POH-stah?

• money orders?	• dei vaglia postali?	• day VAH-lyah poh-STAH-lee?
• stamps?	• dei francobolli?	• day frahn-koh-BOHL-lee?
Is there mail for me?	C'è posta per me?	cheh POH-stah pehr meh?
I'd also like to buy . . .	Vorrei anche comprare . . .	vohr-RAY AHN-keh kohm-PRAH-reh . . .
• airmail paper and envelopes.	• fogli e buste per posta aerea.	• FOH-lyee eh BOO-steh pehr POH-stah ah-EH-reh-ah.
• aerograms.	• aerogrammi.	• ah-eh-ro-GRAHM-mee
• a collection of stamps.	• una collezione di francobolli.	• OO-nah kohl-leh-TSYOH-neh dee frahn-koh-BOHL-lee
Where is . . .	Dov'è . . .	doh-VEH . . .
• the mailbox?	• la cassetta della posta . . . (or) la buca?	• lah kahs-SEHT-tah DEHL-lah POH-stah . . . lah BOO-kah?
• the stamp machine?	• il distributore di francobolli?	• eel dee-stree-boo-TOH-reh dee frahn-koh-BOHL-lee?

TELEGRAMS

There is usually a window at the post office for sending tele-grams. Some hotels conveniently provide telegram service as well. *ITALCABLE* transmits telegrams abroad; both domestic and international telegrams can be dictated over the phone.

Which window is it for telegrams?	Qual è lo sportello per i telegrammi?	kwah-LEH loh spohr-TEHL-loh pehr ee teh-leh-GRAHM-mee?
I would like to send a telegram.	Vorrei mandare un telegramma.	vohr-RAY mahn-DAH-reh oon teh-leh-GRAHM-mah
How much is it per word?	Quanto costa a parola?	KWAHN-toh KOH-stah ah pah-ROH-lah?

127

| Could you give me a telegram form? | **Mi può dare un modulo?** | mee pwoh DAH-reh oon MOH-doo-loh? |
| I'd like to wire some money. | **Vorrei inviare del denaro.** | vohr-RAY een-V'YAH-reh dehl deh-NAH-roh |

THE MEDIA

Books and Newspapers

Libri e Giornali

LEE-bree eh johr-NAH-lee

Do you have . . . in English?	**Ha . . . in inglese?**	ah . . . een een-GLEH-zeh?
• newspapers	• **giornali**	• johr-NAH-lee
• magazines	• **riviste**	• ree-VEE-steh
• books	• **libri**	• LEE-bree
• any publications	• **pubblicazioni**	• poob-blee-kah-TSYOH-nee

Radio and Television

Radio e Televisione

RAH-dyoh eh teh-leh-vee-ZYOH-neh

Is there . . . station?	**C'è una stazione . . .**	cheh OO-nah stah-TSYOH-neh . . .
• an English-language	• **in inglese?**	• een een-GLEH-zeh?
• a music	• **che trasmette musica?**	• keh trah-SMEHT-teh MOO-zee-kah?
• a news	• **che trasmette notizie?**	• keh trah-SMEHT-teh noh-TEE-tsyeh?
• a weather	• **che trasmette le previsioni del tempo?**	• keh trah-SMEHT-teh leh preh-vee-ZYOH-nee dehl TEHM-poh?
What number is it on the dial?	**Su che programma è?**	soo keh proh-GRAHM-mah eh?
What TV channel is it on?	**Su che canale è?**	soo keh kah-NAH-leh eh?
What time is the program?	**A che ora comincia la trasmissione?**	ah keh OH-rah koh-MEEN-chah lah trah-smees-SYOH-neh?

COMMUNICATIONS

128

11/SIGHT-SEEING

Before your trip, you should read something about Italy. In addition to guidebooks, your travel agent or national tourist offices can provide information that will help you plan a sight-seeing itinerary. Ask at your hotel for a guide to the city and activities of the week.

DIALOGUE: TOURING THE CITY (*IN GIRO PER LA CITTÀ*)

Turista:	**Quali posti mi consiglia di visitare?**	KWAH-lee POH-stee mee kohn-SEE-lyah dee vee-zee-TAH-reh?
Impiegato:	**Ci sono molte cose interessanti da vedere.**	chee SOH-noh MOHL-teh KOH-seh een-teh-rehs-SAHN-tee dah veh-DEH-reh
Turista:	**È lontano il centro storico?**	eh lohn-TAH-noh eel CHEHN-troh STOH-ree-koh?
Impiegato:	**No. Può prendere l'autobus qui all'angolo. Porta direttamente in centro.**	noh. pwoh PREHN-deh-reh LOW-toh-boos kwee ahl-LAHN-goh-loh. POHR-tah dee-reht-tah-MEHN-teh een CHEHN-troh
Turista:	**Ci sono molti monumenti antichi?**	chee SOH-noh MOHL-tee moh-noo-MEHN-tee ahn-TEE-kee?
Impiegato:	**Sì. Chiese, palazzi, gallerie, e c'è anche il Museo Archeologico.**	see. KYEH-zeh, pah-LAHT-tsee, gahl-leh-REE-eh, eh cheh AHN-keh eel moo-ZEH-oh ahr-keh-oh-LOH-jee-coh

129

Turista:	**Grazie delle informazioni.**	GRAH-tsyeh DEHL-leh een fohr-mah-TSYOH-nee

Tourist:	What places do you recommend visiting?
Hotel clerk:	There are many interesting things to see.
Tourist:	Is the historic district far from here?
Hotel clerk:	No. You can take a bus just at the corner. It goes right to the historic district.
Tourist:	Are there many ancient monuments?
Hotel clerk:	Yes. Churches, palaces, galleries, and you can also find the Archaeological Museum.
Tourist:	Thanks for the information.

FINDING THE SIGHTS

Where is the tourist office?	**Dov'è l'ufficio turistico?**	doh-VEH loof-FEE-choh too-REE-stee-koh?
Can you suggest . . .	**Può raccomandarmi . . .**	pwoh rahk-koh-mahn-DAHR-mee . . .
• a guided tour?	• **un giro organizzato?**	• oon JEE-roh ohr-gah-need-DZAH-toh
• an excursion?	• **una gita?**	• OO-nah JEE-tah?
Are there English-speaking guides?	**Ci sono guide che parlano inglese?**	chee SOH-noh GWEE-deh keh PAHR-lah-noh een-GLEH-zeh?
We would like a tour guide . . .	**Vorremmo una guida . . .**	vohr-REHM-moh OO-nah GWEE-dah . . .
• for a day.	• **per una giornata.**	• pehr OO-nah johr-NAH-tah
• for an afternoon.	• **per un pomeriggio.**	• pehr oon poh-meh-REED-joh
When does the tour begin?	**Quando comincia il giro?**	KWAHN-doh koh-MEEN-chah eel JEE-roh?
How long does the excursion take?	**Quanto dura la gita?**	KWAHN-toh DOO-rah lah JEE-tah?

English	Italian	Pronunciation
Is breakfast/lunch included?	**La colazione/il pranzo è compresa(-o)?**	lah koh-lah-TSYOH-neh/eel PRAHN-dzoh eh kohm-PREH-zah (-zoh)?
How much is the excursion, everything included?	**Quanto costa la gita, tutto compreso?**	KWAHN-toh KOH-stah lah JEE-tah, TOOT-toh kohm-PREH-zoh?
Do you tip the guide?	**Si lascia la mancia alla guida?**	see LAH-shah lah MAHN-chah AHL-lah GWEE-dah?
Where does the tour begin?	**Da dove comincia il giro?**	dah DOH-veh koh-MEEN-chah eel JEE-roh?
When do we return to the hotel?	**A che ora si ritorna in albergo?**	ah keh OH-rah see ree-TOHR-nah een ahl-BEHR-goh?
I'd like to see the . . .	**Vorrei vedere . . .**	vohr-RAY veh-DEH-reh
• abbey	• **l'abbazia.**	• lahb-bah-TSEE-ah
• art gallery.	• **la galleria d'arte.**	• lah gahl-leh-REE-ah DAHR-teh
• botanical gardens.	• **il giardino botanico.**	• ee jahr-DEE-noh boh-TAH-nee-koh
• business district.	• **il quartiere degli affari.**	• eel kwahr-TYEH-reh DEH-lyee ahf-FAH-ree
• castle.	• **il castello.**	• eel kah-STEHL-loh
• catacombs.	• **le catacombe.**	• leh kah-tah-KOHM-beh
• cathedral.	• **la cattedrale.**	• lah kaht-teh-DRAH-leh
• caves.	• **le grotte.**	• leh GROHT-teh
• cemetery.	• **il cimitero.**	• eel chee-mee-TEH-roh
• central square.	• **la piazza principale.**	• lah PYAHT-tsah preen-chee-PAH-leh
• chapel.	• **la cappella.**	• lah kahp-PEHL-lah
• church.	• **la chiesa.**	• lah KYEH-zah
• cloister.	• **il chiostro.**	• eel KYOH-stroh
• convent.	• **il convento.**	• eel kohn-VEHN-toh

131

• downtown.	• il centro città.	• eel CHEHN-troh cheet-TAH
• flea market.	• il mercato delle pulci.	• eel mehr-KAH-toh DEHL-leh POOL-chee
• fortress.	• la fortezza.	• lah fohr-TEHT-tsah
• fountains.	• le fontane.	• leh fohn-TAH-neh
• government headquarters.	• il palazzo comunale.	• eel pah-LAHT-tsoh koh-moo-NAH-leh
• harbor.	• il porto.	• eel POHR-toh
• historic sites.	• i luoghi storici.	• ee LWOH-ghee STOH-ree-chee
• library.	• la biblioteca.	• lah bee-blyoh-TEH-kah
• market.	• il mercato.	• eel mehr-KAH-toh
• monastery.	• il monastero.	• eel moh-nah-STEH-roh
• monuments.	• i monumenti.	• ee moh-noo-MEHN-tee
• museum . . . of art. of modern art.	• il museo . . . d'arte. d'arte moderna.	• eel moo-ZEH-oh . . . DAHR-teh DAHR-teh moh-DEHR-nah
of natural sciences.	di scienze naturali.	dee SHEHN-tseh nah-too-RAH-lee
• old city.	• la città vecchia.	• lah cheet-TAH VEHK-kyah
• opera house.	• il teatro dell'opera.	• eel teh-AH-troh dehl-LOH-peh-rah
• park.	• il parco.	• eel PAHR-koh
• public gardens.	• i giardini pubblici.	• ee jahr-DEE-nee POOB-blee-chee
• royal palace.	• il palazzo reale.	• eel pah-LAHT-tsoh reh-AH-leh
• ruins	• le rovine.	• leh roh-VEE-neh
• shopping district.	• il centro commerciale.	• eel CHEHN-troh kohm-mehr-CHAH-leh
• square.	• la piazza.	• lah PYAHT-tsah
• stadium.	• lo stadio.	• loh STAH-dyoh
• statue of . . .	• la statua di . . .	• lah STAH-twah dee . . .

• synagogue.	• la sinagoga.	• lah see-nah-GOH-gah
• theatre.	• il teatro.	• eel teh-AH-troh
• tomb of . . .	• la tomba di . . .	• lah TOHM-bah dee . . .
• tower.	• la torre.	• lah TOHR-reh
• university.	• l'università.	• loo-nee-vehr-see-TAH
• zoo.	• lo zoo.	• loh DZOH-oh
Would you take our picture?	Ci fa una foto?	chee fah OO-nah FOH-toh?
One more shot!	Ancora una!	ahn-KOH-rah OO-nah!
Smile!	Sorridete!	soh-ree-DEH-teh!

AT THE MUSEUM

Practically every Italian city has museums and art galleries. Opening times may vary from place to place, but generally their hours are from 9:30 A.M. to 4:00 P.M. on weekdays, 9:30 A.M. to 1:00 P.M. on Sundays and holidays. They are usually closed on Mondays.

When does the museum open/close?	Quando apre/chiude il museo?	KWAHN-doh AH-preh/KYOO-deh eel moo-ZEH-oh?
Is it open on Sundays?	È aperto la domenica?	eh ah-PEHR-toh lah doh-MEH-nee-kah?
How much is the admission?	Quanto costa l' ingrèsso?	KWAHN-toh KOH-stah leen-GREHS-soh?
Can I take pictures?	Si possono fare fotografie?	see POHS-soh-noh FAH-reh foh-toh-grah-FEE-eh?
I'm interested in . . .	Mi interesso di . . .	mee een-teh-REHS-soh dee . . .
• antiques.	• antichità.	• ahn-tee-kee-TAH
• anthropology.	• antropologia.	• ahn-troh-poh-loh-JEE-ah
• archaeology.	• archeologia.	• ahr-keh-oh-loh-JEE-ah

133

. . . art.	• arte . . .	• AHR-teh . . .
classical	classica.	KLAHS-see-kah
medieval	medievale.	meh-dyeh-VAH-leh
modern	moderna.	moh-DEHR-nah
Renaissance	rinascimentale.	ree-nah-shee-mehn-TAH-leh
• natural history.	• storia naturale.	• STOH-ryah nah-too-RAH-leh
• painting.	• pittura.	• peet-TOO-rah
• sculpture.	• scultura.	• skool-TOO-rah

IN THE OLD PART OF TOWN

How many churches are there?	Quante chiese ci sono?	KWAHN-teh KYEH-zeh chee SOH-noh?
Is that church old?	È antica quella chiesa?	eh ahn-TEE-kah KWEHL-lah KYEH-zah?
What religion is it?	Di che culto è?	dee keh COOL-toh eh?
Are there many monuments nearby?	Ci sono molti monumenti qui vicino?	chee SOH-noh MOHL-tee moh-noo-MEHN-tee kwee vee-CHEE-noh?
What does that commemorate?	Che cosa commemora?	keh KOH-zah kohm-MEH-moh-rah?
Whose statue is that?	Di chi è quella statua?	dee kee eh KWEHL-lah STAH-twah?
Who was he/she?	Chi è?	kee eh?

IN THE COUNTRY

Where are the most beautiful landscapes?	Dove si ammirano i paesaggi più belli?	DOH-veh see ahm-MEE-rah-noh ee pah-eh-SAHD-jee pyoo BEHL-lee?
Is there a scenic route to . . . ?	C'è una strada panoramica che porta a . . . ?	cheh OO-nah STRAH-dah pah-noh-RAH-mee-kah keh POHR-tah ah . . . ?
How far is it?	Quanto dista?	KWAHN-to DEE-stah?

English	Italian	Pronunciation
Is there any place to eat there?	C'è un posto per mangiare?	cheh oon POH-stoh pehr mahn-JAH-reh?
Are there restrooms?	Ci sono le toelette?	chee SOH-noh leh toh-eh-LEHT-teh?
I like . . .	Mi piacciono . . .	mee PYAHT-choh-noh . . .
• birds.	• gli uccelli.	• lyee oot-CHEHL-lee
• cliffs.	• le scogliere.	• leh skoh-LYEH-reh
• fields.	• i campi.	• ee KAHM-pee
• flowers.	• i fiori.	• ee FYOH-ree
• forests.	• le foreste.	• leh foh-REH-steh
• heights.	• le cime.	• leh CHEE-meh
• hills.	• le colline.	• leh kohl-LEE-neh
• meadows.	• i prati.	• ee PRAH-tee
• mountains.	• le montagne.	• leh mohn-TAH-nyeh
• peaks.	• i picchi.	• ee PEEK-kee
• plants.	• le piante.	• leh PYAHN-teh
• waterfalls.	• le cascate.	• leh kah-SKAH-teh
• woods.	• i boschi.	• ee BOH-skee
I also like . . .	Mi piacciono anche . . .	mee PYAHT-choh-noh AHN-keh . . .
• cottages.	• i cottage.	• ee KOHT-tehdj
• farms.	• le fattorie.	• leh faht-toh-REE-eh
• country houses.	• le case di campagna.	• leh KAH-zeh dee kahm-PAH-nyah
• inns.	• le locande.	• leh loh-KAHN-deh
• villages.	• i villaggi.	• ee veel-LAHD-jee
• vineyards.	• le vigne.	• leh VEE-nyeh
Look! There's a . . .	Guarda! C'è . . .	GWAHR-dah! cheh . . .
• beach.	• una spiaggia.	• OO-nah SPYAHD-jah
• bridge.	• un ponte.	• oon POHN-teh
• castle.	• un castello.	• oon kah-STEHL-loh
• farmhouse.	• una casa colonica.	• OO-nah KAH-zah koh-LOH-nee-kah
• lake.	• un lago.	• oon LAH-goh
• pond.	• uno stagno.	• OO-noh STAH-nyoh
• river.	• un fiume.	• oon FYOO-meh
The view is . . .	Il panorama è . . .	eel pah-noh-RAH-mah eh . . .

• breathtaking.	• **incantevole.**	• een-kahn-TEH-voh-leh
• magnificent.	• **magnifico.**	• mah-NYEE-fee-koh

RELIGIOUS SERVICES

Because Italy is a Roman Catholic country, churches and cathedrals abound. Most of the great cathedrals on the traveler's circuit are also fully functioning and can be thoroughly appreciated by attending one of the regular masses or a religious service. Remember that you have to dress properly or else you will be refused entrance. No shorts, tank tops, or strapless dresses are allowed. Protestant churches and synagogues can be located by looking in the yellow pages, *le pagine gialle* (leh PAH-jee-neh JAHL-leh).

I'd like to visit . . .	**Vorrei visitare . . .**	vohr-RAY vee-zee-TAH-reh . . .
• a Catholic church.	• **una chiesa cattolica.**	• OO-nah KYEH-zah kaht-TOH-lee-kah
• a mosque.	• **una moschea.**	• OO-nah moh-SKEH-ah
• a Protestant church.	• **una chiesa protestante.**	• OO-nah KYEH-zah proh-teh-STAHN-teh
• a synagogue.	• **una sinagoga.**	• OO-nah see-nah-GOH-gah
When does the . . . begin?	**Quando cominicia . . .**	KWAHN-doh koh-MEEN-chah . . .
• mass	• **la messa?**	• lah MEHS-sah?
• service	• **la funzione?**	• lah foon-TSYOH-neh?
I'm looking for an English-speaking . . .	**Cerco un . . . che parli inglese.**	CHEHR-koh oon . . . keh PAHR-lee een-GLEH-seh
• minister.	• **ministro**	• mee-NEE-stroh
• priest.	• **prete**	• PREH-teh
• rabbi.	• **rabbino**	• rahb-BEE-noh

12/SHOPPING

Italy is a shopper's paradise. The variety and quality of Italian goods are exceptional. Leather and silk are traditional good buys, and are somewhat less expensive than the same articles in the United States. Among the better-known designers, try Ferragamo and Gucci for leather goods, shoes, and scarves; Bruno Magli for shoes; Fendi for furs and accessories. For both haute couture collections, *alta moda* (AHL-tah MOH-dah), and ready-to-wear apparel, look for Armani, Versace, Ferrè, and Valentino sold in boutiques. More basic apparel and household goods may be found in department stores, *grandi magazzini* (GRAHN-dee mah-gahd-ZEE-nee).

Milan's Via Montenapoleone, Via de' Tornabuoni in Florence, Rome's Via Condotti, and Piazza San Marco in Venice offer the finest shopping in general, but many other cities have specialties that interest tourists. Each region features fine craft products that can be purchased from the local artisan's shops, *botteghe* (boht-TEH-geh). Venice is renowned for its glassware from Murano and fine laces from Burano. Look for gold, leather, and straw-ware in Florence. Naples is known for its handcrafted mother-of-pearl and coral objects. For richly decorated ceramics, majolica, and pottery, the city of Faenza in Romagna is world famous, but you can also find them in the regions of Umbria, Marches, Liguria, and Tuscany.

Business hours may vary from one region to another. In general, stores are open from 9:00–9:30 A.M. to 12:30–1:00 P.M. and from 3:30–4:00 P.M. to 7:30–8:00 P.M., although in tourist areas some stores stay open all day long. Shops are closed on Sundays, as well as a half-day during the week, usually Monday mornings or Wednesday, Thursday, or Saturday afternoons.

Prices are fixed at all stores *negozi* (neh-GOH-tsee), although small shops and handicraft establishments may give a discount if you make a sizable purchase. Look for the big sales in August and after Christmas, when you'll see signs in the windows proclaiming *saldi* (SAHL-dee), *sconti* (SKOHN-tee), *occasioni* (ohk-kah-SYOH nee), *liquidazione* (lee-kwee-dah-TSYOH-neh), or *ven-dita promozionale* (VEHN-dee-tah proh-moh-tsyoh-NAH-leh).

In general, Italian stores do not give refunds and they often cannot exchange goods because of their limited stock, so make sure of the fit and quality before buying anything. Also, ask for a receipt, *ricevuta fiscale* (ree-cheh-VOO-tah fee-SKAH-leh), so you can apply for a rebate on the *I.V.A.* (EE-vah), the value-added tax, although don't be surprised if you don't get it back. Be forewarned about having your purchases shipped home from the shop. It's best to carry everything with you.

DIALOGUE: AT THE LEATHER STORE
(*IN UN NEGOZIO DI ARTICOLI DI PELLE*)

Cliente:	**Buon giorno. Vorrei vedere una borsa per mia moglie e un paio di scarpe per me.**	bwohn JOHR-noh, vohr-RAY veh-DEH-reh OO-nah BOHR-sah pehr MEE-ah MOH-lyeh eh oon PAH-yoh dee SKAHR-peh pehr meh
Commessa:	**Buon giorno signore. Abbiamo diversi tipi di borse e di scarpe. Che modello preferisce?**	bwohn JOHR-noh see-NYOH-reh. ahb-BYAH-moh dee-VEHR-see TEE-pee dee BOHR-seh eh dee SKAHR-peh. keh moh-DEHL-loh preh-feh-REE-sheh
Cliente:	**Per me un paio di mocassini neri e per mia moglie una borsetta di coccodrillo verde.**	pehr meh oon PAH-yoh dee moh-kahs-SEE-nee NEH-ree eh pehr MEE-ah MOH-lyeh OO-nah bohr-SEHT-tah dee kohk-koh-DREEL-loh VEHR-deh
Commessa:	**Che numero porta?**	keh NOO-meh-roh POHR-tah?
Cliente:	**Quarantatrè.**	kwah-rahn-tah-TREH

Commessa:	**Un momento. Ecco la borsetta per la Sua signora e i mocassini per Lei. Vanno bene?**	oon moh-MEHN-toh. EHK-koh lah bohr-SEHT-tah pehr lah SOO-ah see-NYOH-rah eh ee moh-kahs-SEE-nee pehr lay. VAHN-noh BEH-neh?
Cliente:	**Sì, sono meravigliosi e la borsa è magnifica. Le scarpe le può mettere in un sacchetto. Per la borsetta, può farmi una confezione regalo, per cortesia?**	see, SOH-noh meh-rah-vee-LYOH-zee.eh lah BOHR-sah eh mah-NYEE-fee-kah. Leh SKAHR-peh leh pwoh MEH teh-reh een oon sahk-KEHT-toh pehr lah bohr-SEHT-tah, pwoh FAHR-mee OO-nah kohn-feh-TSYOH-neh reh-GAH-loh, pehr kohr-teh-ZEE-ah?
Commessa:	**Certamente. Grazie e arrivederLa.**	chehr-tah-MEHN-teh. GRAH-tsyeh eh ahr-ree-veh-DEHR-lah

. . . .

Customer:	Good morning. I'd like to see a handbag for my wife and a pair of shoes for me.
Salesperson:	Good morning sir. We have different types of bags and shoes. What style would you prefer?
Customer:	A pair of black loafers for me and a green alligator handbag for my wife.
Salesperson:	What's your size?
Customer:	Forty-three (nine and a half).
Salesperson:	Just a moment please. Here's the handbag for your wife and here are your loafers. Do they fit?
Customer:	Yes, they are gorgeous, and the handbag is magnificent. You may put my shoes in a bag. Could you gift-wrap my wife's handbag please?
Salesperson:	Certainly. Thank you and goodbye.

TYPES OF STORES

I'm looking for a/an . . .	Cerco . . .	CHEHR-koh . . .
antique shop.	un antiquario.	oon ahn-tee-KWAH-ryoh
art gallery.	una galleria d'arte.	OO-nah gahl-leh-REE-ah DAHR-teh
bakery.	un panificio.	oon pah-nee-FEE-choh
bookstore.	una libreria.	OO-nah lee-breh-REE-ah
camera shop.	un negozio di articoli fotografici. (or) . . . di foto-ottica.	oon neh-GOH-tsyoh dee ahrt-TEE-koh-lee foh-toh-GRAH-fee-chee . . . dee FOH-toh OHT-tee-kah
clothing store.	un negozio d'abbigliamento	oon neh-GOH-tsyoh dahb-bee-lyah-MEH-N-toh
delicatessen.	una salumeria.	OO-nah sah-loo-meh-REE-ah
department store.	un grande magazzino.	oon GRAHN-deh mah-gahd-DZEE-noh
drugstore.	una farmacia.	OO-nah fahr-mah-CHEE-ah
gift shop.	un negozio di articoli da regalo.	oon neh-GOH-tsyoh dee ahr-TEE-koh-lee dah reh-GAH-loh
grocery store.	un negozio di alimentari. (or) una drogheria.	oon neh-GOH-tsyoh dah-lee-mehn-TAH-ree OO-nah droh-geh-REE-ah
jeweler.	una gioielleria.	OO-nah joh-yehl-leh-REE-ah
leather goods store.	una pelletteria.	OO-nah pehl-leht-teh-REE-ah
market.	un mercato.	oon mehr-KAH-toh

- newsstand.
- souvenir shop.

- un'edicola.
- un negozio di souvenir.

- oo-neh-DEE-koh-lah
- oon neh-GOH-tsyoh dee soo-veh-NEER

GENERAL SHOPPING EXPRESSIONS

English	Italian	Pronunciation
Excuse me.	Scusi.	SKOO-zee
Can you help me?	Mi può aiutare?	mee pwah ah-yoo-TAH-reh?
Where can I find . . . ?	Dove si trova . . . ?	DOH-veh see TROH-vah . . . ?
I'm just browsing.	Do solo un'occhiata.	doh SOH-loh oo-nohk-KYAH-tah
Can you show me . . .	Può mostrarmi . . .	pwoh moh-STRAHR-mee . . .
• this?	• questo?	• KWEH-stoh?
• that?	• quello?	• KWEHL-loh?
• the one in the window?	• quello in vetrina?	• KWEHL-loh een veh-TREE-nah?
• something better?	• qualcosa di migliore?	• kwahl-KOH-zah dee mee-LYOH-reh?
• a different color?	• un colore diverso?	• oon koh-LOH-reh dee-VEHR-soh?
• a different style?	• un altro modello?	• oon AHL-troh moh-DEHL-loh?
I'd like a gift for . . .	Vorrei un regalo per . . .	vohr-RAY oon reh-GAH-loh pehr . . .
• an adult.	• un adulto.	• oon ah-DOOL-toh
• a child.	• un bambino.	• oon bahm-BEE-noh
• a girl of seventeen.	• una ragazza di diciassette anni.	• OO-nah rah-GAHT-tsah dee dee-chahs-SEHT-teh AHN-nee
How much is it in . . .	Quant'è in . . .	kwahn-TEH een . . .
• dollars?	• dollari?	• DOHL-lah-ree?
• lire?	• lire?	• LEE-reh?
Can you write down the price for me?	Mi può scrivere il prezzo?	mee pwoh SCREE-veh-reh eel PREHT-tsoh?
It's very expensive.	È molto caro.	eh MOHL-toh KAH-roh

141

Do you have something less expensive?	Ha qualcosa di meno caro?	ah kwahl-KOH-zah dee MEH-noh KAH-roh?
Can you give me a discount?	Mi può fare lo sconto?	mee pwoh FAH-reh loh SKOHN-toh?
I do not want to pay more than . . .	Non voglio pagare più di . . .	nohn VOH-lyoh pah-GAH-reh pyoo dee . . .
I'll take it.	Lo prendo.	loh PREHN-doh
I'll take two.	Ne prendo due.	neh PREHN-doh DOO-eh
That will be all.	È tutto.	eh TOOT-toh
Can I pay . . .	Posso pagare . . .	POHS-soh pah-GAH-reh . . .
• in dollars?	• in dollari?	• een DOHL-lah-ree?
• with traveler's checks?	• con travellers cheques?	• kohn TRAH-vehl-lehr chehk?
• with a credit card?	• con la carta di credito?	• kohn lah KAHR-tah dee KREH-dee-toh?
Do I have to pay the value-added tax?	Devo pagare l'I.V.A.?	DEH-voh pah-GAH-reh LEE-vah?
May I have a bag?	Mi dà un sacchetto?	mee dah oon sahk-KEHT-toh?
It's a gift. Can you wrap it?	È un regalo. Me lo può incartare?	eh oon reh-GAH-loh. meh loh pwoh een-kahr-TAH-reh?
Can you . . .	Me lo può . . .	meh loh pwoh . . .
• order it?	• ordinare?	• ohr-dee-NAH-reh?
• send it?	• spedire?	• speh-DEE-reh?
• deliver to this address?	• far recapitare a questo indirizzo?	• fahr reh-kah-pee-TAH-reh ah KWEH-stoh een-dee-REET-tsoh?
This is damaged. Do you have another one?	È rovinato. Ne ha un altro?	eh roh-vee-NAH-toh. neh ah oon AHL-troh?
Is it out of stock?	Lo avete esaurito?	loh ah-VEH-teh eh-zow-REE-toh?
Can I exchange this?	Lo posso cambiare?	loh POHS-soh kahm-BYAH-reh?

English	Italian	Pronunciation
Here's my receipt.	Ecco la ricevuta.	EHK-koh lah ree-cheh-VOO-tah
I'd like my money back.	Vorrei indietro i soldi.	vohr-RAY een-DYEH-troh ee SOHL-dee
Sorry. I'll look somewhere else.	Mi dispiace. Cercherò da un'altra parte.	mee dee-SPYAH-cheh. chehr-keh-ROH dah oo-NAHL-trah PAHR-teh

CLOTHING

English	Italian	Pronunciation
I'd like to buy . . .	Vorrei comperare . . .	vohr-RAY kohm-peh-RAH-reh . . .
• a bathing cap.	• una cuffia da bagno.	• OO-nah KOOF-fyah dah BAH-nyoh
• a bathing suit.	• un costume da bagno.	• oon koh-STOO-meh dah BAH-nyoh
• a bathrobe.	• un accappatoio.	• oon ahk-kahp-pah-TOH-yoh
• a belt.	• una cintura.	• OO-nah cheen-TOO-rah
• a blouse.	• una camicetta.	• OO-nah kah-mee-CHET-tah
• a bomber jacket.	• un giubbotto.	• oon joob-BOHT-toh
• a bra.	• un reggiseno.	• oon rehd-jee-SEH-noh
• some briefs.	• degli slip.	• DEH-lyee zleep
• a cap.	• un berretto.	• oon behr-REHT-toh
• a coat.	• un cappotto.	• oon kahp-POHT-toh
• a dress.	• un vestito.	• oon veh-STEE-toh
• an evening dress.	• un abito da sera.	• oon AH-bee-toh dah SEH-rah
• gloves.	• dei guanti.	• day GWAHN-tee
• a gown.	• una veste.	• OO-nah VEH-steh
• a handbag.	• una borsetta.	• OO-nah bohr-SEHT-tah
• a handkerchief.	• un fazzoletto.	• oon faht-tsoh-LEHT-toh
• a hat.	• un cappello.	• oon kahp-PEHL-loh
• a jacket.	• una giacca.	• OO-nah JAHK-kah
• jeans.	• dei jeans.	• day jeens

143

• a nightgown.	• una camicia da notte.	• OO-nah kah-MEE-chah dah NOHT-teh
• overalls.	• una tuta.	• OO-nah TOO-tah
• an overcoat.	• un soprabito.	• oon soh-PRAH-bee-toh
• pajamas.	• un pigiama.	• oon pee-JAH-mah
• panties.	• delle mutandine.	• DEHL-leh moo-tahn-DEE-neh
• pants.	• dei pantaloni.	• day pahn-tah-LOH-nee
• pantyhose.	• dei collant.	• day kohl-LAHN
• a petticoat.	• una sottoveste.	• OO-nah soht-toh-VEH-steh
• a raincoat.	• un impermeabile.	• oon eem-pehr-meh-AH-bee-leh
• a (long, woolen) scarf.	• una sciarpa.	• OO-nah SHAR-pah
• a (square, silk) scarf.	• un foulard.	• oon foo-LAHR
• a . . . shirt.	• una camicia . . .	• OO-nah kah-MEE-chah . . .
long-sleeved	con le maniche lunghe.	kohn leh MAH-nee-keh LOON-gheh
short-sleeved	con le maniche corte.	kohn leh MAH-nee-keh KOHR-teh
sleeveless	senza maniche.	SEHN-tsah MAH-nee-keh
• (a pair of) shoes.	• un paio di scarpe.	• oon PAH-yoh dee SKAHR-peh
• shorts.	• dei pantaloni corti.	• day pahn-tah-LOH-nee KOHR-tee
• a skirt.	• una gonna. (or) una sottana.	• OO-nah GOHN-nah OO-nah soht-TAH-nah
• a slip.	• una sottoveste.	• OO-nah soht-toh-VEH-steh
• socks.	• dei calzini.	• day kahl-TSEE-nee
• a sports jacket.	• una giacca sportiva.	• OO-nah JAHK-kah spohr-TEE-vah
• stockings.	• delle calze.	• DEHL-leh KAHL-tseh
• a (man's) suit.	• un abito.	• oon AH-bee-toh

144

• a (woman's) suit.	• **un tailleur.**	• oon tah-YUHR
• suspenders.	• **delle bretelle.**	• DEHL-leh breh-TEHL-leh
• a sweater.	• **un maglione.**	• oon mah-LYOH-neh
• a T-shirt.	• **una maglietta.** *(or)* **una T shirt.**	• OO-nah mah-LYET-tah OO-nah tee shehrt
• a tank top.	• **una canottiera.**	• OO-nah kah-noht-TYEH-rah
• a tie.	• **una cravatta.**	• OO-nah krah-VAHT-tah
• a turtleneck sweater.	• **un maglione con il collo alto.**	• oon mah-LYOH-neh kohn eel KOHL loh AHL-toh
• an umbrella.	• **un ombrello.**	• oon ohm-BREHL-loh
• underpants.	• **delle mutande.**	• DEHL-leh moo-TAHN-deh
• an undershirt.	• **una canottiera.**	• OO-nah kah-noht-TYEH-rah
• underwear.	• **della biancheria intima.**	• DEHL-lah byahn-keh-REE-ah EEN-tee-mah
• a vest.	• **un gilet.**	• oon jee-LEH
• a V-neck pullover.	• **un pullover con il collo a V.**	• oon pool-LOH-vehr cohn eel KOHL-loh ah voo
My size is . . .	**Porto una misura . . .**	POHR-toh OO-nah mee-ZOO-rah . . .
• small.	• **piccola.**	• PEEK-koh-lah
• medium.	• **media.**	• MEH-dyah
• large.	• **grande.** *(or)* **large.**	• GRAHN-deh lahrj
• extra large.	• **extra large.**	• EHK-strah lahrj
I wear size 40.	**Porto il quaranta.**	POHR-toh eel kwah-RAHN-tah
Can I try it on?	**Posso provarlo?**	POHS-soh proh-VAHR-loh?
It fits well.	**Mi sta bene.**	mee stah BEH-neh
It does not fit me.	**Non mi sta bene.**	nohn mee stah BEH-neh

145

Can this be altered?	Lo/la può aggiustare?	loh/lah pwoh ahd-joo-STAH-reh?
Do you have a skirt that's . . .	Avere una gonna . . .	ah-VEH-teh OO-nah GOHN-nah . . .
• longer?	• più lunga?	• pyoo LOON-gah?
• shorter?	• più corta?	• pyoo KOHR-tah?
• bigger?	• più grande?	• pyoo GRAHN-deh?
• smaller?	• più piccola?	• pyoo PEEK-koh-lah?
These pants are . . .	Questi pantaloni sono . . .	KWEH-stee pahn-tah-LOH-nee SOH-noh . . .
• too tight.	• troppo stretti.	• TROHP-poh STREHT-tee
• too loose.	• troppo larghi.	• TROHP-poh LAHR-ghee

Colors and Patterns

I think you would look nice in . . .	La vedo bene in . . .	lah VEH-doh BEH-neh een . . .
• beige.	• beige.	• behzh
• black.	• nero.	• NEH-roh
• blue.	• blu.	• bloo
• brown.	• marrone.	• mahr-ROH-neh
• gray.	• grigio.	• GREE-joh
• green.	• verde.	• VEHR-deh
• orange.	• arancione.	• ah-rahn-CHOH-neh
• pink.	• rosa.	• ROH-zah
• purple.	• viola.	• VYOH-lah
• red.	• rosso.	• ROHS-soh
• white.	• bianco.	• BYAHN-koh
• yellow.	• giallo.	• JAHL-loh
I would like to see something . . .	Vorrei vedere qualcosa . . .	vohr-RAY veh-DEH-reh kwahl-KOH-sah . . .
• lighter.	• di più chiaro.	• dee pyoo KYAH-roh
• darker.	• di più scuro.	• dee pyoo SKOO-roh
• in a solid color.	• in tinta unita.	• een TEEN-tah oo-NEE-tah
• with stripes.	• a righe.	• ah REE-geh

146

• with polka dots.	• a pois.	• ah pwah
• in plaid.	• di scozzese.	• dee skoht-TSEH-zeh
• checked.	• a scacchi.	• ah SKAHK-kee

Materials

I don't like this material.	**Non mi piace questo tessuto.**	nohn mee PYAH-cheh KWEH-stoh tehs-SOO-toh
I prefer something in . . .	**Preferisco qualcosa in . . .**	preh-feh-REE-skoh kwahl-KOH-zah een . . .
• corduroy.	• **velluto a coste.**	• vehl-LOO-toh ah KOH-steh
• cotton.	• **cotone.**	• koh-TOH-neh
• denim.	• **tela.**	• TEH-lah
• gabardine.	• **gabardine.**	• gah-bahr-DEEN
• lace.	• **pizzo.**	• PEET-tsoh
• leather.	• **pelle.**	• PEHL-leh
• linen.	• **lino.**	• LEE-noh
• nylon.	• **nylon.**	• NAHY-lohn
• poplin.	• **popeline.**	• POHP-leen
• satin.	• **raso.**	• RAH-zoh
• silk.	• **seta.**	• SEH-tah
• suede.	• **camoscio.**	• kah-MOH-shoh
• terrycloth.	• **spugna.**	• SPOO-nyah
• velvet.	• **velluto.**	• vehl-LOO-toh
• wool.	• **lana.**	• LAH-nah
• worsted.	• **lana pettinata.**	• LAH-nah peht-tee-NAH-tah

SHOES

I'd like a pair of . . .	**Vorrei un paio di . . .**	vohr-RAY oon PAH-yoh dee . . .
• boots.	• **stivali.**	• stee-VAH-lee
• flats.	• **scarpe col tacco basso.**	• SKAHR-peh kohl TAHK-koh BAHS-soh
• half-boots.	• **stivaletti.**	• stee-vah-LEHT-tee

147

• high heels.	• **scarpe col tacco alto**	• SKAHR-peh kohl TAHK-koh AL IL-toh
• shoes.	• **scarpe.**	• SKAHR-peh
• sneakers.	• **scarpe da tennis.**	• SKAHR-peh dah TEHN-nees
They fit me well.	**Mi vanno bene.**	mee VAHN-noh BEH-neh
They don't fit.	**Non mi vanno bene.**	nohn mee VAHN-noh BEH-neh
They're too . . .	**Sono troppo . . .**	SOH-noh TROHP-poh . . .
• big.	• **grandi.**	• GRAHN-dee
• large.	• **larghe.**	• LAHR-geh
• narrow.	• **strette.**	• STREHT-teh
• small.	• **piccole.**	• PEEK-koh-leh
Do you have a larger/smaller size?	**Ha un numero più grande/piccolo?**	ah oon NOO-meh-roh pyoo GRAHN-deh PEEK-koh-loh?
I do not know my size.	**Non so il numero.**	nohn soh eel NOO-meh-roh
I'd like the same in black.	**Vorrei le stesse in nero.**	vohr-RAY leh STEHS-seh een NEH-roh

WOMEN'S CLOTHING SIZES*

Coats, Dresses, Suits, Skirts, Slacks								
U.S.	4	6	8	10	12	14	16	18
Italy	36	38	40	42	44	46	48	50

Blouses, Sweaters							
U.S.	30	32	34	36	38	40	42
Italy	38	40	42	44	46	48	50

Shoes							
U.S.	5–5½	6	6½–7	7½	8	8½	9	9½–10
Italy	35	36	37	38	38½	39	40	41

MEN'S CLOTHING SIZES*

Suits, Coats
U.S.	34	36	38	40	42	44	46	48
Italy	44	46	48	50	52	54	56	58

Sweaters
U.S.	XS-36	S/38	M/40	L/42	XL/44
Italy	42/2	44/3	46-48/4	50/5	52-54/6

Shirts
U.S.	14	14½	15	15½	15¾	16	16½	17	17½	18
Italy	36	37	38	39	40	41	42	43	44	45

Socks
U.S.	9½	10	10½	11	11½	12
Italy	36-37	38-39	40-41	42-43	44-45	46

Shoes
U.S.	6½	7	7½	8	8½	9	9½	10	10½	11	11½
Italy	39	39½	40	41	42	42½	43	43½	44	44½	45

*We recommend trying on all clothing before buying because sizes vary and do not always correlate exactly with U.S. sizes. Also, it is less customary in Italy to return clothing purchased, except at large department stores in major cities.

THE JEWELRY STORE

I'd like to see . . .	Vorrei vedere . . .	vohr-RAY veh-DEH-reh . . .
• a bracelet.	• un braccialetto.	• oon braht-chah-LEHT-toh
• a brooch.	• una spilla.	• OO-nah SPEEL-lah
• a chain.	• una catenina.	• OO-nah kah-teh-NEE-nah
• a cigarette case.	• un portasigarette.	• oon pohr-tah-see-gah-REHT-teh
• a clock.	• un orologio.	• oon oh-roh-LOH-joh
• some cufflinks.	• dei gemelli.	• day jeh-MEHL-lee
• some earrings.	• degli orecchini.	• DEH-lyee oh-rehk-KEE-nee
• a gem.	• una pietra preziosa.	• OO-nah PYEH-trah preh-TSYOH-zah

149

• a necklace.	• una collana.	• OO-nah kohl-LAH-nah
• a pin.	• una spilla.	• OO-nah SPEEL-lah
• a ring.	• un anello.	• oon ah-NEHL-loh
• an engagement ring.	• un anello di fidanzamento.	• oon ah-NEHL-loh dee fee-dahn-tsah-MEHN-toh
• a wedding ring.	• una fede (or) una vera.	• OO-nah FEH-deh OO-nah VEH-rah
• a tie clip.	• un fermacravatte.	• oon fehr-mah-krah-VAHT-teh
• a tie pin.	• una spilla da cravatta.	• OO-nah SPEEL-lah dah krah-VAHT-tah
• a watch.	• un orologio da polso.	• oon oh-roh-LOH-joh dah POHL-so
• a watchstrap.	• un cinturino.	• oon cheen-too-REE-noh
Do you have this . . .	L'avete . . .	lah-VEH-teh . . .
• in 18 carat gold?	• in oro a diciotto carati?	• een OH-roh ah dee-CHOHT-toh kah-RAH-tee?
• gold-plated?	• placcato in oro?	• plahk-KAH-toh een OH-roh?
• in platinum?	• in platino?	• een PLAH-tee-noh?
• in silver?	• in argento?	• een ahr-JEHN-toh?
• in stainless steel?	• in acciaio inossidabile?	• een aht-CHAH-yoh ee-nohs-see-DAH-bee-leh?
Can you repair this watch?	Può riparare questo orologio?	pwoh ree-pah-RAH-reh KWEH-stoh oh-roh-LOH-joh?
How many carats is this?	Quanti carati è?	KWAHN-tee kah-RAH-tee-eh?
What is this made out of?	Di che cosa è fatto?	dee keh KOH-zah eh FAHT-toh?
It's . . .	È . . .	eh . . .
• an amethyst.	• un'ametista.	• oo-nah-meh-TEE-stah
• copper.	• di rame.	• dee RAH-meh
• coral.	• di corallo.	• dee koh-RAHL-loh

150

• crystal.	• di cristallo.	• dee kree-STAHL-loh
• a diamond.	• un diamante.	• oon dyah-MAHN-teh
• an emerald.	• uno smeraldo.	• OO-noh zmeh-RAHL-doh
• ivory.	• d'avorio.	• dah-VOH-ryoh
• jade.	• di giada.	• dee JAH-dah
• onyx.	• d'onice.	• DOH-nee-cheh
• a pearl.	• una perla.	• OO-nah PEHR-lah
• a ruby.	• un rubino.	• oon roo-BEE-noh
• a sapphire.	• uno zaffiro.	• OO-noh dzahf-FEE-roh
• a topaz.	• un topazio.	• oon toh-PAH-tsyoh

THE PHOTO SHOP

Do you sell . . .	Vendete . . .	vehn-DEH-teh . . .
• cameras?	• macchine fotografiche?	• MAHK-kee-neh foh-toh-GRAH-fee-keh?
• movie cameras?	• cineprese?	• chee-neh-PREH-zeh?
• filters?	• filtri?	• FEEL-tree?
• batteries?	• pile?	• PEE-leh?
Do you have . . .	Avete . . .	ah-VEH-teh . . .
• a light meter?	• un esposimetro?	• oon eh-spoh-ZEE-meh-troh?
• a lens?	• un obiettivo?	• oon oh-byeht-TEE-voh?
• a lens cap?	• un copriobiettivo?	• oon koh-pree-oh-byeht-TEE-voh?
• a telephoto lens?	• un teleobiettivo?	• oon teh-leh-oh-byeht-TEE-voh?
• a wide-angle lens?	• un grandangolare?	• oon grahn-dahn-goh-LAH-reh?
I'd like a roll of . . .	Vorrei una pellicola . . .	vohr-RAY OO-nah pehl-LEE-koh-lah . . .
• film for prints.	• per stampe.	• pehr STAHM-peh
• film for slides.	• per diapositive.	• pehr dyah-poh-zee-TEE-veh
• color film.	• a colori.	• ah koh-LOH-ree
• black-and-white film.	• in bianco e nero.	• een BYAHN-koh eh NEH-roh

151

• .35 millimeter film.	• **trentacinque millimetri.**	• trehn-tah-CHEEN-kweh meel-LEE-meh-tree
• 36 exposures.	• **per trentasei pose.**	• pehr trehn-tah-SAY POH-zeh
How long does it take?	**Quanto tempo ci vuole?**	KWAHN-toh TEHM-poh chee voo-OH-leh?
I'd like . . .	**Vorrei . . .**	vohr-RAY . . .
• two prints of each negative.	• **due stampe di ogni negativa.**	• DOO-eh STAHM-peh dee OH-nyee neh-gah-TEE-vah
• an enlargement of this photo.	• **un ingrandimento di questa foto.**	• oon een-grahn-dee-MEHN-toh dee KWEH-stah FOH-toh
• prints with a . . .	• **foto su carta . . .**	• FOH-toh soo KAHR-tah . . .
• glossy finish.	• **lucida.**	• LOO-chee-dah
• matt finish.	• **opaca.**	• oh-PAH-kah
When will they be ready?	**Quando sono pronte?**	KWAHN-doh SOH-noh PROHN-teh?
Do you do camera repairs?	**Riparate macchine fotografiche?**	ree-pah-RAH-teh MAHK-kee-neh foh-toh-GRAH-fee-keh?

BOOKS, MAGAZINES, AND PAPER GOODS

In an Italian bookstore, *libreria* (lee-breh-REE-ah), you can usually find popular and scholarly books, as well as guides, manuals, and art and photography books. Writing supplies are found at the stationery store, *cartoleria* (kahr-toh-leh-REE-ah). Newspapers and magazines can be found at any outdoor newsstand, *edicola* (eh-DEE-koh-lah).

I'm looking for . . .	**Cerco . . .**	CHEHR-koh . . .
• a bookstore.	• **una libreria.**	• OO-nah lee-breh-REE-ah
• a newsstand.	• **un'edicola.**	• oo-neh-DEE-koh-lah
• a stationery store.	• **una cartoleria.**	• OO-nah kahr-toh-leh-REE-ah

Is there a bookstore that carries . . . in English?	C'e una libreria che vende . . . in inglese?	cheh OO-nah lee-breh-REE-ah keh VEHN-deh . . . een een-GLEH-zeh?
• books	• libri	• LEE-bree
• magazines	• riviste	• ree-VEE-steh
• newspapers	• giornali	• johr-NAH-lee
Do you have the book . . . by . . . ?	Ha il libro . . . di . . . ?	ah eel LEE-broh . . . dee . . . ?
I'd like a book on . . .	Vorrei un libro di . . .	vohr-RAY oon LEE-broh dee . . .
The title is . . .	È intitolato . . .	eh een-tee-toh-LAH-toh . . .
The author is . . .	L'autore è . . .	low-TOH-reh eh . . .
Do you have it in paperback?	L'avete in edizione tascabile?	lah-VEH-teh een eh-dee-TSYOH-neh tah-SKAH-bee-leh?
Do you have this guidebook in English?	Avete questa guida in inglese?	ah-VEH-teh KWEH-stah GWEE-dah een een-GLEH-zeh?
Do you have an Italian-English dictionary?	Avete un dizionario italiano-inglese?	ah-VEH-teh oon dee-tsyoh-NAH-ryoh ee-tah-LYAH-noh/een-GLEH-zeh?
Do you have . . .	Avete . . .	ah-VEH-teh . . .
• a pocket dictionary?	• un dizionario tascabile?	• oon dee-tsyoh-NAH-ryoh tah-SKAH-bee-leh?
• a map?	• una mappa?	• OO-nah MAHP-pah?
• a city map?	• una pianta della città?	• OO-nah PYAHN-tah DEHL-lah cheet-TAH
• a road map?	• una carta stradale?	• OO-nah KAHR-tah strah-DAH-leh?
• a travel guide?	• una guida turistica?	• OO-nah GWEE-dah too-REE-stee-kah?
I'd like . . .	Vorrei . . .	vohr-RAY . . .
• a ballpoint pen.	• una biro. (or) una penna a sfera.	• OO-nah BEE-roh • OO-nah PEHN-nah ah-SFEH-rah

153

• a calendar.	• un calendario.	• oon kah-lehn-DAH-ryoh
• envelopes.	• delle buste.	• DEHL-leh BOO-steh
• an eraser.	• una gomma.	• OO-nah GOHM-mah
• a fountain pen.	• una stilografica.	• OO-nah stee-loh-GRAH-fee-kah
• a marker.	• un pennarello.	• oon pehn-nah-REHL-loh
• a notebook.	• un quaderno.	• oon kwah-DEHR-noh
• paperclips.	• delle graffette.	• DEHL-leh grahf-FEHT-teh
• a pencil.	• una matita.	• OO-nah mah-TEE-tah
• a pencil sharpener.	• un temperino.	• oon tehm-peh-REE-noh
• a pocket calculator.	• una calcolatrice tascabile.	• OO-nah kahl-koh-lah-TREE-cheh tah-SKAH-bee-leh
• a ruler.	• una riga.	• OO-nah REE-gah
• scotch tape.	• dello scotch.	• DEHL-loh skohch
• a stapler.	• una cucitrice.	• OO-nah koo-chee-TREE-cheh
• staples.	• dei punti metallici.	• day POON-tee meh-TAHL-lee-chee
• stationery.	• della carta da lettere.	• DEHL-lah KAHR-tah dah LEHT-teh-reh
• string.	• dello spago.	• DEHL-loh SPAH-goh
• a typewriter.	• una macchina da scrivere.	• OO-nah MAHK-kee-nah dah SCREE-veh-reh
• a typewriter ribbon.	• un nastro.	• oon NAH-stroh
• wrapping paper.	• della carta da pacchi.	• DEHL-lah KAHR-tah dah PAHK-kee
• a writing pad.	• un bloc notes.	• oon blohk NOH-tehs

TOILETRIES

Perfume and cosmetics are available at many major department stores. You can also find them at a *profumeria* (proh-foo-meh-REE-ah). Other toiletries may be found in a *drogheria* (droh-geh-REE-ah) or in a *farmacia* (fahr-mah-CHEE-ah).

Do you have . . .	Avete . . .	ah-VEH-teh . . .
• after-shave lotion?	• una lozione dopobarba?	• OO-nah loh-TSYOH-neh doh-poh-BAHR-bah?
• bobby pins?	• delle mollette?	• DEHL-leh mohl-LEHT-teh?
	(or) delle forcine?	DEHL-leh fohr-CHEE-neh?
• a brush?	• una spazzola?	• OO-nah SPAHT-tsoh-lah?
• bubble bath?	• un bagnoschiuma?	• oon bah-nyoh-SKYOO-mah?
• cleansing cream?	• una crema detergente?	• OO-nah KREH-mah deh-tehr-JEHN-teh?
• cologne?	• dell'acqua di colonia?	• dehl-LAHK-kwah dee koh-LOH-nyah?
• a comb?	• un pettine?	• oon PEHT-tee-neh?
• curlers?	• dei bigodini?	• day bee-goh-DEE-nee?
• a deodorant?	• un deodorante?	• oon deh-oh-doh-RAHN-teh?
• diapers?	• dei pannolini?	• day pahn-noh-LEE-nee?
• an emery board?	• una limetta per unghie?	• OO-nah lee-MEHT-tah pehr OON-gyeh?
• an eye liner?	• un eye liner?	• oon ahy LAHY-nehr?
• an eye pencil?	• una matita per occhi?	• OO-nah mah-TEE-tah pehr OHK-kee?
• eye shadow?	• un ombretto?	• oon ohm-BREHT-toh?
• face powder?	• della cipria?	• DEHL-lah CHEE-pryah?
• foundation?	• un fondo tinta?	• oon FOHN-doh TEEN-tah?
• hairspray?	• della lacca?	• DEHL-lah LAHK-kah?

155

• hand cream?	• una crema per le mani?	• OO-nah KREH-mah pehr leh MAH-nee?
• lipstick?	• un rossetto?	• oon rohs-SEHT-toh?
• makeup?	• dei cosmetici?	• day koh-ZMEH-tee-chee?
• mascara?	• del mascara?	• dehl mah-SKAH-rah?
• a mirror?	• uno specchio?	• OO-noh SPEHK-kyoh?
• moisturizing cream?	• una crema idratante?	• OO-nah KREH-mah ee-drah-TAHN-teh?
• mouthwash?	• del collutorio?	• dehl kohl-loo-TOH-ryoh?
• a nail clipper?	• un tronchesino?	• oon trohn-keh-ZEE-noh?
• nail polish?	• dello smalto?	• DEHL-loh ZMAHL-toh?
• nail polish remover?	• del solvente per unghie? (or) dell'acetone?	• dehl sohl-VEHN-teh pehr OON-gyeh? • dehl-lah-cheh-TOH-neh?
• nail scissors?	• delle forbicine da unghie?	• DEHL-leh fohr-bee-CHEE-neh dah OON-gyeh?
• perfume?	• del profumo?	• dehl proh-FOO-moh?
• prophylactics?	• dei profilattici?	• day proh-fee-LAHT-tee-chee?
• a razor?	• un rasoio?	• oon rah-ZOH-yoh?
• razor blades?	• delle lamette da barba?	• DEHL-leh lah-MEHT-teh dah BAHR-bah?
• rouge?	• del fard?	• dehl fahrd?
• safety pins?	• delle spille da balia?	• DEHL-leh SPEEL-leh dah BAH-lyah?
• sanitary napkins?	• degli assorbenti igienici?	• DEH-lyee ahs-sohr-BEHN-tee ee-JEH-nee-chee?
• scissors?	• delle forbici?	• DEHL-leh FOHR-bee-chee?
• setting lotion?	• un fissatore per capelli?	• oon fees-sah-TOH-reh pehr kah-PEHL-lee?

• shampoo?	• uno shampoo?	OO-noh SHAHM-poh?
• shaving cream?	• una crema da barba?	OO-nah KREH-mah dah BAHR-bah?
• soap?	• una saponetta?	OO-nah sah-poh-NEHT-tah?
• suntan lotion?	• una crema solare?	OO-nah KREH-mah soh-LAH-reh?
• talcum powder?	• del talco?	dehl TAHL-koh?
• tampons?	• dei tamponi?	day tahm-POH-nee?
• tissues?	• dei fazzolettini di carta?	day faht-tsoh-leht-TEE-nee dee KAHR-tah?
• toilet paper?	• della carta igienica?	DEHL-lah KAHR-tah ee-JEH-nee-kah?
• a toothbrush?	• uno spazzolino da denti?	OO-noh spaht-tsoh-LEE-noh dah DEHN-tee?
• toothpaste?	• del dentifricio?	dehl dehn-tee-FREE-choh?
• tweezers?	• delle pinzette?	DEHL-leh peen-TSEHT-teh?

FOOD SHOPPING

I'd like . . .	Vorrei . . .	vohr-RAY . . .
• six cans of Coke.	• sei lattine di coca.	SAY laht-TEE-neh dee KOH-kah.
• a box of chocolates.	• una scatola di cioccolatini.	OO-nah SKAH-toh-lah dee chohk-koh-lah-TEE-nee
• a bottle of mineral water.	• una bottiglia di acqua minerale.	OO-nah boht-TEE-lyah dee AHK-kwah mee-neh-RAH-leh
• a dozen eggs.	• una dozzina di uova.	OO-nah dohd-DZEE-nah dee WOH-vah
• a jar of pickles.	• un vasetto di sottaceti.	oon vah-SEHT-toh dee soht-tah-CHEH-tee
• a kilo of potatoes.	• un chilo di patate.	oon KEE-loh dee pah-TAH-teh

157

• a liter of milk.	• **un litro di latte.**	• oon LEE-troh dee LAHT-teh
• a piece of cheese.	• **un pezzo di formaggio.**	• oon PFHT-tsoh dee fohr-MAHD-joh
I'd also like some . . .	**Vorrei anche . . .**	vohr-RAY AHN-keh . . .
• cereal.	• **dei cereali.**	day-cheh-reh-AH-lee
• coffee.	• **del caffè.**	• dehl kahf-FEH
• cookies/crackers.	• **dei biscotti.**	• day bee-SKOHT-tee
• cold cuts.	• **dell'affettato.**	• dehl-lahf-feht-TAH-toh

WEIGHTS AND MEASURES

Metric Weight	**U.S.**
1 gram (g)	0.035 ounce
28.35 grams	1 ounce
100 grams	3.5 ounces
454 grams	1 pound
1 kilogram (kilo)	2.2 pounds

Liquids	**U.S.**
1 liter (l)	4.226 cups
1 liter	2.113 cups
1 liter	1.056 quarts
3.785 liters	1 gallon

Dry Measures	**U.S.**
1 litre	0.908 quart
1 decalitre	1.135 pecks
1 hectolitre	2.837 bushels

One inch = 2.54 centimeters
One centimeter = .39 inch

	in.	feet	yards
1 mm.	0.039	0.003	0.001
1 cm.	0.39	0.03	0.01
1 dm.	3.94	0.32	0.10
1 m.	39.40	3.28	1.09

.39 (# of centimeters) = (# of inches)
.54 (# of inches) = (# of centimeters)

	mm.	cm.	m.
1 in.	25.4	2.54	0.025
1 ft.	304.8	30.48	0.304
1 yd.	914.4	91.44	0.914

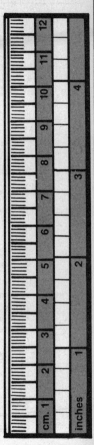

159

13/ACTIVITIES AND ENTERTAINMENT

In Italy, people spend their free time in a variety of ways. You will see people sitting in parks or cafés, reading a magazine or a newspaper, drinking espresso, chatting, or just watching other people. Italy's rich cultural life includes movies, theater, ballet, opera, and concerts.

Italians are avid sports enthusiasts, both as participants and spectators. If you feel like getting some exercise yourself, you can rent a bicycle, or go skiing, hiking, or swimming if the season permits.

DIALOGUE: SWIMMING (*A NUOTARE*)

Marcello:	**Che caldo!**	keh KAHL-doh!
Sofia:	**Sì. Perché non andiamo a nuotare?**	see. pehr-KEH nohn ahn-DYAH-moh ah nwoh-TAH-reh?
Marcello:	**Buona idea! Andiamo al mare o in piscina?**	BWOH-nah ee-DEH-ah! ahn-DYAH-moh ahl MAH-reh oh een pee-SHEE-nah?
Sofia:	**A dire il vero io preferisco il mare. Ma non è pericoloso in questa zona?**	ah DEE-reh eel VEH-roh EE-oh preh-feh-REE-skoh eel MAH-reh, mah nohn eh peh-ree-koh-LOH-zoh een KWEH-stah DZOH-nah?
Marcello:	**No, il mare oggi è piuttosto calmo.**	noh, eel MAH-reh OHD-jee eh pyoot-TOH-stoh KAHL-moh
Sofia:	**Bene. Allora ci vediamo in spiaggia tra cinque minuti.**	BEH-neh. ahl-LOH-rah chee veh-DYAH-moh een SPYAHD-jah trah CHEEN-kweh mee-NOO-tee.

| Marcello: | **D'accordo. E non dimenticare l'abbronzante. Il sole picchia forte.** | dahk-KOHR-doh. eh nohn dee-mehn-tee-KAH-reh lahb-brohn-DZAHN-teh. eel SOH-leh PEEK-kyah FOHR-teh |

. . . .

Marcello:	It's so hot out!
Sofia:	Yes. Why don't we go swimming?
Marcello:	Good idea! Shall we go to the beach or to the pool?
Sofia:	To tell you the truth I love the sea. But isn't it dangerous around here?
Marcello:	No, today the sea is quite calm.
Sofia:	Good. Then I'll see you on the beach in five minutes.
Marcello:	Right. And don't forget the suntan lotion. The sun is very strong.

SPORTS

At the Beach

Let's go swimming!	**Andiamo a nuotare!**	ahn-DYAH-moh ah nwoh-TAH-reh!
Where are the finest beaches?	**Dove sono le spiagge più belle?**	DOH-veh SOH-noh leh SPYAHD-jeh pyoo BEHL-leh?
How do I get there?	**Come ci si arriva?**	KOH-meh chee see ahr-REE-vah?
Is it a private or public beach?	**È una spiaggia pubblica o privata?**	eh OO-nah SPYAHD-jah POOB-blee-kah oh pree-VAH-tah?
Where is the lifeguard?	**Dov'è il bagnino?**	doh-VEH eel bah-NYEE-noh?
Is it dangerous for children?	**È pericoloso per i bambini?**	eh peh-ree-koh-LOH-zoh pehr ee bahm-BEE-nee?

161

The sand is hot but the water is cool.	La sabbia scotta ma l'acqua è fresca.	lah SAHB-byah SKOHT-tah mah LAHK-kwah eh FREH-skah
Are there dangerous currents?	Ci sono correnti pericolose?	chee SOH-noh kohr-REHN-tee peh-ree-koh-LOH-zeh?
No, there are only waves.	No, ci sono solo onde.	noh chee SOH-noh SOH-loh OHN-deh
Look at the big waves!	Guarda che cavalloni!	GWAHR-dah keh kah-vahl-LOH-nee!
I'd like to rent . . .	Vorrei noleggiare . . .	vohr-RAY noh-lehd-JAH-reh . . .
• a beach chair.	• un lettino. (or) uno sdraio.	• oon leht-TEE-noh OO-noh SDRAH-yoh
• a beach towel.	• un telo da spiaggia.	• oon TEH-loh dah SPYAHD-jah
• a cabana.	• una cabina.	• OO-nah kah-BEE-nah
• a rowboat.	• una barca a remi.	• OO-nah BAHR-kah ah REH-mee
• a rowboat (light double raft).	• un moscone. (or) un pattino.	• oon moh-SKOH-neh • oon paht-TEE-noh
• a sailboard.	• una tavola a vela.	• OO-nah TAH-voh-lah ah VEH-lah
• a sailboat.	• una barca a vela.	• OO-nah BAHR-kah ah VEH-lah
• skin-diving equipment.	• attrezzatura per pesca subacquea.	• aht-treht-tsah-TOO-rah pehr PEH skah soo-BAHK-kweh-ah
• a surfboard.	• una tavola da surf. (or) un surfboard.	• OO-nah TAH-voh-lah dah sehrf • oon SEHRF-bohrd
• an umbrella.	• un ombrellone.	• oon ohm-brehl-LOH-neh
• waterskis.	• degli sci d'acqua.	• DEH-lyee shee DAHK-kwah

Poolside

Where is the pool?	Dov'è la piscina?	doh-VEH lah pee-SHEE-nah?

162

Is the pool . . .	La piscina è . . .	lah pee-SHEE-nah eh . . .
• heated?	• riscaldata?	• ree-skahl-DAH-tah?
• indoors?	• coperta?	• koh-PEHR-tah?
• outdoors?	• scoperta?	• skoh-PEHR-tah?
When does the pool open/close?	A che ora apre/chiude la piscina?	ah keh OH-rah AH-preh/KYOO-deh lah pee-SHEE-nah?

Soccer

Soccer, *il calcio* (eel KAHL-choh), is Italy's national sport, and is played both by children and adults. Professional teams are passionately followed each Sunday in stadiums all over Italy. The soccer championship season starts in mid-September and continues until the end of May/beginning of June.

Let's go to the stadium!	Andiamo allo stadio!	ahn-DYAH-moh AHL-loh STAH-dyoh!
I'd like to see a soccer match.	Vorrei vedere una partita di calcio.	vohr-RAY veh-DEH-reh OO-nah pahr-TEE-tah dee KAHL-choh
Who's playing?	Chi gioca?	kee JOH-kah?
Which is the best team?	Qual è la squadra migliore?	kwah-LEH lah SKWAH-drah mee-LYOH-reh?
Is the stadium near here?	È vicino lo stadio?	eh vee-CHEE-noh loh STAH-dyoh?
How much do the tickets cost?	Quanto costano i biglietti?	KWAHN-toh KOH-stah-noh ee bee-LYEHT-tee?
When does the match begin?	Quando comincia la partita?	KWAHN-doh koh-MEEN-chah lah pahr-TEE-tah?
Are there better seats?	Ci sono posti migliori?	chee SOH-noh POH-stee mee-LYOH-ree?
What's the score?	Qual'è il risultato?	kwah-LEH eel ree-zool-TAH-toh?
Who won?	Chi ha vinto?	kee ah VEEN-toh?

163

Skiing

Would you like to go skiing?	Vuole andare a sciare?	voo-OH-leh ahn-DAH-reh ah shee-AH-reh?
What's the best ski area?	Qual è la stazione sciistica migliore?	kwah-LEH lah stah-TSYOH-neh shee-EE-stee-kah mee-LYOH-reh?
I like Cortina.	Mi piace Cortina.	mee PYAH-cheh kohr-TEE-nah
Are there slopes for beginners?	Ci sono piste per principianti?	chee SOH-noh PEE-steh pehr preen-chee-PYAHN-tee?
I'd like to take some lessons.	Vorrei prendere qualche lezione.	vohr-RAY PREHN-deh-reh KWAHL-keh leh-TSYOH-neh
How are the weather conditions?	Come sono le condizioni del tempo?	KOH-meh SOH-noh leh kohn-dee-TSYOH-nee dehl TEHM-poh
There's lots of snow.	C'è molta neve.	cheh MOHL-tah NEH-veh
Where's the ski lift?	Dov'è la sciovia?	doh-VEH lah shee-oh-VEE-ah?
I'd like to rent . . .	Vorrei noleggiare . . .	voh-RAY noh-lehd-JAH-reh . . .
• skis.	• degli sci.	• DEH-lyee shee
• ski boots.	• degli scarponi da sci.	• DEH-lyee skahr-POH-nee dah shee

Other Sports

I like . . .	Mi piace . . .	mee PYAH-cheh . . .
• baseball.	• il baseball.	• eel BAY-sbohl
• cycling.	• il ciclismo.	• eel chee-KLEE-zmoh
• deep-sea diving.	• la pesca subacquea.	• lah PEH-skah soo-BAHK-kweh-ah
• football.	• il football americano.	• eel FOOT-bohl ah-meh-ree-KAH-noh
• rugby.	• il rugby.	• eel RAHG-bee
• swimming.	• il nuoto.	• eel NWOH-toh

164

• volleyball.	• la pallavolo.	• lah pahl-lah-VOH-loh
Let's go see . . .	Andiamo a vedere . . .	ahn-DYAH-moh ah veh-DEH-reh . . .
• a horse race.	• una corsa di cavalli.	• OO-nah KOHR-sah dee kah-VAHL-lee
• a tennis match.	• una partita di tennis.	• OO-nah pahr-TEE-tah dee TEHN-nees
Would you like to play . . .	Vuole giocare . . .	voo-OH-leh joh-KAH-reh . . .
• golf?	• a golf?	• ah gohlf?
• tennis?	• a tennis?	• ah TEHN-nees?
Where can I find . . .	Dove posso trovare . . .	DOH-veh POHS-soh troh-VAH-reh . . .
• a golf course?	• un campo da golf?	• oon KAHM-poh dah gohlf?
• a tennis court?	• un campo da tennis?	• oon KAHM-poh dah TEHN-nees?
• a skating rink?	• una pista di pattinaggio?	• OO-nah PEE-stah dee paht-tee-NAHD-joh?
How much is it . . .	Quanto costa . . .	KWAHN-toh KOH-stah . . .
• per hour?	• all'ora?	• ahl-LOH-rah?
• per day?	• al giorno?	• ahl JOHR-noh?
We need to buy some balls.	Dobbiamo comprare delle palle.	dohb-BYAH-moh kohm-PRAH-reh DEHL-leh PAHL-leh
I need a racket.	Ho bisogno di una racchetta.	oh bee-ZOH-nyoh dee OO-nah rahk-KEHT-tah
You play very well.	Gioca benissimo.	JOH-kah beh-NEES-see-moh

MOVIES

Italy, a leader in cinematic art, hosts several film festivals. Among them, the most famous is the Venice International Film Festival at the *Biennale,* taking place the last week of August and the first week of September. There you can preview some of the movies of the coming season, both Italian and foreign.

Let's go to the movies!	**Andiamo al cinema!**	ahn-DYAH-moh ahl CHEE-neh-mah!
What's playing?	**Che cosa danno?**	keh KOH-zuh DAHN-noh?
Is it in Italian or English?	**È in italiano o in inglese?**	eh een ee-tah-LYAH-noh oh een een-GLEH-zeh?
With subtitles?	**Con le didascalie?**	kohn leh dee-dah-skah-LEE-eh?
Is it dubbed?	**È doppiato?**	eh dohp-PYAH-toh?
I prefer to see the original version.	**Preferisco vedere la versione originale.**	preh-feh-REE-skoh veh-DEH-reh lah vehr-ZYOH-neh oh-ree-jee-NAH-leh
What kind of film is it?	**Che genere di film è?**	keh JEH-neh-reh dee feelm eh?
I'd like to see . . .	**Mi piacerebbe vedere . . .**	mee pyah-cheh-REHB-beh veh-DEH-reh . . .
• an action movie.	• **un film d'azione.**	• oon feelm dah-TSYOH-neh
• an adventure movie.	• **un film d'avventura.**	• oon feelm dahv-vehn-TOO-rah
• a comedy.	• **un film comico.**	• oon feelm KOH-mee-koh
• a detective story.	• **un film poliziesco.**	• oon feelm poh-lee-TSYEH-skoh
• a drama.	• **un film drammatico.**	• oon feelm drahm-MAH-tee-koh
• a horror movie.	• **un film dell'orrore.**	• oon feelm dehl-lohr-ROH-reh
• a love story.	• **una storia d'amore.**	• OO-nah STOH-ryah dah-MOH-reh
• a musical.	• **un musical.**	• oon MYOO-zee-kahl
• a political movie.	• **un film politico.**	• oon feelm poh-LEE-tee-koh
• a science fiction movie.	• **un film di fantascienza.**	• oon feelm dee fahn-tah-SHEHN-tsah
• a tearjerker.	• **un film sentimentale.**	• oon feelm sehn-tee-menhn-TAH-leh
• a thriller.	• **un giallo.**	• oon JAHL-loh

166

| • a war movie. | • **un film di guerra.** | • oon feelm dee GWEHR-rah |
| • a western. | • **un western.** | • oon WEH-stehrn |

THEATER, CONCERTS, OPERA, AND BALLET

The performing arts, particularly opera, are an essential part of Italian culture. The celebrated Teatro alla Scala in Milan is perhaps the most famous opera house in the world. In the summer, spectacular operas are performed outdoors at the Arena Sferisterio in Macerata (July) and at the Terme di Caracalla in Rome (July/August). In the breathtaking Arena di Verona, before the performance begins, it is customary for the audience to light up small candles that flicker like stars. Pesaro offers a Rossini Opera Festival beginning in mid-August; Torre del Lago, near Lucca, features Puccini's operas in the open-air theater in August, and Ravenna presents both opera and ballet in the majestic Rocca di Brancaleone, an ancient fortress built by the Venetians. Two of the most important festivals of the performing arts are the Maggio Musicale Fiorentino (opera, concerts, ballet, drama), held in Florence in May/June, and the Festival of Two Worlds (art exhibits, ballet, concerts, drama, opera) in Spoleto from mid-June to mid-July. Also notable are the Music and Drama Festival, a review of films, music, and stage plays held in Taormina's Greek theater in July and August, and the Shakespeare Festival at the Roman theater of Verona. The famous International Ballet Festival is held at Nervi near Genoa in July.

What's playing at the theater?	**Che cosa danno a teatro?**	keh KOH-zah DAHN-noh ah teh-AH-troh?
What kind of play is it?	**Che tipo di spettacolo è?**	keh TEE-poh dee speht-TAH-koh-loh eh?
Who is . . .	**Chi è . . .**	kee eh . . .
• the author?	• **l'autore?**	• low-TOH-reh?
• the director?	• **il regista?**	• eel reh-JEE-stah?
Are there tickets for tonight?	**Ci sono biglietti per questa sera?**	chee SOH-noh bee-LYEHT-tee pehr KWEH-stah SEH-rah?

How much are they?	Quanto costano?	KWAHN-toh KOH-stah-noh?
I'd like . . .	Vorrei . . .	vohr-RAY . . .
• an orchestra seat.	• un posto in platea.	• oon POH-stoh een plah-TEH-ah
• a mezzanine seat.	• un posto in prima galleria.	• oon POH-stoh een PREE-mah gahl-leh-REE-ah
• a balcony seat.	• un posto in seconda galleria.	• oon POH-stoh een seh-KOHN-dah gahl-leh-REE-ah
• seats up front.	• dei posti davanti.	• day POH-stee dah-VAHN-tee
• seats in back.	• dei posti di dietro.	• day POH-stee dee DYEH-troh
• seats on the side.	• dei posti laterali.	• day POH-stee lah-teh-RAH-lee
• tickets for the matinee.	• dei biglietti per lo spettacolo del pomeriggio.	• day bee-LYEHT-tee pehr loh speht-TAH-koh-loh dehl poh-meh-REED-joh
• tickets for the evening.	• dei biglietti per lo spettacolo serale.	• day bee-LYEHT-tee pehr loh speht-TAH-koh-loh seh-RAH-leh
A program, please.	Un programma, per favore.	oon proh-GRAHM-mah, pehr fah-VOR-reh
I'd like to see . . .	Vorrei vedere . . .	vohr-RAY veh-DEH-reh . . .
• a ballet.	• un balletto.	• oon bahl-LEHT-toh
• a comedy.	• una commedia.	• OO-nah kohm-MEH-dyah
• a concert.	• un concerto.	• oon kohn-CHEHR-toh
• an opera.	• un'opera.	• oo-NOH-peh-rah
• an operetta.	• un'operetta.	• oo-noh-peh-REHT-tah
• a musical.	• una commedia musicale.	• OO-nah kohm-MEH-dyah moo-zee-KAH-leh

• a variety show.	• una rivista di varietà.	• OO-nah ree-VEE-stah dee vah-ryeh-TAH
Who's playing?	Chi recita?	kee REH-chee-tah?
Who's singing?	Chi canta?	kee KAHN-tah?
Who's dancing?	Chi balla?	kee BAHL-lah?
Who's the conductor?	Chi è il direttore d'orchestra?	kee eh eel dee-reht-TOH-reh dohr-KEH-strah?

CLUBS, DISCOS, AND CABARETS

In Italy, particularly in large cities, some restaurants are also nightclubs, where you can have dinner and see a show. On weekends, many nightclubs may have live music. Cabarets and boîtes are scattered around town. Reservations are sometimes needed if you plan to visit better-known clubs, or if there are featured shows. For the younger crowds there are discos, which often play American-style music.

Why don't we go dancing tonight!	Perché non andiamo a ballare questa sera!	pehr-KEH nohn ahn-DYAH-moh ah bahl-LAH-reh KWEH-stah SEH-rah!
I like dancing a lot.	Mi piace molto ballare.	mee PYAH-cheh MOHL-toh bah-LAH-reh
Can you suggest . . .	Può consigliarmi . . .	pwoh kohn-see-LYAHR-mee . . .
• a good disco?	• una buona discoteca?	• OO-nah BWOH-nah dee-skoh-TEH-kah?
• a good nightclub?	• un buon night-club?	• un bwohn "night club"?
Good evening.	Buona sera.	BWOH-nah SEH-rah
We would like a table . . .	Vorremmo un tavolo . . .	vohr-REHM-moh oon TAH-voh-loh . . .
• near the dance floor.	• vicino alla pista.	• vee-CHEE-noh AHL-lah PEE-stah
• near the stage.	• vicino alla scena.	• vee-CHEE-noh AHL-lah SHEH-nah

169

DAYS, MONTHS, AND SEASONS

Days of the Week	Giorni della settimana	JOHR-nee DEHL-lah seht-tee-MAH-nah
What day is it today?	Che giorno è oggi?	keh JOHR-noh eh OHD-jee?
Today is . . .	Oggi è . . .	OHD-jee eh . . .
• Monday.	• lunedì.	• loo-neh-DEE
• Tuesday.	• martedì.	• mahr-teh-DEE
• Wednesday.	• mercoledì.	• mehr-koh-leh-DEE
• Thursday.	• giovedì.	• joh-veh-DEE
• Friday.	• venerdì.	• veh-nehr-DEE
• Saturday.	• sabato.	• SAH-bah-toh
• Sunday.	• domenica.	• doh-MEH-nee-kah

Months of the Year	Mesi dell'anno	MEH-zee dehl-LAHN-noh
January	gennaio	jehn-NAH-yoh
February	febbraio	fehb-BRAH-yoh
March	marzo	MAHR-tsoh
April	aprile	ah-PREE-leh
May	maggio	MAHD-joh
June	giugno	JOO-nyoh
July	luglio	LOO-lyoh
August	agosto	ah-GOH-stoh
September	settembre	seht-TEHM-breh
October	ottobre	oht-TOH-breh
November	novembre	noh-VEHM-breh
December	dicembre	dee-CHEM-breh

Seasons	Le stagioni	leh stah-JOH-nee
spring	la primavera	lah pree-mah-VEH-rah
summer	l'estate	leh-STAH-teh
autumn	l'autunno	low-TOON-noh
winter	l'inverno	leen-VEHR-noh

THE DATE

What's today's date?	**Quanti ne abbiamo oggi?**	KWAHN-tee neh ahb-BYAH-moh OHD-jee?
Today is . . .	**Oggi è . . .**	OHD-jee eh . . .
• January 29, 1990.	• **il ventinove gennaio millenovecentonovanta.**	• eel vehn-tee-NOH-veh jehn-NAH-yoh MEEL-leh-noh-veh-CHEHN-toh-noh-VAHN-tah
• Monday, April 1.	• **lunedì, primo aprile.***	• loo-neh-DEE PREE-moh ah-PREE-leh

*The ordinal number *il primo* (the first) is used for the first day of each month. Otherwise, regular cardinal numbers are used for dates.

AGE

How old are you?	**Quanti anni ha?**	KWAHN-tee AHN-nee ah?
I'm 27.	**Ho ventisette anni.**	oh vehn-tee-SEHT-teh AHN-nee
How old is he/she?	**Quanti anni ha lui/lei?**	KWAHN-tee AHN-nee ah LOO-ee/lay?
He/she is 30.	**Ha trent'anni.**	ah trehn-TAHN-nee
I was born in . . . (year)	**Sono nato(-a) nel . . .**	SOH-noh NAH-toh (-tah) nehl . . .
I'm younger/older than he/she is.	**Sono più giovane/vecchio (-a) di lui/lei.**	SOH-noh pyoo JOH-vah-neh/VEHK-kyoh (-kyah) dee LOO-ee/lay
His/her birthday is March 6, 1953.	**Il suo compleanno è il sei marzo millenoventocinquantatrè.**	eel SOO-oh kohm-pleh-AHN-noh eh eel say MAHR-tsoh MEEL-leh-noh-veh-CHEHN-toh-cheen-kwahn-tah-TREH

171

now	ora/adesso	OH-rah/ah-DEHS-soh
earlier	più presto/prima	pyoo PREH-stoh/PREE-mah
later	più tardi/dopo	pyoo TAHR-dee/DOH-poh
before	prima	PREE-mah
after	dopo	DOH-poh
soon	presto	PREH-stoh
once	una volta	OO-nah VOHL-tah
in the morning	di mattina	dee maht-TEE-nah
at noon	a mezzogiorno	ah mehd-dzoh-JOHR-noh
in the afternoon	di pomeriggio	dee poh-meh-REED-joh
in the evening	di sera	dee SEH-rah
at night	di notte	dee NOHT-teh
at midnight	a mezzanotte	ah mehd-dzah-NOHT-teh
yesterday	ieri	YEH-ree
today	oggi	OHD-jee
tomorrow	domani	doh-MAH-nee
the day before yesterday	ieri l'altro	YEH-ree LAHL-troh
the day after tomorrow	dopodomani	doh-poh-doh-MAH-nee
this week	questa settimana	KWEH-stah seht-tee-MAH-nah
next week	la settimana prossima	lah seht-tee-MAH-nah PROHS-see-mah
last week	la settimana scorsa	lah seht-tee-MAH-nah SKOHR-sah
every week	ogni settimana	OH-nyee seht-tee-MAH-nah
in a week (from now).	fra una settimana	frah OO-nah seht-tee-MAH-nah
in a week (actual time)	in una settimana	een OO-nah seht-tee-MAH-nah
every day	ogni giorno	OH-nyee JOHR-noh
in three days	fra tre giorni	frah treh JOHR-nee

two days ago	**due giorni fa**	DOO-eh JOHR-nee fah
on Saturday	**sabato**	SAH-bah-toh
on Saturdays	**il sabato**	eel SAH-bah-toh
on weekends	**il fine settimana** *(or)* **il weekend**	eel FEE-neh seht-tee-MAH-nah eel wee-KEHND
on weekdays	**durante la settimana**	doo-RAHN-teh lah seht-tee-MAH-nah
a working day	**un giorno feriale**	oon JOHR-noh feh-RYAH-leh
a day off (from work)	**un giorno di permesso**	oon JOHR-noh dee pehr-MEHS-soh
a day off (a free day)	**un giorno libero**	oon JOHR-noh LEE-beh-roh
in January	**in gennaio**	een jehn-NAH-yoh
last January	**gennaio scorso**	jehn-NAH-yoh SKOHR-soh
next January	**gennaio prossimo**	jehn-NAH-yoh PROHS-see-moh
each month	**ogni mese**	OH-nyee MEH-zeh
every month	**tutti i mesi**	TOOT-tee ee MEH-zee
since August	**da agosto**	dah ah-GOH-stoh
in summer	**in estate**	een eh-STAH-teh
this month	**questo mese**	KWEH-stoh MEH-zeh
last month	**il mese scorso**	eel MEH-zeh SKOHR-soh
next year	**l'anno prossimo**	LAHN-noh PROHS-see-moh
every year	**ogni anno**	OH-nyee AHN-noh
In what year . . .	**In che anno . . .**	een keh AHN-noh . . .
In 1990 . . .	**Nel milleno-vecentono-vanta . . .**	nehl MEEL-leh-noh-veh-CHEHN-toh-noh-VAHN-tah . . .
In the nineteenth century . . .	**Nel diciannovesimo secolo . . .**	nehl dee-chahn-noh-VEH-zee-moh SEH-koh-loh . . .
In the sixties . . .	**Negli anni sessanta . . .**	NEH-lyee AHN-nee sehs-SAHN-tah . . .

173

WEATHER

The protection provided by the Alps against the cold northern winds and the influence of sea that moderates the harshness of winter bless Italy with a generally mild climate. However, the weather varies a great deal according to the location. Around the Ligurian Riviera, the southern coasts, and Sicily, the climate is quite mild in the winter, whereas it is cold in northern Italy, especially in the Alps. In the Po Valley and the Apennines, winters are humid and foggy. Summers are hot and humid almost everywhere. However, a pleasant breeze at sea-side resorts mitigates the temperature there, while in the mountains the weather is nice and cool.

What's the weather today?	Che tempo fa oggi?	keh TEHM-poh fah OHD-jee?
It's a nice day.	Fa bel tempo.	fah behl TEHM-poh
It's a nasty day.	Fa brutto tempo. (or) . . . cattivo . . .	fah BROOT-toh TEHM-poh . . . kaht-TEE-voh . . .
It's raining.	Piove.	PYOH-veh
It's pouring.	Piove a catinelle.	PYOH-veh ah kah-tee-NEHL-leh
It's snowing.	Nevica.	NEH-vee-kah
It's . . .	Fa . . .	fah . . .
• cold.	• freddo.	• FREHD-doh
• cool.	• fresco.	• FREH-skoh
• hot.	• caldo.	• KAHL-doh
It's cloudy.	È nuvoloso.	eh-noo-voh-LOH-zoh
It's . . .	C'è . . .	cheh . . .
• foggy.	• nebbia.	• NEHB-byah
• sunny.	• il sole.	• eel SOH-leh
It's windy.	Tira vento.	TEE-rah VEHN-toh
What's the forecast for tomorrow?	Quali sono le previsioni del tempo di domani?	KWAH-lee SOH-noh leh preh-vee-ZYOH-nee dehl TEHM-poh dee doh-MAH-nee?
Is it going to rain?	Pioverà?	pyoh-veh-RAH?

174

Centigrade	Fahrenheit
°C	°F
100	212
40	105
37	98.6
35	
30	90
25	80
20	70
15	60
10	50
5	40
0	32
	30
−5	20
−10	10
−15	0
−20	

TEMPERATURE CONVERSION

To Convert Centigrade to Fahrenheit

$(\frac{9}{5})C° + 32 = F°$

1. Divide by 5.
2. Multiply by 9.
3. Add 32.

To Convert Fahrenheit to Centigrade

$(F° - 32)\frac{5}{9} = C°$

1. Subtract 32.
2. Divide by 9.
3. Multiply by 5.

HOLIDAYS

The following are public holidays in Italy—they are either religious or national. Be aware that when a holiday falls on a Thursday or on a Tuesday, many businesses close for a four-day weekend. This practice of filling the gap is called *fare il ponte* (FAH-reh eel POHN-teh), literally, building the bridge. Keep holidays in mind when planning your trip, because stores, public offices, and banks will be closed on the following dates:

January 1	**Capodanno** (kah-poh-DAHN-noh)	New Year's Day
January 6	**Epifania** (eh-pee-fah-NEE-ah)	Epiphany
March/April	**Pasqua** (PAH-skwah)	Easter
March/April	**Lunedì dell'Angelo/ Pasquetta** (loo-neh-DEE dehl-LAHN-jeh-loh/pah-SKWEHT-tah)	Easter Monday
April 25	**Anniversario della Liberazione** (ahn-nee-vehr-SAH-ryoh DEHL-lah lee-beh-rah-TSYOH-neh)	Liberation Day
May 1	**Giornata del Lavoro** (johr-nah-tah dehl lah-VOH-roh)	Labor Day
August 15	**Assunzione/ Ferragosto** (ahs-soon-TSYOH-neh/fehr-rah-GOH-stoh)	Assumption Day
November 1	**Ognissanti** (oh-nyees-SAHN-tee)	All Saints Day
December 8	**Immacolata Concezione** (eem-mah-koh-LAH-tah kohn-cheh-TSYOH-neh)	Immaculate Conception
December 25	**Natale** (nah-TAH-leh)	Christmas
December 26	**Santo Stefano** (SAHN-toh STEH-fa-no)	Saint Steven

Best wishes!	**Auguri!**	ow-GOO-ree!
Merry Christmas!	**Buon Natale!**	bwohn nah-TAH-leh!
Happy New Year!	**Buon Anno!**	bwohn AHN-noh!
Happy Easter!	**Buona Pasqua!**	BWOH-nah PAH-skwah!
Happy holidays!	**Buone vacanze!**	BWOH-neh vah-KAHN-tseh!
Happy birthday!	**Buon compleanno!**	bwohn kohm-pleh-AHN-noh!
Happy name day!	**Buon onomastico!**	bwohn oh-noh-MAH-stee-koh!
Happy anniversary!	**Buon anniversario!**	bwohn ahn-nee-vehr-SAH-ryoh!
Congratulations!	**Congratulazioni!**	kohn-grah-too-lah-TSYOH-nee!

NATIONAL ORIGINS

Where do you come from?	**Da dove viene?** *(or)* **Di dov'è?**	dah DOH-veh VYEH-neh? dee doh-VEH?
I come from Italy.	**Vengo dall'Italia.** *(or)* **Sono italiano (-a).**	VEHN-goh dahl-lee-TAH-lyah SOH-noh ee-tah-LYAH-noh(-nah)
I come from . . .	**Vengo . . .**	VEHN-goh . . .
• Switzerland.	• **dalla Svizzera.**	• DAHL-lah ZVEET-tseh-rah
• Egypt.	• **dall'Egitto.**	• dahl-leh-JEET-toh

Note: 1. To express the idea of *from,* use *dal* before a masculine country beginning with a consonant, use *dalla* before a feminine country beginning with a consonant, *dall'* before a masculine or feminine country beginning with a vowel, *dalle* before a feminine country that is plural, and *dagli* before a masculine country that is plural (like the United States).

2. For *in* or *to,* use *in* with both masculine and feminine countries that are singular, no matter how they begin; *alle* with feminine plural countries; *negli* with masculine plural countries.

3. For cities, use *da* alone to express *from*—*vengo da Roma* (VEHN-goh dah ROH-mah)—and use *a* alone to express *to*—*vado a Milano* (VAH-doh ah mee-LAH-noh).

• Austria.	• **dall'Austria.**	• dahl-LOW-stryah
• Portugal.	• **dal Portogallo.**	• dahl pohr-toh-GAHL-loh
• the Bahamas.	• **dalle Bahamas.**	• DAHL-leh bah-HAH-mahz
• the United States.	• **dagli Stati Uniti.**	• DAH-lyee STAH-tee oo-NEE-tee

I'm going to . . .	**Vado . . .**	VAH-doh . . .
• Germany.	• **in Germania.**	• een jehr-MAH-nyah
• Mexico.	• **in Messico.**	• een MEHS-see-koh
• the Azores.	• **alle Azorre.**	• AHL-leh ah-DZOHR-reh
• the United States.	• **negli Stati Uniti.**	• NEH-lyee STAH-tee oo-NEE-tee

CONTINENTS

Africa	**l'Africa**	LAH-free-kah
Asia	**l'Asia**	LAH-zyah
Australia	**l'Australia**	low-STRAH-lyah
Europe	**l'Europa**	leh-oo-ROH-pah
North America	**l'America del Nord**	lah-MEH-ree-kah dehl nohrd
South America	**l'America del Sud**	lah-MEH-ree-kah dehl sood

COUNTRIES AND NATIONALITIES

Country	Paese (pah-EH-zeh)	Nationality/ Nazionalità (nah-tsyoh-nah-lee-TAH)
Algeria	**l'Algeria** (lahl-jeh-REE-ah)	**algerino(-a)** (ahl-jeh-REE-noh[-nah])
Argentina	**l'Argentina** (lahr-jehn-TEE-nah)	**argentino(-a)** (ahr-jehn-TEE-noh[-nah])
Australia	**l'Australia** (low-STRAH-lyah)	**australiano(-a)** (ow-strah-LYAH-noh[-nah])
Austria	**l'Austria** (LOW-stryah)	**austriaco(-a)** (ow-STREE-ah-koh[-kah])

Belgium	**il Belgio** (eel BEHL-joh)	**belga** (BEHL-gah)
Bolivia	**la Bolivia** (lah boh-LEE-vyah)	**boliviano(-a)** (boh-lee-VYAH-noh [-nah])
Brazil	**il Brasile** (eel brah-ZEE-leh)	**brasiliano(-a)** (brah-zee-LYAH-noh [-nah])
Canada	**il Canada** (eel KAH-nah-dah)	**canadese** (kah-nah-DEH-zeh)
Chile	**il Cile** (eel CHEE-leh)	**cileno(-a)** (chee-LEH-noh[-nah])
China	**la Cina** (lah CHEE-nah)	**cinese** (chee-NEH-zeh)
Colombia	**la Colombia** (lah koh-LOHM-byah)	**colombiano(-a)** (koh-lohm-BYAH-noh [-nah])
Costa Rica	**la Costa Rica** (lah KOH-stah REE-kah)	**costaricano(-a)** (koh-stah-ree-KAH-noh[-nah])
Cuba	**Cuba** (KOO-bah)	**cubano(-a)** (koo-BAH-noh[-nah])
Denmark	**la Danimarca** (lah dah-nee-MAHR-kah)	**danese** (dah-NEH-zeh)
Dominican Republic	**la Repubblica Dominicana** (lah reh-POOB-blee-kah doh-mee-nee-KAH-nah)	**dominicano(-a)** (doh-mee-nee-KAH-noh[-nah])
Ecuador	**l'Ecuador** (leh-kwah-DOHR)	**ecuadoriano(-a)** (eh-kwah-dohr-YAH-noh[-nah])
Egypt	**l'Egitto** (leh-JEET-toh)	**egiziano(-a)** (eh-jee-TSYAH-noh [-nah])
England	**l'Inghilterra** (leen-geel-TEHR-rah)	**inglese** (een-GLEH-zeh)
Finland	**la Finlandia** (lah feen-LAHN-dyah)	**finlandese** (feen-lahn-DEH-zeh)

179

France	la Francia (lah FRAHN-chah)	francese (frahn-CHEH-zeh)
Germany	la Germania (lah jehr-MAH-nyah)	todesco(-a) (teh-DEH-skoh[-skoh])
Greece	la Grecia (lah GREH-chah)	greco(-a) (GREH-koh[-kah])
Holland	l'Olanda (lah-LAHN-dah)	olandese (oh-lahn-DEH-zeh)
Iceland	l'Islanda (lee-SLAHN-dah)	islandese (ee-slahn-DEH-zeh)
India	l'India (LEEN-dyah)	indiano(-a) (een-DYAH-noh[-nah])
Ireland	l'Irlanda (leer-LAHN-dah)	irlandese (eer-lahn-DEH-zeh)
Israel	Israele (ee-zrah-EH-leh)	israeliano(-a) (ee-zrah-eh-LYAH-noh [-nah])
Italy	l'Italia (lee-TAH-lyah)	italiano(-a) (ee-tah-LYAH-noh [-nah])
Japan	il Giappone (eel jahp-POH-neh)	giapponese (jahp-poh-NEH-zeh)
Mexico	il Messico (eel MEHS-see-koh)	messicano(-a) (mehs-see-KAH-noh [-nah])
Morocco	il Marocco (eel mah-ROHK-koh)	marocchino(-a) (mah-rohk-KEE-noh [-nah])
New Zealand	la Nuova Zelanda (lah NWOH-vah dzeh-LAHN-dah)	zelandese (dzeh-lahn-DEH-zeh)
Norway	la Norvegia (lah nohr-VEH-jah)	norvegese (nohr-veh-JEH-zeh)
Panama	Panama (PAH-nah-mah)	panamense (pah-nah-MEHN-zeh)
Paraguay	il Paraguay (eel pah-rah-GWAHY)	paraguaiano(-a) (pah-rah-gwah-YAH-noh[-nah])
Peru	il Perù (eel peh-ROO)	peruviano(-a) (peh-roo-VYAH-noh [-nah])

Poland	la Polonia	polacco(-a)
	(lah poh-LOH-nyah)	(poh-LAHK-koh[-kah])
Portugal	il Portogallo	portoghese
	(eel pohr-toh-GAHL-loh)	(pohr-toh-GEH-zeh)
Puerto Rico	Porto Rico	portoricano(-a)
	(POHR-toh REE-koh)	(pohr-toh-ree-KAH-noh[-nah])
Russia	la Russia	russo(-a)
	(lah ROOS-syah)	(ROOS-soh[-sah])
Spain	la Spagna	spagnolo(-a)
	(lah SPAH-nyah)	(spah-NYOH-loh[-lah])
Sweden	la Svezia	svedese
	(lah ZVEH-tsyah)	(zveh-DEH-zeh)
Switzerland	la Svizzera	svizzero(-a)
	(lah ZVEET-tseh-rah)	(ZVEET-tseh-roh[-rah])
Thailand	la Tailandia	tailandese
	(lah tahy-LAHN-dyah)	(tahy-lahn-DEH-zeh)
Tunisia	la Tunisia	tunisino(-a)
	(lah too-nee-SEE-ah)	(too-nee-SEE-noh [-nah])
Turkey	la Turchia	turco(-a)
	(lah toor-KEE-ah)	(TOOR-koh[-kah])
United States	gli Stati Uniti	americano(-a)
	(lyee STAH-tee oo-NEE-tee)	(ah-meh-ree-KAH-noh [-nah])
Uruguay	l'Uruguay	uruguaiano(-a)
	(loo-roo-GWAHY)	(oo-roo-gwah-YAH-noh[-nah])
Venezuela	il Venezuela	venezuelano(-a)
	(eel veh-neh-TZWEH-lah)	(veh-neh-tzweh-LAH-noh[-nah])

LANGUAGES

Name of languages, *lingue* (LEEN-gweh), or idioms, *idiomi* (ee-DYOH-mee), are usually the same as the masculine form of the nationality. For example, the words for the German and Spanish languages are *tedesco* (teh-DEH-skoh) and *spagnolo* (spah-NYOH-loh). Likewise, to say "I speak Italian" you say *Parlo italiano* (PAHR-loh ee-tah-LYAH-noh), or for "I speak English" you say *Parlo inglese* (PAHR-loh een-GLEH-zeh). Remember that the indefinite article is used with names of languages but commonly omitted after the verb *parlare* (to speak):

I speak Italian.	**Parlo italiano.**	PAHR-loh ee-tah-LYAH-noh
I like Italian.	**Mi piace l'italiano.**	mee PYAH-cheh lee-tah-LYAH-noh

OCCUPATIONS

Professions	Professioni	proh-fehs-SYOH-nee
architect	**architetto**	ahr-kee-TEHT-toh/tah
artist	**artista***	ahr-TEE-stah
cardiologist	**cardiologo**	kahr-DYOH-loh-goh/gah
dentist	**dentista**	dehn-TEE-stah
doctor	**dottore/dottoressa**	doh-TOH-reh/doh-toh-REHS-sah
	(or) medico	MEH-dee-koh
engineer	**ingegnere**	een-jeh-NYEH-reh
eye doctor (opthalmologist)	**oculista**	oh-koo-LEE-stah
lawyer	**avvocato**	ahv-voh-KAH-toh
neurologist	**neurologo**	neh-oo-ROH-loh-goh
painter	**pittore/pittrice**	peet-TOH-reh/peet-TREE-cheh
sculptor	**scultore/scultrice**	skool-TOH-reh/skool-TREE-cheh
writer	**scrittore/scrittrice**	skreet-TOH-reh/skreet-TREE-cheh

*The masculine form of some professions is used by women as well as men. Masculine forms ending in -a also can be used for both men and women.

Occupations	Occupazioni	ohk-koo-pah-TSYOH-nee
accountant	commercialista	kom-mehr-chah-LEE-stah
baker	fornaio(-a)	fohr-NAH-yoh(-yah)
blacksmith	fabbro	FAHB-broh
butcher	macellaio(-a)	mah-chehl-LAH-yoh (-yah)
carpenter	falegname	fah-leh-NYAH-meh
chef	chef	shehf
clerk	impiegato(-a)	eem-pyeh-GAH-toh (-tah)
cook	cuoco(-a)	KWOH-koh(-kah)
electrician	elettricista	eh-leht-tree-CHEE-stah
locksmith	fabbro ferraio	FAHB-broh fehr-RAH-yoh
maid	cameriera	kah-meh-RYEH-rah
nurse	infermierme(-a)	een-fehr-MYEH-reh (-rah)
plumber	idraulico	ee-DROW-lee-koh
salesperson	commesso(-a)	kohm-MEHS-soh(-sah)
shoemaker	calzolaio	kahl-tsoh-LAH-yoh
shopkeeper	negoziante	neh-goh-TSYAHN-teh
waiter/waitress	cameriere(-a)	kah-meh-RYEH-reh (-rah)

EMERGENCIES

Look!	Guardi!	GWAHR-dee!
Listen!	Ascolti!	ah-SKOHL-tee!
	(or) Senta!	SEHN-tah!
Watch out!	Attenzione!	aht-tehn-TSYOH-neh!
Fire!	Al fuoco!	ahl FWOH-koh!
Help!	Aiuto!	ah-YOO-toh!
Stop!	Fermo!	FEHR-moh!
	(or) Alt!	ahlt!
Stop him!	Fermatelo!	fehr-MAH-teh-loh!
Thief!	Al ladro!	ahl LAH-droh!
Call the police!	Chiami la polizia!	KYAH-mee lah poh-lee-TSEE-ah!

183

Cull the fire department!	**Chiami i pompieri!**	KYAH-mee ee pohm-PYEH-ree!
I'm sick!	**Sto male!**	stoh MAH-leh!
Call a doctor!	**Chiami un dottore!**	KYAH-mee oon doht-TOH-reh!
It's an emergency!	**È un'emergenza!**	eh oo-neh-mehr-JEHN-tsah!
I'm lost!	**Mi sono perso!**	mee SOH-noh PEHR-soh!
Can you help me?	**Mi può aiutare?**	mee PWOH ah-yoo-TAH-reh?
Leave me alone!	**Mi lasci in pace!**	mee LAH-shee een PAH-cheh!
Someone/They stole my . . .	**Mi hanno rubato . . .**	mee AHN-noh roo-BAH-to . . .
• camera.	• **la macchina fotografica.**	• lah MAHK-kee-nah foh-toh-GRAH-fee-kah
• handbag.	• **la borsetta.**	• lah bohr-SEHT-tah
• money.	• **i soldi.**	• ee SOHL-dee
• suitcase.	• **la valigia.**	• lah vah-LEE-jah
• wallet.	• **il portafoglio.**	• eel pohr-tah-FOH-lyoh
• watch.	• **l'orologio.**	• loh-roh-LOH-joh
I've lost my . . .	**Ho perso . . .**	oh PEHR-soh . . .
• car keys.	• **le chiavi della macchina.**	• leh KYAH-vee DEHL-lah MAHK-kee-nah
• credit cards.	• **le carte di credito.**	• leh KAHR-teh dee KREH-dee-toh

184

15/GRAMMAR IN BRIEF

With this book, you can find and use essential phrases without formal study of Italian grammar. However, by learning some of the basic grammatical patterns, you will be able to construct an unlimited number of your own sentences and greatly increase your range of expression.

DEFINITE ARTICLES

Articles have different forms to agree with nouns in gender—masculine or feminine—and in number—singular or plural.

Masculine Singular

il (noun begins with a consonant)

il libro (the book)

l' (noun begins with a vowel)

l'albero (the tree)

lo (noun begins with s + consonant, or z)

lo stadio, lo zingaro (the stadium, the gypsy)

Masculine Plural

il becomes i
l' and lo become gli

i libri (the books)
gli alberi, gli stadi, gli zingari (the trees, the stadiums, the gypsies)

Feminine Singular

la (noun begins with any consonant)

la casa, la sala, la scuola, la zia (the house, the hall, the school, the aunt)

l' (noun begins with a vowel)

l'agenda (the agenda)

Feminine Plural

le (for all forms)

le case, le sale, le scuole, le zie (the houses, the halls, the schools, the aunts)

INDEFINITE ARTICLES

Masculine Singular

un (before nouns beginning with vowels and consonants)

un amico, un libro, un sasso (a friend, a book, a stone)

uno (before nouns beginning with s + consonant or z)

uno studente, uno zio (a student, an uncle)

Masculine Plural

dei (before nouns beginning with a consonant)

dei libri, dei sassi (some books, some stones)

degli (before nouns beginning with a vowel, s + consonant, or z)

degli amici, degli studenti, degli zii (some friends, some students, some uncles)

Feminine Singular

un' (before nouns beginning with a vowel)

un'amica, un'automobile (a friend, a car)

una (before nouns beginning with *any* consonant)

una casa, una sala, una scuola, una zia (a house, a hall, a school, an aunt)

Feminine Plural

delle (before vowels and consonants)

delle amiche, delle case, delle sale, delle scuole, delle zie (some friends, some houses, some halls some schools, some aunts)

The following chart summarizes the forms of the articles:

Definite—"the"	Singular	Plural
Masculine	il	i
	l', lo	gli
Feminine	l', la	le

Indefinite	Singular—"a, an"	Plural—"some"
Masculine	un, uno	dei/degli
Feminine	un', una	delle

186

NOUNS

All nouns in Italian are either masculine or feminine (there is no neuter). As a general rule, all masculine nouns end in -*o* in the singular and -*i* in the plural. All feminine nouns end in -*a* in the singular and -*e* in the plural. However, there are also nouns ending in -*e* in the singular, which may be either masculine or feminine. Whether masculine or feminine, they both end in -*i* in the plural. When you come across nouns ending in -*e*, it's advisable to learn them with the proper definite article so that you will immediately recognize the gender.*

	Singular	Plural
m. (book)	**il libro**	**i libri**
f. (house)	**la casa**	**le case**
m. (flower)	**il fiore**	**i fiori**
f. (car)	**l'automobile**	**le automobili**

*m. and f. refer to masculine and feminine.

ADJECTIVES

Descriptive Adjectives

Adjectives agree in gender and number with the noun they modify. They usually follow the noun:

il ragazzo italiano (the Italian boy)
il vino bianco (the white wine)

They *always* follow the noun when modified by the adverb *molto* (very):

una ragazza molto bella (a very beautiful girl)

When the adjective ends in -*e* it does not change to agree with the noun in gender:

un uomo intelligente (an intelligent man)
una donna intelligente (an intelligent woman)

To make an adjective plural, follow the same rules given for the nouns:

187

Singular	Plural
ragazzo Italiano (Italian boy)	**ragazzi italiani** (Italian boys)
ragazzo spagnola (Spanish girl)	**ragazze spagnole** (Spanish girls)
bambino francese (French child [m.])	**bambini francesi** (French children)
bambina inglese (English child [f.])	**bambine inglesi** (English children)

If an adjective modifies two or more nouns of different gender, the masculine plural form must be used, and the article repeated before each noun:

I giornali e le riviste sono interessanti. (The papers and magazines are interesting.)

Some common adjectives may precede the noun. They are:

bello (beautiful), **brutto** (ugly), **buono** (good), **cattivo** (bad), **grande** (big), **piccolo** (small), **giovane** (young), **vecchio** (old)

Demonstrative Adjectives

Questo (this, these):

questo, questa (this)   **questi, queste** (these)

Quello (that, those) has several different forms that follow the pattern of the definite articles (for reference see the chart on p. 186):

quel, quell', quello, quella (that)	**quei, quegli, quelle** (those)
quel libro (that book)	**quei libri** (those books)
quell'amico (that friend)	**quegli amici/studenti** (those friends/students)
quello studente (that student)	
quella casa (that house)	**quelle case** (those houses)

Possessive Adjectives

Possessive adjectives denote ownership. In Italian they agree in gender and number with the thing possessed, not with the possessor as they do in English. They precede the noun.

| | Singular | | Plural | |
	Masculine	**Feminine**	**Masculine**	**Feminine**
my	il mio	la mia	i miei	le mie
your (familiar sing.)	il tuo	la tua	i tuoi	le tue
your (polite sing.)	il Suo	la Sua	i Suoi	le Sue
his/her	il suo	la sua	i suoi	le sue
our	il nostro	la nostra	i nostri	le nostre
your (familiar plural)	il vostro	la vostra	i vostri	le vostre
your (polite plural)	il Loro	la Loro	i Loro	le Loro
their	il loro	la loro	i loro	le loro

Here are some examples:

la mia camera (my room)
la sua casa (his/her house)
il suo appartamento (his/her apartment)
i nostri libri (our books)
le loro valigie (their suitcases)

In some expressions, the possessive adjective is used without the definite article and is placed after the noun:

a casa mia/tua/sua (at my/your/his/her place)
da parte Sua (on your behalf [polite form])
È colpa sua. (It's his/her fault.)

Important: Possessive adjectives are used without the article with a singular, unmodified noun expressing family relationship, except for *their*, which always requires the article:

mio padre (my father), **tua madre** (your mother), **suo fratello** (his/her brother), **nostra sorella** (our sister), **vostra zia** (your aunt), but **il loro cugino** (their cousin)

If the noun denoting family relationship is modified by an adjective or a suffix, then the possessive retains the article.

il mio caro padre (my dear father), **la mia cara madre** (my dear mother), **il mio fratellino** (my little brother)

Possessive adjectives are less used in Italian than they are in English, especially when possession is evident and particularly with parts of the body or articles of clothing:

Ho lasciato i guanti a casa. (I left my gloves at home.)
Mi fa male la testa. (My head aches.)

COMPARATIVES

Italian has three comparatives: equality *(uguaglianza)*, majority *(maggioranza)*, and minority *(minoranza)*.

1. Comparison of Equality (as . . . as)   adjective + *come:*

Il mio appartamento è grande come il tuo. (My apartment is as large as yours.)

2. Comparison of Majority (-er . . . than/more . . . than) and Comparison of Minority (less . . . than/fewer . . . than)

(a) *più* (more)/*meno* (less) . . . *di* (by itself or combined with the definite article) when two different persons or items are compared:

Questa ragazza è più alta di Maria. (This girl is taller than Maria.)
Il mio libro è più interessante del tuo. (My book is more interesting than yours.)

(b) *più* (more)/*meno* (less) . . . *che,* when two words are compared and related to the same subject:

Questa ragazza è più elegante che bella. (This girl is more elegant than beautiful.)

(c) *più* (more)/*meno* (less) . . . *di quel/quello che* + verb:

Studia più di quel/quello che tu pensi. (He studies more than you think.)

SUPERLATIVES

Italian has two superlatives:

1. Relative Superlative, superlativo relativo (the most/the least/the . . . -est. The relative superlative is formed by placing the appropriate definite article before *più* or *meno*. The second term, of/in, is translated with *di*, either by itself or combined with the definite article:

Quest'uomo è il più ricco del mondo. (This man is the richest in the world.)
Lei è la più/meno famosa delle sorelle. (She is the most/least famous of the sisters.)

2. Absolute Superlative, superlativo assoluto (very + adjective). Italians are very fond of the *-issimo* form, which agrees in gender and number:

È un quadro bellissimo. (It's a very beautiful painting.)
È una rivista interessantissima. (It's a very interesting magazine.)

Of course, you can also use the invariable adverb *molto* (very) before the adjective:

È un quadro molto bello. (It's a very beautiful painting.)
È una stampa molto vecchia. (It's a very old print.)

Irregular Comparatives and Superlatives
Some adjectives have irregular comparatives and superlatives in addition to the regular forms.

Positive	Comparative	Relative Superlative	Absolute Superlative
good	better	the best	very good
buono (regular)	**più buono(-a)**	**il(la) più buono(-a)**	**buonissimo**
(irregular)	**migliore**	**il/la migliore**	**ottimo**
bad	worse	the worst	very bad
cattivo (regular)	**più cattivo(-a)**	**il(la) più cattivo(-a)**	**cattivissimo (-a)**
(irregular)	**peggiore**	**il/la peggiore**	**pessimo(-a)**

Positive	Comparative	Relative Superlative	Absolute Superlative
big/great	bigger/greater	the biggest/ greatest	very big/great
grande (regular)	**più grande**	**il/la più grande**	**grandissimo (-a)**
(irregular)	**maggiore**	**il/la maggiore**	**massimo(-a)**
small/little	smaller	the smallest	very small
piccolo (regular)	**più piccolo (-a)**	**il(la) più piccolo(-a)**	**piccolissimo (-a)**
(irregular)	**minore**	**il/la minore**	**minimo(-a)**

lento	**lenta**	**lentamente**
serio	**seria**	**seriamente**

Remember, *maggiore* and *minore* are also used to express age:

mio fratello maggiore (my older brother)
mia sorella minore (my younger sister)

ADVERBS

In English, *-ly* is added to an adjective to form an adverb. Italian forms adverbs by adding *-mente* to the feminine form of the adjective:

If the adjective ends in *-le* or *-re*, the final *e* is dropped before adding *-mente*:

facile	**facilmente**
particolare	**particolarmente**

Note that some common adverbs have their own form, or the same form as the adjectives:

Their Own Form		Adjective Form	
allora	then	**chiaro**	clearly
ancora	yet	**forte**	loud
bene	well	**giusto**	right

così	so	**piano**	slow
già	already	**sodo**	hard (as in *lavorare sodo*—to work hard)
insieme	together	**veloce**	fast
male	badly	**vicino**	near
meglio	better		
peggio	worse		
sempre	always		
spesso	often		
subito	at once		
tardi	late		

PRONOUNS

Pronouns stand for or replace nouns. They perform several distinct functions.

Subject Pronouns

These pronouns are the subjects of sentences or clauses, and are usually found at the beginning of the sentence. In Italian, subject pronouns are usually omitted because the verb ending indicates who is performing the action:

Vado al cinema. (I am going to the movies.)
Mangiamo il gelato. (We eat ice cream.)

Direct Object Pronouns

They represent persons or things that receive the action of the verb. They answer the question Whom? or What? They are used with transitive verbs, that is, with those verbs that take an object:

Vedi Maria? Sì *la* **vedo questo pomeriggio.** (Do you see Maria? Yes, I'll see her this afternoon.)
Capisci l'italiano? Sì, *lo* **capisco un po'.** (Do you understand Italian? Yes, I understand it a little.)

As seen from the above examples, Italian direct object pronouns are usually placed before the conjugated verb. With an infinitive, however, they follow and are attached to the infinitive, which drops the final *-e*:

193

Ti piace guardare la televisione? Sì, mi piace guardar*la*. (Do you like to watch television? Yes, I like to watch it.)

Indirect Object Pronouns
They receive the action of the verb indirectly: the action is done to or for the indirect object. They answer the question To whom? or For whom?

Parlo a Mario. *Gli* parlo. (I speak to him.)
Parlo a Maria. *Le* parlo. (I speak to her.)

The placement of indirect object pronouns is the same as for direct objects. They usually precede a conjugated verb, the only exception being *loro* (to them), which always follows:

Parlo agli amici. *Gli* parlo. (I speak to my friends. I speak to them.)

Again, with an infinitive the indirect object pronoun is attached to the infinitive, which drops the final *-e*. With *loro*, the infinitive may retain its final *-e* (optional) and the pronoun is never attached:

Ho bisogno di veder*la*. (I need to see her.)
Preferisco parlar(e) loro. (I prefer to speak to them.)

Pronouns as Objects of Prepositions
They always follow the preposition:

Vado con lei. (I'm going with her.)
Lo faccio per te. (I'm doing this for you.)

The following chart shows the forms of all the pronouns mentioned above.

Subject		Direct Object		Indirect Object		After a Preposition	
I	**io**	me	**mi**	to me	**mi**	me	**me**
you (familiar)	**tu**	you	**ti**	to you	**ti**	you	**te**
you (polite)	**Lei**	you	**La**	to you	**Le**	you	**Lei**

he	**lui**	him	**lo**	to him	**gli**	him	**lui**
she	**lei**	her	**la**	to her	**le**	her	**lei**
we	**noi**	us	**ci**	to us	**ci**	us	**noi**
you (familiar)	**voi**	you	**vi**	to you	**vi**	you	**voi**
you (polite)	**Loro**	you	**Li** (m.) **Le** (f.)	to you	. . . **Loro**	you	**Loro**
they	**loro**	them	**li** (m.) **le** (f.)	to them	. . . **loro**	them	**loro**

Note: Tu, Lei, voi, Loro. Italian has preserved a distinction between familiar and formal "you" both in the singular and in the plural.

Dare del tu, or to use the *tu* form with someone, is reserved for children, close friends, and relatives. *Dare del Lei*, or to use the *Lei* polite form, is reserved for people with whom you are not familiar, people you have just met, people whose name is preceded by a title such as Mr. or Dr., and finally with people you hold in esteem and reverence. Never confuse the *tu* and the *Lei* forms. Therefore, if you are addressing a friend of yours and want to ask "How are you?" you will say, *Come stai (tu)?* If you are addressing a doctor or lawyer, you will say, *Come sta (Lei)?* In the plural the *voi* and *Loro* forms have now become almost interchangeable in favor of *voi: Come state (voi)?*

Relative Pronouns
In English, relative pronouns are often omitted. In Italian they must always be expressed. They are:

che	who, whom, which, that (invariable; refers to persons and things): **l'uomo che parla** (the man who speaks) **i libri che devo leggere** (the books I must read)
cui	whom, that, which (always after a preposition; refers to persons and things and is invariable): **l'appartamento in cui vivo** (the apartment I live in) **l'uomo a cui parlo** (the man I'm talking to)

195

il/la cui, i/le cui	whose, of which (used to express possession; the article agrees in gender and number with the noun following cui, that is, with the person or thing possessed):
	il signore la cui moglie è italiana (the man whose wife is Italian)
	l'edificio i cui inquilini sono in vacanza (the building whose tenants are on vacation)
il/la quale, i/le quali	(the one) who, whom (used instead of che to avoid ambiguity; the article will express the gender and number of the antecedent, the subject of the sentence):
	L'amico di Maria il quale arriva oggi (Mary's friend who is arriving today)
	La sorella di Paolo la quale è al mare (Paul's sister who is at the seaside)

Interrogative Pronouns

chi	who, whom (invariable)
che, che cosa, cosa	what (invariable and interchangeable)
quale/quali	which (one/ones)
quanto(-a), quanti(-e)	how much, how many
Chi parla italiano?	Who speaks Italian?
Che cosa hai visto?	What did you see?
Quali hai letto?	Which ones did you read?
Quanti hanno parlato?	How many did speak?

Demonstrative Pronouns

They are less complicated than the demonstrative adjectives because *questo* (this) and *quello* (that) as pronouns only have four regular forms, according to gender and number.

Singular		Plural	
questo, questa	this (one)	**questi, queste**	these (ones)
quello, quella	that (one)	**quelli, quelle**	those (ones)

Questo è buono e quello è cattivo. (This one is good, and that one is bad.)

Queste sono belle e quelle sono brutte. (These are beautiful, and those are ugly.)

NEGATIVE SENTENCES

To form the negative in Italian place the word *non* in front of the verb. For example:

Parlo Italiano. (I speak Italian.)
Non parlo italiano. (I don't speak Italian.)

Other words that are used with the negative *non* are:

affatto (at all)	**Non sono affatto contento.** (I am not at all happy.)
ancora (yet)	**Non ho ancora mangiato.** (I haven't eaten yet.)
mai (never)	**Non ha mai soldi.** (He never has money.)
nulla/niente (nothing)	**Non sanno niente.*** (They don't know anything/They know nothing.)
nessuno (no one)	**Non conosco nessuno.*** (I don't know anyone./I know no one.)
neanche/nemmeno/neppure (not even)	**Non vengo neanche se mi preghi.** (I won't come, not even if you beg me.)
più (more, longer)	**Non abita più qui.** (He doesn't live here any more.)

As you may have noticed from the examples, Italian uses double negatives. At times there can be as many and three negatives in a sentence:

Non ha detto niente a nessuno. (He did not say anything to anyone. Literally: He did not say nothing to no one.)

*Notice that both sapere and conoscere mean to know. Sapere is used when referring to facts, conoscere when referring to people and places. Also note that the personal pronoun is not used here. The meaning is implied by the particular verb conjugation.

QUESTIONS

Questions are easy to form in Italian. The simplest way is to raise the intonation of your voice at the end of a statement to indicate a question, as you would do in English:

197

| Statement (flat voice) | **Andiamo al ristorante.** (We are going to the restaurant.) |
| Question (raising voice) | **Andiamo al ristorante?** (Shall we go to the restaurant?) |

Wh- questions are another major category. These are the questions that in English begin with *wh-*:

who?	**chi?**	**Chi arriva oggi?** (Who is arriving today?)
what?	**che cosa?**	**Che cosa leggi?** (What are you reading?)
where?	**dove?**	**Dove vai a quest'ora?** (Where are you going at this time?)
when?	**quando?**	**Quando parte il treno?** (When does the train leave?)
why?	**perché?**	**Perché mangi adesso?** (Why are you eating now?)

These questions are formed as follows:

wh- word + verb + subject

PREPOSITIONS

The most common prepositions in Italian are:

to	**a**	ah
from	**da**	dah
of	**di**	dee
in	**in**	een
on	**su**	soo
	(or) sopra	SOH-prah
with	**con**	kohn
about	**circa**	CHEER-kah
	(or) di	dee
according to	**secondo**	seh-KOHN-doh
across	**attraverso**	aht-trah-VEHR-soh
after	**dopo**	DOH-poh
against	**contro**	KOHN-troh
among/between	**tra**	trah
	(or) fra	frah
at	**a**	ah

GRAMMAR

at (plus name of person or profession)*	**da**	dah
besides	**inoltre**	ee-NOHL-treh
by/for	**per**	pehr
during	**durante**	doo-RAHN-teh
except	**eccetto**	eht-CHEHT-toh
over	**sopra**	SOH-prah
through	**attraverso**	aht-trah-VEHR-soh
	(or) per	pehr
towards	**verso**	VEHR-soh
under	**sotto**	SOHT-toh
without	**senza**	SEHN-tsah

*At the doctor's would be translated dal (da + il) dottore. At Marco's (house) is da Marco.

CONTRACTIONS

In Italian some prepositions combine with the definite article to make one word. The most common are:

Prepositions	Articles						
	+il	+lo	+l'	+la	+i	+gli	+le
a (to)	al	allo	all'	alla	ai	agli	alle
da (from)	dal	dallo	dall'	dalla	dai	dagli	dalle
di (of)	del	dello	dell'	della	dei	degli	delle
in (in)	nel	nello	nell'	nella	nei	negli	nelle
su (on)	sul	sullo	sull'	sulla	sui	sugli	sulle

Note the following idiomatic forms:

alla radio (on the radio)
alla televisione (on TV)
al telefono (on the phone)
sul giornale (in the newspaper)

VERBS

There are three verb conjugations in Italian. In the infinitive, all verbs end in either *-are*, *-ere*, or *-ire*. Verbs ending in *-ire* fall into two categories: the regular ones (those whose ending *-ire* is usually preceded by two consonants such as *dormire—rm* before *ire* (to sleep), and the so-called *isco* verbs, namely those whose ending -*ire* is only preceded by one consonant, such as *capire—p* before *ire* (to understand). The *isco* verbs add -*isc*- between the stem of the verb, *cap-* in this case, and the ending for all forms except *noi* (we) and *voi* (you).

	1st Conjugation	2nd Conjugation	3rd Conjugation	
	Parlare (to speak)	Ripetere (to repeat)	Dormire (to sleep)	Capire (-*isc*) (to understand)
(io)	parlo	ripeto	dormo	capisco
(tu)	parli	ripeti	dormi	capisci
(lui/lei/Lei)	parla	ripete	dorme	capisce
(noi)	parliamo	ripetiamo	dormiamo	capiamo
(voi)	parlate	ripetete	dormite	capite
(loro/Loro)	parlano	ripetono	dormono	capiscono

For the third-person plural, *loro*, the stress is on the stem: *parlano* (PAHR-lah-noh), *ripetono* (ree-PEH-toh-noh), *dormono* (DOHR-moh-noh), and *capiscono* (kah-PEE-skoh-noh). All regular verbs follow this pattern.

	Essere (to be)	Avere (to have)	Andare (to go)	Venire (to come)
(io)	sono	ho	vado	vengo
(tu)	sei	hai	vai	vieni
(lui/lei/Lei)	è	ha	va	viene
(noi)	siamo	abbiamo	andiamo	veniamo
(voi)	siete	avete	andate	venite
(loro/Loro)	sono	hanno	vanno	vengono

	Dare (to give)	Dire (to say/tell)	Fare (to do)	Stare (to be/stay)
(io)	do	dico	faccio	sto
(tu)	dai	dici	fai	stai

(lui/lei/Lei)	dà	dice	fa	sta
(noi)	diamo	diciamo	facciamo	stiamo
(voi)	date	dite	fate	state
(loro/Loro)	danno	dicono	fanno	stanno

Irregular Verbs

Some commonly used verbs do not follow the patterns given above and have irregular forms. Here are conjugations of a few of the most common irregular verbs.

	Dovere (must)	Potere (to be able/can)	Volere (want)
(io)	devo (debbo)	posso	voglio
(tu)	devi	puoi	vuoi
(lui/lei/Lei)	deve	può	vuole
(noi)	dobbiamo	possiamo	vogliamo
(voi)	dovete	potete	volete
(loro/Loro)	devono (or) debbono	possono	vogliono

Past Tense

To express an action in the past Italian usually recurs to the structure called *passato prossimo* (present perfect):

subject + present tense of *essere* or *avere* + past participle of main verb

The past participle is formed by adding the appropriate ending to the stem:

Infinitive	Ending	Past Participle
parl-are	-ato	parlato
ripet-ere	-uto	ripetuto
cap-ire	-ito	capito

In this past tense, all verbs are conjugated with either *avere* (to have) or *essere* (to be). All transitive verbs (verbs that take an object) are conjugated with *avere* (whether the object is expressed or not). The past participle is invariable:

| We ate (an apple). | **Abbiamo mangiato (una mela).** |
| I sang an Italian song. | **Ho cantato una canzone italiana.** |

All intransitive verbs (verbs that do not take an object), such as verbs of motion, are conjugated with the auxiliary *essere*. In this case, the past participle always agrees in gender and number with the subject. Here's a list of the most common verbs conjugated with *essere*:

Verb	Infinitive	Past Participle
to arrive/to leave	**arrivare/partire**	**arrivato(-a)/ partito(-a)**
to enter/to leave (go out)	**entrare/uscire**	**entrato(-a)/ uscito(-a)**
to go up/to go down	**salire/scendere**	**salito(-a)/ sceso(-a)**
to go/to come	**andare/venire**	**andato(-a)/ venuto(-a)**
to remain/to return	**rimanere/ritornare**	**rimasto(-a)/ ritornato(-a)**
to be born/to die	**nascere/morire**	**nato(-a)/morto(-a)**

| Mary left for Bologna. | **Maria è partita per Bologna.** |
| The boys have just arrived. | **I ragazzi sono appena arrivati.** |

Irregular Past Participles
Some of the most commonly used Italian verbs have irregular past participles. A number of these are listed below. They are all conjugated with the auxiliary *avere,** and the past participle, as mentioned above, is invariable.

Verb	Infinitive	Past Participle
to ask	**chiedere**	**chiesto**
to be	**essere**	**stato(-a)**
to choose	**scegliere**	**scelto**
to do/to make	**fare**	**fatto**
to drink	**bere**	**bevuto**

to light	accendere	acceso
to offer	offrire	offerto
to open	aprire	aperto
to put	mettere	messo
to read	leggere	letto
to say/to tell	dire	detto
to take	prendere	preso
to turn off	spegnere	spento
to write	scrivere	scritto
We had (took) coffee.	**Abbíamo preso il caffè.**	
I wrote many cards.	**Ho scritto molte cartoline.**	

*Note that *essere* is always conjugated with the auxiliary *essere*, and its past participle is *stato(-a)*, just like the past participle of *stare* (to stay):

I have been **Sono stato(-a).**

Avere has a regular past participle and is conjugated with the auxiliary *avere*:

She has had. **Ha avuto.**

Future Tense

The Future tense expresses a future action and is the equivalent of the English "I will" or "I'm going to" + infinitive. The easiest way to form the future in Italian is as follows: drop the final *e* of the infinitive and add the endings -*o*, -*ai*, -*a*, -*emo*, -*ete*, -*anno*. Verbs ending in -*are* change the stem from -*ar* to -*er* and then add the endings.*

Parlare	Ripetere	Dormire	Finire
parlerò	ripeterò	dormirò	finirò
parlerai	ripeterai	dormirai	finirai
parlerà	ripeterà	dormirà	finirà
parleremo	ripeteremo	dormiremo	finiremo
parlerete	ripeterete	dormirete	finirete
parleranno	ripeteranno	dormiranno	finiranno

*The stem for conjugating the future tense of *essere* is *sar-*, and for *avere*, *avr-*.

I'll remember my beautiful holidays in Italy.	**Ricorderò le mie belle vacanze in Italia.**
We'll buy some shoes in Florence.	**Compreremo delle scarpe a Firenze.**

Reflexive Verbs

Reflexive verbs are those in which the action of the verb reflects back on the subject. In Italian, reflexive verbs are conjugated with reflexive pronouns, as follows:

subject pronoun (optional) + reflexive pronoun + conjugated verb

Subject	Reflexive Pronoun	Verb (*lavarsi,* to wash oneself)
io	mi	lavo
tu	ti	lavi
lui/lei/Lei	si	lava
noi	ci	laviamo
voi	vi	lavate
loro/Loro	si	lavano

Mi lavo tutte le mattine. (I wash myself every morning.)
Si rade un giorno sì e un giorno no. (He shaves every other day.)

In compound tenses, reflexive verbs are conjugated with *essere* and the past participle must agree in gender and number:

(Lei) Si è alzata e si è vestita. (She got up and got dressed.)

The reflexive is used in Italian with parts of the body and articles of clothing. The English possessive is replaced by the definite article:

Mi lavo le mani. (I wash my hands.)
Si mette il cappotto. (She puts her coat on.)

With a compound tense and an object in the sentence, the past participle preferably agrees with the subject rather than with the object:

204

Mario si è lavato la faccia. (Mario washed his face.)
Carla si è messa i guanti. (Carla put her gloves on.)

Here, *lavato* agrees with Mario, not *la faccia*, and *messa* agrees with Carla, not with *i guanti*. Some common verbs can be made reflexive by dropping the final -*e* and by adding -*si* to the infinitive. For example:

alzare	to lift	**alzarsi**	to get up
chiamare	to call	**chiamarsi**	to be named
lavare	to wash	**lavarsi**	to wash oneself
svegliare	to wake (someone) up	**svegliarsi**	to wake up
vestire	to dress	**vestirsi**	to get dressed

Verbs *Essere* and *Stare*

The verb "to be" is expressed in Italian by two different verbs: *essere* and *stare* (see irregular verbs section for conjugation). *Essere* is used most of the time. *Stare* is used:

1. In courtesy expressions to express how one feels with an adverb like *bene* or *male*, such as *Come sta?* (How are you?), and their answers *Sto bene/male/così così.* (I'm well/not well/so so.) However, with an adjective, one must use *essere: Sono stanco.* (I am tired.), *Sono contenta.* (I am happy.)
2. To form the progressive tense, to describe an action in progress:

Sto parlando. (I am speaking.)
Stai scrivendo. (You are writing.)
Sta dormendo. (He is sleeping.)

Note: the gerund is formed as follows:

-*are* verbs drop -*are* from the infinitive and add -*ando (parl-are/parl-ando).*
-*ere* and -*ire* verbs drop -*ere* and -*ire* and add -*endo (scriv-ere/scriv-endo; dorm-ire/dorm-endo).*

Special Uses of *Avere* and *Fare*

In Italian, some idiomatic forms are expressed with the verb *avere* (to have) + noun to describe a state of being, whereas in

English the same idioms are usually expressed with "to be" + adjective. For example, "I am hungry" is expressed in Italian as "I have hunger," *Ho fame.*

avere . . . anni	to be . . . years old
avere . . .	to be . . .
• bisogno di . . .	• in need of . . .
• caldo	• warm
• fame	• hungry
• freddo	• cold
• fretta	• in a hurry
• paura	• afraid
• sete	• thirsty
• sonno	• sleepy
avere voglia di . . .	to feel like . . .

Fare (to make) is also used to express "to be," but it refers to weather conditions, and it's always used in the third-person singular:

Che tempo fa? (What's the weather like?)
Fa bel tempo. (The weather is nice.)

To Like *(Piacere)*

Piacere is the equivalent of "to like." However, its construction is different from the English "to like" and more similar to the expression "to be pleasing to." To get it right in Italian, you have to change the sentence around, and use **piace** if the object is singular, **piacciono** if the object is plural.

"I like pasta," becomes "Pasta is pleasing to me." **Mi piace la pasta.**
"I like books," becomes "Books are pleasing to me." **Mi piacciono i libri.**

If the subject of the English sentence is a person, his/her name will be introduced in Italian by the preposition *a*:

A Maria piacciono i fiori. (Mary likes flowers.)
A Carlo piace il calcio. (Carlo likes soccer.)

206

With a noun, the preposition *a* is contracted with the appropriate definite article:

Ai ragazzi piace nuotare.* (The boys like swimming.)
Alle ragazze piace andare a ballare.* (The girls like to go dancing.)

*With infinitives describing an activity such as *nuotare* and *ballare*, one always uses the third-person singular *piace*: *Mi piace leggere*. (I like to read.)

Here's an easy chart to remember *piacere*:

I like	**mi piace/piacciono**
you (familiar) like	**ti piace/piacciono**
you (polite) like	**Le piace/piacciono**
he likes	**gli piace/piacciono**
she likes	**le piace/piacciono**
we like	**ci piace/piacciono**
you like (familiar)	**vi piace/piacciono**
you like (polite)	**piace/piacciono Loro***
they like	**piace/piacciono loro***

*Remember that *loro* and *Loro* always follow the verb: *Questo libro piace (a) loro.* (They like this book.)

ENGLISH-ITALIAN DICTIONARY

The gender of nouns is indicated by m. (masculine) or f. (feminine). Nouns commonly used in the plural are shown in the plural form and are followed by the notation pl.

Adjectives appear in their masculine singular forms. Notice that all adjectives ending in -e may be either masculine or feminine.

Verbs ending in -si are reflexive and are followed by the notation (refl.).

A

a; an un, un', uno (m.), un', una (f.) *(oon, OO-noh, OO-nah)*

able, be potere *(poh-TEH-reh)*

about circa *(CHEER-kah)*

above su, sopra *(soo, SOH-prah)*

abroad all'estero *(ahl-LEH-steh-roh)*

accept accettare *(aht-cheht-TAH-reh)*

accident incidente (m.) *(een-chee-DEHN-teh)*

accompany accompagnare *(ahk-kohm-pah-NYAH-reh)*

according to secondo *(seh-KOHN-doh)*

acquaintance conoscenza (f.) *(koh-noh-SHEHN-tsah)*

across attraverso *(aht-trah-VEHR-soh)*

address indirizzo (m.) *(een-dee-REET-tsoh)*

admission, admittance entrata (f.), ingresso (m.) *(ehn-TRAH-tah, een-GREHS-soh)*

afraid, be avere paura di *(ah-VEH-reh pah-OO-rah dee)*

after dopo *(DOH-poh)*

afternoon pomeriggio (m.) *(poh-meh-REED-joh)*

again ancora, di nuovo *(ahn-KOH-rah, dee NWOH-voh)*

against contro *(KOHN-troh)*

age età (f.) *(eh-TAH)*

agency agenzia (f.) *(ah-jehn-TSEE-ah)*

ago fa (with expressions of time) *(fah)*

agree essere d'accordo *(EHS-seh-reh dahk-KOHR-doh)*

aid aiuto (m.) *(ah-YOO-toh)*

first aid pronto soccorso (m.) *(PROHN-toh sohk-KOHR-soh)*

air aria (f.) *(AH-ryah)*

air-conditioning aria condizionata (f.) *(AH-ryah kohn-dee-tsyoh-NAH-tah)*

airmail posta aerea (f.) *(POH-stah ah-EH-reh-ah)*

airplane aereo (m.) *(ah-EH-reh-oh)*

airport aeroporto (m.) *(ah-eh-roh-POHR-toh)*

alarm clock sveglia (f.) *(ZVEH-lyah)*

all tutto *(TOOT-toh)*

allow permettere *(pehr-MEHT-teh-reh)*

almost quasi *(KWAH-zee)*

alone solo *(SOH-loh)*

already già *(jah)*

also anche *(AHN-keh)*

always sempre *(SEHM-preh)*

A.M. di mattina *(dee maht-TEE-nah)*

am, I sono, sto *(SOH-noh, stoh)*

American americano(-a) *(ah-meh-ree-KAH-noh)(-nah)*

among tra, fra *(trah, frah)*

amuse divertire, divertirsi (refl.) *(dee-vehr-TEE-reh, dee-vehr-TEER-see)*

and e *(eh)*

another un altro *(oon AHL-troh)*

answer risposta (f.) *(ree-SPOH-stah)*

   to answer rispondere *(ree-SPOHN-deh-reh)*

any qualsiasi *(kwahl-SEE-ah-see)*

anybody, anyone qualcuno *(kwahl-KOO-noh)*

anything qualcosa *(kwahl-KOH-sah)*

apartment appartamento (m.) *(ahp-pahr-tah-MEHN-toh)*

apologize scusarsi (refl.) *(skoo-ZAHR-see)*

appetite appetito (m.), fame (f.) *(ahp-peh-TEE-toh, FAH-meh)*

appetizers antipasto (m.) *(ahn-tee-PAH-stoh)*

apple mela (f.) *(MEH-lah)*

appointment appuntamento (m.) *(ahp-poon-tah-MEHN-toh)*

area code prefisso (indicativo) (m.) *(preh-FEES-soh een-dee-kah-TEE-voh)*

arm braccio (m.) *(BRAHT-choh)*

around attorno *(aht-TOHR-noh)*

arrival arrivo (m.) *(ahr-REE-voh)*

arrive arrivare *(ahr-ree-VAH-reh)*

art arte (f.) *(AHR-teh)*

art gallery galleria d'arte (f.) *(gahl-leh-REE-ah DAHR-teh)*

as come *(KOH-meh)*

ashtray portacenere (m.) *(pohr-tah-CHEH-neh-reh)*

ask chiedere *(KYEH-deh-reh)*

aspirin aspirina (f.) *(ah-spee-REE-nah)*

at a *(ah)*

attention attenzione (f.) *(aht-tehn-TSYOH-neh)*

automatic automatico *(ow-toh-MAH-tee-koh)*

automobile automobile (f.), macchina (f.) *(ow-toh-MOH-bee-leh, MAHK-kee-nah)*

autumn autunno (m.) *(ow-TOON-noh)*

avoid evitare *(eh-vee-TAH-reh)*

awful terribile *(tehr-REE-bee-leh)*

B

baby bebè (m./f.) *(beh-BEH)*

   babysitter bambinaia (f.) *(bahm-bee-NAH-yah)*

back (body part) schiena (f.) *(SKYEH-nah)*

   (behind) dietro a *(DYEH-troh ah)*

bacon pancetta affumicata (f.) *(pahn-CHEHT-tah ahf-foo-mee-KAH-tah)*

209

bad cattivo *(kaht-TEE-voh)*

badly male *(MAH-leh)*

bag borsa (f.) *(BOHR-sah)*

  handbag borsetta
  (f.) *(bohr-SEHT-tah)*

  (valise) valigia (f.) *(vah-LEE-jah)*

baggage bagaglio (m.) *(bah-GAH-lyoh)*

  baggage locker custodia
  automatica (f.) *(koo-STOH-dyah ow-toh-MAH-tee-kah)*

baked al forno *(ahl FOHR-noh)*

bakery panificio (m.) *(pah-nee-FEE-choh)*

bandage benda (f.), fascia
(f.) *(BEHN-dah, FAH-shah)*

bank banca (f.) *(BAHN-kah)*

bar bar (m.), caffè
(m.) *(bahr, kahf-FEH)*

barber barbiere (m.) *(bahr-BYEH-reh)*

bargain affare (m.) *(ahf-FAH-reh)*

bath bagno (m.) *(BAH-nyoh)*

bathe bagnarsi (refl.) *(bah-NYAHR-see)*

bathing suit costume da
bagno (m.) *(koh-STOO-meh
dah BAH-nyoh)*

bathrobe accappatoio
(m.) *(ahk-kahp-pah-TOH-yoh)*

bathroom stanza da bagno
(f.), bagno (m.) *(STAHN-tsah
dah BAH-nyoh, BAH-nyoh)*

battery pila (f.) *(PEE-lah)*

be essere *(EHS-seh-reh)*

beach spiaggia (f.) *(SPYAHD-jah)*

beans fagioli (m.pl.) *(fah-JOH-lee)*

beard barba (f.) *(BAHR-bah)*

beautiful bello *(BEHL-loh)*

beauty parlor istituto di
bellezza (m.) *(ee-stee-TOO-toh dee behl-LEHT-tsah)*

because perché *(pehr-KEH)*

become diventare *(dee-vehn-TAH-reh)*

bed letto (m.) *(LEHT-toh)*

bedroom camera da letto
(f.) *(KAH-meh-rah dah LEHT-toh)*

beef manzo (m.) *(MAHN-dzoh)*

beer birra (f.) *(BEER-rah)*

before prima *(PREE-mah)*

begin cominciare *(koh-meen-CHAH-reh)*

beginning inizio (m.) *(ee-NEE-tsyoh)*

behind dietro, indietro *(DYEH-troh, een-DYEH-troh)*

  (late) in ritardo *(een ree-TAHR-doh)*

believe credere *(KREH-deh-reh)*

bellboy fattorino (m.) *(faht-toh-REE-noh)*

below sotto *(SOHT-toh)*

belt cintura (f.) *(cheen-TOO-rah)*

beneath sotto *(SOHT-toh)*

beside accanto a *(ahk-KAHN-toh ah)*

best il/la migliore *(eel/lah
mee-LYOH-reh)*

better (adj.) migliore *(mee-LYOH-reh)*

  (adv.) meglio *(MEH-lyoh)*

between tra, fra *(trah, frah)*
beyond oltre *(OHL-treh)*
big grande *(GRAHN-deh)*
bill conto (m.) *(KOHN-toh)*
birthday compleanno (m.) *(kohm-pleh-AHN-noh)*
bite morso (m.) *(MOHR-soh)*
  to bite mordere *(MOHR-deh-reh)*
bitter amaro *(ah-MAH-roh)*
black nero *(NEH-roh)*
blanket coperta (f.) *(koh-PEHR-tah)*
block (city) isolato (m.) *(ee-zoh-LAH-toh)*
blond biondo *(BYOHN-doh)*
blood sangue (m.) *(SAHN-gweh)*
blouse camicetta (f.) *(kah-mee-CHEHT-tah)*
blue blu *(bloo)*
boarding pass carta d'imbarco (f.) *(KAHR-tah deem-BAHR-koh)*
boat barca (f.), battello (m.) *(BAHR-kah, baht-TEHL-loh)*
body corpo (m.) *(KOHR-poh)*
boiled bollito *(bohl-LEE-toh)*
bone osso (m.) *(OHS-soh)*
book libro (m.) *(LEE-broh)*
  book of tickets carnet (m.) *(kahr-NEH)*
  guidebook guida (f.) *(GWEE-dah)*
bookstore libreria (f.) *(lee-breh-REE-ah)*
boot stivale (m.) *(stee-VAH-leh)*
booth cabina (f.) *(kah-BEE-nah)*

border frontiera (f.) *(frohn-TYEH-rah)*
born nato *(NAH-toh)*
borrow prendere a prestito *(PREHN-deh-reh ah PREH-stee-toh)*
bother infastidire, seccare, dare fastidio a *(een-fah-stee-DEE-reh, sehk-KAH-reh, DAHR-eh fah-STEE-dyoh ah)*
  don't bother non si preoccupi *(nohn see preh-OHK-koo-pee)*
bottle bottiglia (f.) *(boht-TEE-lyah)*
box scatola (f.) *(SKAH-toh-lah)*
box office botteghino (m.) *(boht-teh-GHEE-noh)*
boy ragazzo (m.) *(rah-GAHT-tsoh)*
bracelet braccialetto (m.) *(braht-chah-LEHT-toh)*
brain cervello (m.) *(chehr-VEHL-loh)*
brakes freni (m.pl.) *(FREH-nee)*
bread pane (m.) *(PAH-neh)*
break rompere *(ROHM-peh-reh)*
breakdown (car) guasto (m.), panne (f.) *(GWAH-stoh, PAHN-neh)*
breakfast (prima) colazione (f.) *(PREE-mah koh-lah-TSYOH-neh)*
bridge ponte (m.) *(POHN-teh)*
bring portare *(pohr-TAH-reh)*
broiled alla griglia *(AHL-lah GREE-lyah)*
broken rotto *(ROHT-toh)*

brother fratello (m.) *(frah-TEHL-loh)*

brown marrone *(mahr-ROH-neh)*

brush spazzola (f.) *(SPAHT-tsoh-lah)*

building edificio (m.) *(eh-dee-FEE-choh)*

to burn bruciare, scottare *(broo-CHAH-reh, skoht-TAH-reh)*

bus autobus (m.) *(OW-toh-boos)*

   bus stop fermata d'autobus (f.) *(fehr-MAH-tah DOW-toh-boos)*

business affari (m.pl.) *(ahf-FAH-ree)*

busy occupato *(ohk-koo-PAH-toh)*

but ma *(mah)*

butcher shop macelleria (f.) *(mah-chehl-leh-REE-ah)*

butter burro (m.) *(BOOR-roh)*

button bottone (m.) *(boht-TOH-neh)*

buy comprare *(kohm-PRAH-reh)*

by da, con, in, per *(dah, kohn, een, pehr)*

C

cab taxi (m.) *(TAHK-see)*

cake torta (f.), dolce (m.) *(TOHR-tah, DOHL-cheh)*

call chiamare *(kyah-MAH-reh)*

   (by name) chiamarsi *(kyah-MAHR-see)*

   telephone call chiamata (f.) *(kyah-MAH-tah)*

calm calmo, tranquillo *(KAHL-moh, trahn-KWEEL-loh)*

camera macchina fotografica (f.) *(MAHK-kee-nah foh-toh-GRAH-fee-kah)*

camp campeggio (m.) *(kahm-PEHD-joh)*

can

   (to be able) potere *(poh-TEH-reh)*

cancel annullare, cancellare *(ahn-nool-LAH-reh, kahn-chehl-LAH-reh)*

car automobile (f.), macchina (f.) *(ow-toh-MOH-bee-leh, MAHK-kee-nah)*

   car rental agency autonoleggio (m.) *(ow-toh-noh-LEHD-joh)*

carbonated gassato *(gahs-SAH-toh)*

card (playing) carta (f.) *(KAHR-tah)*

care (caution) attenzione (f.) *(aht-tehn-TSYOH-neh)*

careful attento *(aht-TEHN-toh)*

   to be careful fare attenzione *(FAH-reh aht-tehn-TSYOH-neh)*

carry portare *(pohr-TAH-reh)*

carryon luggage bagaglio a mano (m.) *(bah-GAH-lyoh ah MAH-noh)*

cart carrello (m.) *(kahr-REHL-loh)*

cash contanti (m.pl.) *(kohn-TAHN-tee)*

cash register cassa (f.) *(KAHS-sah)*

to cash incassare *(een-kahs-SAH-reh)*

cashier cassiera(-e) (f., m.) *(kahs-SYEH-rah, -reh)*

castle castello (m.) *(kah-STEHL-loh)*

cat gatto (m.) *(GAHT-toh)*

catch afferrare *(ahf-fehr-RAH-reh)*

cathedral cattedrale (f.) *(kaht-teh-DRAH-leh)*

caution cautela (f.) *(kow-TEH-lah)*

center centro (m.) *(CHEHN-troh)*

certainly certamente *(chehr-tah-MEHN-teh)*

change (money) spiccioli (m.pl.) *(SPEET-choh-lee)*
  to change cambiare *(kahm-BYAH-reh)*

chapel cappella (f.) *(kahp-PEHL-lah)*

charge, cover coperto (m.), consumazione (f.) *(koh-PEHR-toh, kohn-soo-mah-TSYOH-neh)*
  to charge fare pagare *(FAH-reh pah-GAH-reh)*

cheap a buon mercato, economico *(ah bwohn mehr-KAH-toh, eh-koh-NOH-mee-koh)*

check assegno (m.) *(ahs-SEH-nyoh)*

cheese formaggio (m.) *(fohr-MAHD-joh)*

chicken pollo (m.) *(POHL-loh)*

child bambino(-a) (m., f.) *(bahm-BEE-noh)(-nah)*

chin mento (m.) *(MEHN-toh)*

chocolate cioccolato(-a) (m., f.) *(chohk-koh-LAH-toh)(-tah)*

choose scegliere *(SHEH-lyeh-reh)*

church chiesa (f.) *(KYEH-zah)*

cigarette sigaretta (f.) *(see-gah-REHT-tah)*

cinnamon cannella (f.) *(kahn-NEHL-lah)*

city città (f.) *(cheet-TAH)*

class classe (f.) *(KLAHS-seh)*

clean pulito *(poo-LEE-toh)*
  to clean pulire *(poo-LEE-reh)*

climb scalare *(skah-LAH-reh)*

clock orologio (m.) *(oh-roh-LOH-joh)*

close (near) vicino *(vee-CHEE-noh)*
  closed chiuso *(KYOO-soh)*
  to close chiudere *(KYOO-deh-reh)*

closet armadio (m.) *(ahr-MAH-dyoh)*

clothes vestiti (m.pl.) *(veh-STEE-tee)*

cloudy nuvoloso *(noo-voh-LOH-zoh)*

clutch (automobile) frizione (f.) *(free-TSYOH-neh)*

coast costa (f.) *(KOH-stah)*

coat cappotto (m.) *(kahp-POHT-tah)*

coffee caffè (m.) *(kahf-FEH)*
  (with milk) caffellatte (m.) *(kahf-fehl-LAHT-teh)*

coin (money) moneta (f.) *(moh-NEH-tah)*

cold (temperature) freddo (m.) *(FREHD-doh)*
  (illness) raffreddore (m.) *(rahf-frehd-DOH-reh)*

cold cuts affettato (m.) *(ahf-feht-TAH-toh)*

color colore (m.) *(koh-LOH-reh)*

comb, pettine (m.) *(PEHT-tee-neh)*

come venire *(veh-NEE-reh)*
  to come back ritornare *(ree-tohr-NAH-reh)*
  to come in entrare *(ehn-TRAH-reh)*

comfortable comodo *(KOH-moh-doh)*

company compagnia (f.) *(kohm-pah-NYEE-ah)*

complaint reclamo (m.) *(reh-KLAH-moh)*

concert concerto (m.) *(kohn-CHEHR-toh)*

confirm confermare *(kohn-fehr-MAH-reh)*

congratulations congratu-lazioni (f.pl.) *(kohn-grah-too-lah-TSYOH-nee)*

contact lens lente a contatto (f.) *(LEHN-teh ah kohn-TAHT-toh)*

continue continuare *(kohn-tee-NWAH-reh)*

to cook cucinare *(koo-chee-NAH-reh)*

cookies biscotti (m.pl.) *(bee-SKOHT-tee)*

cool fresco *(FREH-skoh)*

corkscrew cavatappi (m.) *(kah-vah-TAHP-pee)*

corn granoturco (m.), mais (m.) *(grah-noh-TOOR-koh, MAH-ees)*

corner angolo (m.) *(AHN-goh-loh)*

correspondence corris-pondenza (f.) *(kohr-ree-spohn-DEHN-tsah)*

cost (amount) costo (m.) *(KOH-stoh)*
  to cost costare *(koh-STAH-reh)*

count contare *(kohn-TAH-reh)*

country (nation) paese (m.) *(pah-EH-zeh)*

countryside campagna (f.) *(kahm-PAH-nyah)*

cousin cugino (m.), cugina (f.) *(koo-JEE-noh, koo-JEE-nah)*

cover (charge) coperto (m.) *(koh-PEHR-toh)*
  covered coperto *(koh-PEHR-toh)*
  to cover coprire *(koh-PREE-reh)*

crazy matto, pazzo *(MAHT-toh, PAHT-tsoh)*

cream crema (f.) *(KREH-mah)*

credit card carta di credito (f.) *(KAHR-tah dee KREH-dee-toh)*

cross attraversare *(aht-trah-vehr-SAH-reh)*

crosswalk passaggio pedonale (m.) *(pahs-SAHD-joh peh-doh-NAH-leh)*

cry piangere *(PYAHN-jeh-reh)*

cucumber cetriolo (m.) *(cheh-tree-OH-loh)*

cup tazza (f.) *(TAHT-tsah)*

currency cambio (m.) *(KAHM-byoh)*
  currency exchange ufficio cambio (m.) *(oof-FEE-choh KAHM-byoh)*

customer cliente (m./f.) *(klee-EHN-teh)*

customs dogana (f.) *(doh-GAH-nah)*

cut taglio (m.) *(TAH-lyoh)*
  to cut tagliare *(tah-LYAH-reh)*

cycling ciclismo (m.) *(chee-CLEE-zmoh)*

D

daily quotidiano *(kwoh-tee-DYAH-noh)*

dance ballo (m.) *(BAHL-loh)*
  to dance ballare *(bahl-LAH-reh)*

danger pericolo (m.) *(peh-REE-koh-loh)*

dangerous pericoloso *(peh-ree-koh-LOH-zoh)*

dark scuro *(SKOO-roh)*

date (calendar) data (f.) *(DAH-tah)*

daughter figlia (f.) *(FEE-lyah)*

day giorno (m.) *(JOHR-noh)*

dead morto *(MOHR-toh)*

dear caro *(KAH-roh)*

death morte (f.) *(MOHR-teh)*

decaffeinated decaffeinato *(deh-kaf-fay-NAH-toh)*

decide decidere *(deh-CHEE-deh-reh)*

declare dichiarare *(dee-kyah-RAH-reh)*

delay ritardo (m.) *(ree-TAHR-doh)*

delicatessen salumeria (f.) *(sah-loo-meh-REE-ah)*

delighted lieto *(LYEH-toh)*

dentist dentista (m./f.) *(dehn-TEE-stah)*

deodorant deodorante (m.) *(deh-oh-doh-RAHN-teh)*

department store grande magazzino (m.) *(GRAHN-deh mah-gahd-DZEE-noh)*

desire desiderio (m.), voglia (f.) *(deh-zee-DEH-ryoh, VOH-lyah)*

desk scrivania (f.) *(skree-vah-NEE-ah)*

dessert dolce (m.) *(DOHL-cheh)*

detour deviazione (f.) *(deh-vyah-TSYOH-neh)*

diamond diamante (m.) *(dyah-MAHN-teh)*

diapers pannolini (m.pl.) *(pahn-noh-LEE-nee)*

dictionary dizionario (m.) *(dee-tsyoh-NAH-ryoh)*

diet dieta (f.) *(DYEH-tah)*

different differente, diverso *(deef-feh-REHN-teh, dee-VEHR-soh)*

difficult difficile *(deef-FEE-chee-leh)*

dine cenare *(cheh-NAH-reh)*

dining room sala da pranzo (f.) *(SAH-lah dah PRAHN-dzoh)*

dinner pranzo (m.), cena (f.) *(PRAHN-dzoh, CHEH-nah)*

direct diretto *(dee-REHT-toh)*

direction direzione (f.) *(dee-reh-TSYOH-neh)*

directory (telephone) elenco telefonico (m.) *(eh-LEHN-koh teh-leh-FOH-nee-koh)*

dirty sporco *(SPOHR-koh)*

discount sconto (m.) *(SKOHN-toh)*

dish piatto (m.) *(PYAHT-toh)*

distance distanza (f.) *(dee-STAHN-tsah)*

do fare *(FAH-reh)*

doctor dottore (m.) *(doht-TOH-reh)*

dog cane (m.) *(KAH-neh)*

dollar dollaro (m.) *(DOHL-lah-roh)*

door porta (f.) *(POHR-tah)*

downstairs dabbasso, giù *(dahb-BAHS-soh, joo)*

downtown centro (m.) *(CHEHN-troh)*

dozen dozzina (f.) *(dohd-DZEE-nah)*

dress vestito (m.) *(veh-STEE-toh)*
   to dress vestirsi (refl.) *(veh-STEER-see)*

drink (beverage) bevanda (f.) *(beh-VAHN-dah)*
   to drink bere *(BEH-reh)*

drive (a car) guidare *(gwee-DAH-reh)*

drugstore farmacia (f.) *(fahr-mah-CHEE-ah)*

dry secco *(SEHK-koh)*
   dry cleaner lavasecco (m.), tintoria (f.) *(lah-vah-SEHK-koh, teen-toh-REE-ah)*

dubbed doppiato *(dohp-PYAH-toh)*

during durante *(doo-RAHN-teh)*

duty-free esente da dogana *(eh-ZEHN-teh dah dah-GAH-nah)*

E

each ogni *(OH-nyee)*

each one ciascuno, ognuno *(chah-SKOO-noh, oh-NYOO-noh)*

ear orecchio (m.) *(oh-REHK-kyoh)*

early presto *(PREH-stoh)*

earring orecchino (m.) *(oh-rehk-KEE-noh)*

easy facile *(FAH-chee-leh)*

eat mangiare *(mahn-JAH-reh)*

eel anguilla (f.) *(ahn-GWEEL-lah)*

egg uovo (m.s.), uova (f.pl.) *(WOH-voh, WOH-vah)*

eggplant melanzana (f.) *(meh-lahn-DZAH-nah)*

electricity elettricità (f.) *(eh-leht-tree-chee-TAH)*

elevator ascensore (m.) *(ah-shehn-SOH-reh)*

elsewhere altrove *(ahl-TROH-veh)*

emergency emergenza (f.) *(eh-mehr-JEHN-tsah)*

empty vuoto *(voo-OH-toh)*

end fine (f.) *(FEE-neh)*
   to end finire *(fee-NEE-reh)*

engine motore (m.) *(moh-TOH-reh)*

enough abbastanza *(ahb-bah-STAHN-tsah)*

entire intero *(een-TEH-roh)*

entrance entrata (f.) *(ehn-TRAH-tah)*

entry prohibited vietato entrare *(vyeh-TAH-toh ehn-TRAH-reh)*

evening sera (f.) *(SEH-rah)*

every ogni *(OH-nyee)*

everybody ognuno, tutti, ciascuno *(oh-NYOO-noh, TOOT-tee, chah-SKOO-noh)*

everything tutto *(TOOT-toh)*
example esempio (m.) *(eh-ZEHM-pyoh)*
excellent eccellente *(eht-chehl-LEHN-teh)*
exchange cambio (m.) *(KAHM-byoh)*
  exchange office ufficio cambio (m.) *(oof-FEE-choh KAHM-byoh)*
  to exchange cambiare *(kahm-BYAH-reh)*
excursion escursione (f.), gita (f.) *(eh-skoor-ZYOH-neh, JEE-tah)*
excuse scusa (f.) *(SKOO-zah)*
  to excuse scusare *(skoo-ZAH-reh)*
exhausted esausto *(eh-ZOW-stoh)*
exit uscita (f.) *(oo-SHEE-tah)*
expensive caro *(KAH-roh)*
express train espresso (m.) *(eh-SPREHS-soh)*
extra extra (m.), supplemento (m.) *(EHK-strah, soop-pleh-MEHN-toh)*
eye occhio (m.) *(OHK-kyoh)*
eyeglasses occhiali (m.pl.) *(ohk-KYAH-lee)*
  sunglasses occhiali da sole (m.pl.) *(ohk-KYAH-lee dah SOH-leh)*

F
face faccia (f.), viso (m.) *(FAHT-chah, VEE-zoh)*
factory fabbrica (f.) *(FAHB-bree-kah)*
to fall cadere *(kah-DEH-reh)*
false falso *(FAHL-soh)*

familiar with, be essere a conoscenza di *(EHS-seh-reh ah koh-noh-SHEHN-tsah dee)*
family famiglia (f.) *(fah-MEE-lyah)*
far lontano *(lohn-TAH-noh)*
farm fattoria (f.) *(faht-toh-REE-ah)*
fast rapida, veloce *(RAH-pee-doh, veh-LOH-cheh)*
fat grasso *(GRAHS-soh)*
father padre (m.) *(PAH-dreh)*
fear paura (f.) *(pah-OO-rah)*
  to fear avere paura di *(ah-VEH-reh pah-OO-rah dee)*
feel sentirsi (refl.) *(sehn-TEER-see)*
fever febbre (f.) *(FEHB-breh)*
few alcuni *(ahl-KOO-nee)*
fill riempire *(ryehm-PEE-reh)*
  fill her up! (car) il pieno! *(eel PYEH-noh!)*
film film (m.), pellicola (f.) *(feelm, pehl-LEE-koh-lah)*
  (cartridge) pellicola (f.) *(pehl-LEE-koh-lah)*
find trovare *(troh-VAH-reh)*
fine (good quality) bello, fine *(BEHL-loh, FEE-neh)*
fine (penalty) multa (f.) *(MOOL-tah)*
fine arts belle arti (f.pl.) *(BEHL-leh AHR-tee)*
finger dito (m.) *(DEE-toh)*
finish finire *(fee-NEE-reh)*
fire fuoco (m.) *(FWOH-koh)*
  (destructive) incendio (m.) *(een-CHEHN-dyoh)*
first primo *(PREE-moh)*
fish pesce (m.) *(PEH-sheh)*

217

to fit (clothes) andar bene *(ahn-DAHR BEH-neh)*

fix riparare *(ree-pah-RAH-reh)*

   fixed price a prezzo fisso *(ah PREHT-tsoh FEES-soh)*

flashlight pila (f.) *(PEE-lah)*

flat piatto, piano *(PYAHT-toh, PYAH-noh)*

   flat tire gomma a terra (f.) *(GOHM-mah ah TEHR-rah)*

flavor sapore (m.) *(sah-POH-reh)*

flea market mercato delle pulci (m.) *(mehr-KAH-toh DEHL-leh POOL-chee)*

flight volo (m.) *(VOH-loh)*

floor piano (m.) *(PYAH-noh)*

flour farina (f.) *(fah-REE-nah)*

flower fiore (m.) *(FYOH-reh)*

fly mosca (f.) *(MOH-skah)*

   to fly volare *(voh-LAH-reh)*

fog nebbia *(NEHB-byah)*

follow seguire *(seh-GWEE-reh)*

food cibo (m.) *(CHEE-boh)*

foot piede (m.) *(PYEH-deh)*

for per *(pehr)*

forbidden proibito, vietato *(proy-BEE-toh, vyeh-TAH-toh)*

foreign forestiero, straniero *(foh-reh-STYEH-roh, strah-NYEH-roh)*

forest foresta (f.) *(foh-REH-stah)*

forget dimenticare *(dee-mehn-tee-KAH-reh)*

fork forchetta (f.) *(fohr-KEHT-tah)*

format formato (m.) *(fohr-MAH-toh)*

forward avanti *(ah-VAHN-tee)*

fountain fontana (f.) *(fohn-TAH-nah)*

fowl pollame (m.), volatile (m.) *(pohl-LAH-meh, voh-LAH-tee-leh)*

free libero *(LEE-beh-roh)*

fresh fresco *(FREH-skoh)*

Friday venerdì (m.) *(veh-nehr-DEE)*

fried fritto *(FREET-toh)*

friendship amicizia (f.) *(ah-mee-CHEE-tsyah)*

from da *(dah)*

front (position) davanti, di fronte *(dah-VAHN-tee, dee FROHN-teh)*

frozen gelato *(jeh-LAH-toh)*

fruit frutta (f.) *(FROOT-tah)*

full pieno *(PYEH-noh)*

to have fun divertirsi (refl.) *(dee-vehr-TEER-see)*

furnished ammobiliato *(ahm-moh-bee-LYAH-toh)*

furniture mobili (m.pl.) *(MOH-bee-lee)*

G

garage garage (m.) *(gah-RAHZH)*

garden giardino (m.) *(jahr-DEE-noh)*

garlic aglio (m.) *(AH-lyoh)*

gas (fuel) benzina (f.) *(behn-DZEE-nah)*

   gas station distributore di benzina (m.) *(dee-stree-boo-TOH-reh dee behn-DZEE-nah)*

gate cancello (m.) *(kahn-CHEHL-loh)*

(airport) uscita (f.) *(oo-SHEE-tah)*

gentleman signore (m.) *(see-NYOH-reh)*

to get (obtain) ottenere *(oht-teh-NEH-reh)*

  to get in/on salire *(sah-LEE-reh)*

  to get off scendere *(SHEHN-deh-reh)*

  to get out uscire *(oo-SHEE-reh)*

  to get up alzarsi (refl.) *(ahl-TSAHR-see)*

gift regalo (m.) *(reh-GAH-loh)*

girl ragazza *(rah-GAHT-tsah)*

give dare *(DAH-reh)*

glass (drinking) bicchiere (m.) *(beek-KYEH-reh)*

glove guanto (m.) *(GWAHN-toh)*

go andare *(ahn-DAH-reh)*

  to go down scendere *(SHEHN-deh-reh)*

  to go up salire *(sah-LEE-reh)*

gold oro (m.) *(OH-roh)*

good buono *(BWOH-noh)*

good-bye arrivederci *(ahr-ree-veh-DEHR-chee)*

grandfather nonno (m.) *(NOHN-noh)*

grandmother nonna (f.) *(NOHN-nah)*

grandson nipote (m.) *(nee-POH-teh)*

grape uva (f.) *(OO-vah)*

grapefruit pompelmo (m.) *(pohm-PEHL-moh)*

grass erba (f.) *(EHR-bah)*

grateful grato *(GRAH-toh)*

grave (burial place) tomba (f.) *(TOHM-bah)*

  (serious) serio *(SEH-ryoh)*

gray grigio *(GREE-joh)*

green verde *(VEHR-deh)*

green beans fagiolini (m.pl.) *(fah-joh-LEE-nee)*

grilled alla griglia *(AHL-lah GREE-lyah)*

grocery drogheria (f.) *(droh-geh-REE-ah)*

ground suolo (m.), terra (f.) *(SWOH-loh, TEHR-rah)*

  ground floor pianterreno (m.) *(pyahn-tehr-REH-noh)*

guest ospite *(OH-spee-teh)*

guide guida (m./f.) *(GWEE-dah)*

  guidebook guida (f.) *(GWEE-dah)*

H

hair capelli (m.pl.) *(kah-PEHL-lee)*

  (body) pelo (m.) *(PEH-loh)*

  hair dryer phon (m.) *(fohn)*

hairbrush spazzola (f.) *(SPAHT-tsoh-lah)*

haircut taglio (m.) *(TAH-lyoh)*

hairdresser parrucchiere (m.) *(pahr-rook-KYEH-reh)*

half metà (f.) *(meh-TAH)*

  (adjective) mezzo *(MEHD-dzoh)*

  half-bottle mezza bottiglia (f.) *(MEHD-dzah boht-TEE-lyah)*

hall porter concierge (m.), portiere (m.) *(kohn-SYEHRZH, pohr-TYEH-reh)*

ham prosciutto (m.) *(proh-SHOOT-toh)*

hand mano (f.) *(MAH-noh)*

handbag borsetta (f.) *(bohr-SEHT-tah)*

handmade fatto a mano *(FAHT-toh ah MAH-noh)*

handsome bello, affascinante *(BEHL-loh, ahf-fah-shee-NAHN-teh)*

hanger (clothes) gruccia (f.) *(GROOT-chah)*

happen accadere, succedere *(ahk-kah-DEH-reh, soot-CHEH-deh-reh)*

happy felice, contento *(feh-LEE-cheh, kohn-TEHN-toh)*

harbor porto (m.) *(POHR-toh)*

hard (difficult) difficile *(deef-FEE-chee-leh)*
 (tough) duro *(DOO-roh)*

have avere *(ah-VEH-reh)*
 to have fun divertirsi (refl.) *(dee-vehr-TEER-see)*
 to have to dovere *(doh-VEH-reh)*

he lui *(LOO-ee)*

head testa (f.) *(TEH-stah)*
 headache mal di testa (m.) *(mahl dee TEH-stah)*

health salute (f.) *(sah-LOO-teh)*

hear sentire *(sehn-TEE-reh)*

heart cuore (m.) *(KWOH-reh)*

heat calore (m.), caldo (m.) *(kah-LOH-reh, KAHL-doh)*

heavy pesante *(peh-ZAHN-teh)*

height altezza (f.) *(ahl-TEHT-tsah)*

hello buongiorno, ciao *(bwohn-JOHR-noh, chow)*
 (on telephone) pronto *(PROHN-toh)*

help aiuto (m.) *(ah-YOO-toh)*
 to help aiutare *(ah-yoo-TAH-reh)*

her, hers (possessive pronoun) il suo/la sua/i suoi/le sue *(eel SOO-oh/lah SOO-ah/ee SWOH-ee/leh SOO-eh)*

herself (pronoun) lei stessa *(lay STEHS-sah)*

herbs odori (m.pl.) *(oh-DOH-ree)*

here qui *(kwee)*

here is/are ecco *(EHK-koh)*

high alto *(AHL-toh)*

highway autostrada (f.) *(ow-toh-STRAH-dah)*

hill collina (f.) *(kohl-LEE-nah)*

him (pronoun—dir. obj., ind. obj., after prep.) lo/gli/lui *(loh/lyee/LOO-ee)*

himself (pronoun) lui stesso *(LOO-ee STEHS-soh)*

his (possessive pronoun) il suo/la sua/i suoi/le sue *(eel SOO-ah/lah SOO-ah/ee SWOH-ee/leh SOO-eh)*

holiday vacanza (f.) *(vah-KAHN-tsah)*

home casa (f.) *(KAH-zah)*

hope speranza (f.) *(speh-RAHN-tsah)*

hors d'oeuvres antipasto (m.) *(ahn-tee-PAH-stoh)*

horse cavallo (m.) *(kah-VAHL-loh)*

hospital ospedale (m.) *(oh-speh-DAH-leh)*

hostel, youth ostello (m.) *(oh-STEHL-loh)*

hot caldo *(KAHL-doh)*

(piquant) piccante *(peek-KAHN-teh)*

hotel hotel (m.), albergo (m.) *(oh-TEHL, ahl-BEHR-goh)*

hour ora (f.) *(OH-rah)*

house casa (f.) *(KAH-zah)*

at the house of a casa di, . . . da *(ah KAH-zah dee, . . . dah)*

how? come? *(KOH-meh?)*

how do you say? come si dice? *(KOH-meh see DEE-cheh?)*

how many? quanti (-e)? *(KWAHN-tee?)(-teh?)*

how much? quanto (-a)? *(KWAHN-toh?)(-tah?)*

hundred cento *(CHEHN-toh)*

hungry, be avere fame *(ah-VEH-reh FAH-meh)*

hurry affrettarsi *(ahf-freht-TAHR-see)*

hurt fare male *(FAH-reh MAH-leh)*

husband marito (m.) *(mah-REE-toh)*

I

I io *(EE-oh)*

ice ghiaccio (m.) *(GYAHT-choh)*

ice cream gelato (m.) *(jeh-LAH-toh)*

if se *(seh)*

ill malato *(mah-LAH-toh)*

illness malattia (f.) *(mah-laht-TEE-ah)*

important importante *(eem-pohr-TAHN-teh)*

impossible impossibile *(eem-pohs-SEE-bee-leh)*

in in *(een)*

included compreso, incluso *(kohm-PREH-zoh, een-KLOO-zoh)*

inform informare *(een-fohr-MAH-reh)*

information informazione (f.) *(een-fohr-mah-TSYOH-neh)*

in-laws suoceri (m.pl.), cognati (m.pl.) *(SWOH-cheh-ree, koh-NYAH-tee)*

inn locanda (f.) *(loh-KAHN-dah)*

inside dentro *(DEHN-troh)*

instead of invece di *(een-VEH-cheh dee)*

insure assicurare *(ahs-see-koo-RAH-reh)*

intelligent intelligente *(een-tehl-lee-JEHN-teh)*

interesting interessante *(een-teh-rehs-SAHN-teh)*

to be interested in interessarsi di (refl.) *(een-teh-rehs-SAHR-see dee)*

intersection incrocio (m.) *(een-KROH-choh)*

into dentro a *(DEHN-troh ah)*

introduce presentare *(preh-zehn-TAH-reh)*

invite invitare *(een-vee-TAH-reh)*

is è *(eh)*

island isola (f.) *(EE-zoh-lah)*

Italian italiano(-a) *(ee-tah-LYAH-noh)(-nah)*

Italy Italia (f.) *(ee-TAH-lyah)*

J

jacket giacca (f.) *(JAHK-kah)*

jam (fruit) marmellata (f.) *(mahr-mehl-LAH-tah)*

221

jar vasetto (m.) *(vah-ZEHT-toh)*

jewelry gioielli (m.pl.) *(joh-YEHL-lee)*

 jewelry store gioielleria (f.) *(joh-yehl-leh-REE-ah)*

job lavoro (m.) *(lah-VOH-roh)*

jogging footing (m.) *(FOO-teeng)*

journey viaggio (m.) *(VYAHD-joh)*

juice succo (m.), sugo (m.) *(SOOK-koh, SOO-goh)*

K

keep tenere *(teh-NEH-reh)*

key chiave (f.) *(KYAH-veh)*

kilogram chilo (m.) *(KEE-loh)*

kilometer chilometro *(kee-LOH-meh-troh)*

kind (nice) gentile *(jehn-TEE-leh)*

 (type) genere (m.), tipo (m.) *(JEH-neh-reh, TEE-poh)*

kiosk chiosco (m.), edicola (f.) *(KYOH-skoh, eh-DEE-koh-lah)*

kiss bacio (m.) *(BAH-choh)*

 to kiss baciare *(bah-CHAH-reh)*

kitchen cucina (f.) *(koo-CHEE-nah)*

knee ginocchio (m.) *(jee-NOHK-kyoh)*

knife coltello (m.) *(kohl-TEHL-loh)*

knock bussare *(boos-SAH-reh)*

know (a fact, how) sapere *(sah-PEH-reh)*

 (a person, a thing) conoscere *(koh-NOH-sheh-reh)*

L

label etichetta (f.) *(eh-tee-KEHT-tah)*

to lack mancare *(mahn-KAH-reh)*

ladies' room signore (f.pl.), donne (f.pl.) *(see-NYOH-reh, DOHN-neh)*

lady signora (f.) *(see-NYOH-rah)*

lake lago (m.) *(LAH-goh)*

lamp lampada (f.) *(LAHM-pah-dah)*

land terra (f.) *(TEHR-rah)*

language lingua (f.) *(LEEN-gwah)*

large largo *(LAHR-goh)*

last (final) ultimo *(OOL-tee-moh)*

 (preceding) scorso *(SKOHR-soh)*

late tardi *(TAHR-dee)*

to laugh ridere *(REE-deh-reh)*

laundromat lavanderia automatica (f.) *(lah-vahn-deh-REE-ah ow-toh-MAH-tee-kah)*

laundry bucato (m.) *(boo-KAH-toh)*

lawyer avvocato (m.) *(ahv-voh-KAH-toh)*

learn imparare *(eem-pah-RAH-reh)*

at least almeno *(ahl-MEH-noh)*

leather cuoio (m.), pelle (f.) *(KWOH-yoh, PEHL-leh)*

leave (behind) lasciare *(lah-SHAH-reh)*

 (to depart) partire *(pahr-TEE-reh)*

left sinistra *(see-NEE-strah)*

leg gamba (f.) *(GAHM-bah)*

lend prestare *(preh-STAH-reh)*

lens lente (f.) *(LEHN-teh)*

less meno *(MEH-noh)*

lesson lezione (f.) *(leh-TSYOH-neh)*

let lasciare *(lah-SHAH-reh)*

letter lettera (f.) *(LEHT-teh-rah)*

library biblioteca (f.) *(bee-blyoh-TEH-kah)*

license licenza (f.) *(lee-CHEHN-tsah)*

life vita (f.) *(VEE-tah)*

lifeguard bagnino (m.) *(bah-NYEE-noh)*

light (weight) leggero *(lehd-JEH-roh)*

   (brightness) luce (f.) *(LOO-cheh)*

like, as come *(KOH-meh)*

   I'd like vorrei *(vohr-RAY)*

   to like piacere *(pyah-CHEH-reh)*

line (of people) fila (f.), coda (f.) *(FEE-lah, KOH-dah)*

linen lino (m.) *(LEE-noh)*

lip labbro (m.) *(LAHB-broh)*

lipstick rossetto (m.) *(rohs-SEHT-toh)*

liquor liquore (m.) *(lee-KWOH-reh)*

list lista (f.) *(LEE-stah)*

listen ascoltare *(ah-skohl-TAH-reh)*

liter litro (m.) *(LEE-troh)*

little (small) piccolo *(PEEK-koh-loh)*

   a little of un po' di *(oon poh dee)*

live vivere *(VEE-veh-reh)*

living room salotto (m.), soggiorno (m.) *(sah-LOHT-toh, sohd-JOHR-noh)*

local locale *(loh-KAH-leh)*

lock serratura (f.) *(sehr-rah-TOO-rah)*

long lungo *(LOON-goh)*

look at guardare *(gwahr-DAH-reh)*

   look for cercare *(chehr-KAH-reh)*

lose perdere *(PEHR-deh-reh)*

lost-and-found oggetti smarriti (m.pl.) *(ohd-JEHT-tee smahr-REE-tee)*

lotion lozione (f.) *(loh-TSYOH-neh)*

lots of (much) molto *(MOHL-toh)*

   (many) molti *(MOHL-tee)*

love amore (m.) *(ah-MOH-reh)*

   to love amare *(ah-MAH-reh)*

low basso *(BAHS-soh)*

luck fortuna (f.) *(fohr-TOO-nah)*

luggage bagaglio (m.) *(bah-GAH-lyoh)*

lunch pranzo (m.) *(PRAHN-dzoh)*

M

machine macchina (f.) *(MAHK-kee-nah)*

madam signora (f.) *(see-NYOH-rah)*

magazine rivista (f.) *(ree-VEE-stah)*

maid domestica (f.), colf (f.) *(doh-MEH-stee-kah, kohlf)*

223

mail posta (f.) *(POH-stah)*
 to mail impostare *(eem-poh-STAH-reh)*
mailbox cassetta della posta (f.) *(kahs-SEHT-tah DEHL-lah POH-stah)*
make fare *(FAH-reh)*
man uomo (m.) *(WOH-moh)*
 men uomini (m.pl.) *(WOH-mee-nee)*
manager direttore (m.), manager (m.) *(dee-reht-TOH-reh, MEH-neh-jehr)*
many molti *(MOHL-tee)*
map (road) carta stradale (f.) *(KAHR-tah strah-DAH-leh)*
market mercato (m.) *(mehr-KAH-toh)*
married sposato *(spoh-ZAH-toh)*
marvelous meraviglioso *(meh-rah-vee-LYOH-zoh)*
match (game) partita (f.) *(pahr-TEE-tah)*
 (light) fiammifero (m.) *(fyahm-MEE-feh-roh)*
matter, it does not non importa *(nohn eem-POHR-tah)*
 what's the matter? cosa c'è? *(KOH-zah cheh?)*
maybe forse *(FOHR-seh)*
me me *(meh)*
meal pasto (m.) *(PAH-stoh)*
mean significare *(see-nyee-fee-KAH-reh)*
meat carne (f.) *(KAHR-neh)*
medicine medicina (f.) *(meh-dee-CHEE-nah)*
meet incontrare *(een-kohn-TRAH-reh)*

(for the first time) conoscere *(koh-NOH-sheh-reh)*
meeting incontro (m.), riunione (f.) *(een-KOHN-troh, ryoo-NYOH-neh)*
melon melone (m.) *(meh-LOH-neh)*
men's room signori (m.pl.), uomini (m.pl.) *(see-NYOH-ree, WOH-mee-nee)*
menu menu (m.) *(meh-NOO)*
merchant negoziante (m./f.), commerciante (m./f.) *(neh-goh-TSYAHN-teh, kohm-mehr-CHAHN-teh)*
middle (center) mezzo (m.), centro (m.) *(MEHD-dzoh, CHEHN-troh)*
midnight mezzanotte (f.) *(mehd-dzah-NOHT-teh)*
mileage chilometraggio (m.) *(kee-loh-meh-TRAHD-joh)*
milk latte (m.) *(LAHT-teh)*
mineral water acqua minerale (f.) *(AHK-kwah mee-neh-RAH-leh)*
minister ministro (m.) *(mee-NEE-stroh)*
minute minuto (m.) *(mee-NOO-toh)*
mirror specchio (m.) *(SPEHK-kyoh)*
Miss signorina (f.) *(see-nyoh-REE-nah)*
miss (the absence of) mancare *(mahn-KAH-reh)*
 (a train) perdere *(PEHR-deh-reh)*
mistake errore (m.), sbaglio (m.) *(ehr-ROH-reh, ZBAH-lyoh)*

moment momento (m.) *(moh-MEHN-toh)*

money soldi (m.pl.), denaro (m.) *(SOHL-dee, deh-NAH-roh)*

(change) spiccioli (m.pl.) *(SPEET-choh-lee)*

money order vaglia postale (m.) *(VAH-lyah poh-STAH-leh)*

month mese (m.) *(MEH-zeh)*

moon luna (f.) *(LOO-nah)*

more più *(pyoo)*

morning mattina (f.) *(maht-TEE-nah)*

mother madre (f.) *(MAH-dreh)*

mountain montagna (f.) *(mohn-TAH-nyah)*

mouth bocca (f.) *(BOHK-kah)*

movies (movie theatre) cinema (m.) *(CHEE-neh-mah)*

Mr. signore (m.) *(see-NYOH-reh)*

Mrs. signora (f.) *(see-NYOH-rah)*

much molto *(MOHL-toh)*

museum museo (m.) *(moo-ZEH-oh)*

mushroom fungo (m.) *(FOON-goh)*

music musica (f.) *(MOO-zee-kah)*

must dovere *(doh-VEH-reh)*

mustard senape (f.) *(SEH-nah-peh)*

my il mio/la mia/i miei/le mie *(eel MEE-oh/lah MEE-ah/ee MYEH-ee/leh MEE-eh)*

N

nail (finger-, toe-) unghia (f.) *(OON-gyah)*

name nome (m.) *(NOH-meh)*

named, to be chiamarsi (refl.) *(kyah-MAHR-see)*

napkin tovagliolo (m.) *(toh-vah-LYOH-loh)*

narrow stretto *(STREHT-toh)*

nationality nazionalità (f.) *(nah-tsyoh-nah-lee-TAH)*

nature natura (f.) *(nah-TOO-rah)*

near vicino *(vee-CHEE-noh)*

nearly quasi *(KWAH-zee)*

necessary necessario *(neh-chehs-SAH-ryoh)*

neck collo (m.) *(KOHL-loh)*

necklace collana (f.) *(kohl-LAH-nah)*

necktie cravatta (f.) *(krah-VAHT-tah)*

need avere bisogno di *(ah-VEH-reh bee-ZOH-nyoh dee)*

neighbor vicino (m.) *(vee-CHEE-noh)*

neighborhood zona (f.), quartiere (m.) *(DZOH-nah, kwahr-TYEH-reh)*

never mai *(MAH-ee)*

new nuovo *(NWOH-voh)*

newspaper giornale (m.) *(johr-NAH-leh)*

newsstand edicola (f.) *(eh-DEE-koh-lah)*

next (adj.) prossimo *(PROHS-see-moh)*

(adv.) poi, dopo *(poy, DOH-poh)*

nice carino, gentile, simpatico *(kah-REE-noh, jehn-TEE-leh, seem-PAH-tee-koh)*

night notte (f.) *(NOHT-teh)*

nightclub locale notturno (m.) (loh-KAH-leh noht-TOOR-noh)

no no (noh)

noise rumore (m.) (roo-MOH-reh)

none nessuno (nehs-SOO-noh)

noon mezzogiorno (m.) (mehd-dzoh-JOHR-noh)

north nord (m.) (nohrd)

nose naso (m.) (NAH-zoh)

no-smoking section sezione non fumatori (f.) (seh-TSYOH-neh nohn foo-mah-TOH-ree)

not non (nohn)

   not at all affatto, per niente (ahf-FAHT-toh, pehr NYEHN-teh)

nothing niente (NYEHN-teh)

notice (announcement) avviso (m.) (ahv-VEE-zoh)

   to notice notare (noh-TAH-reh)

novel (book) romanzo (m.) (roh-MAHN-dzoh)

now ora, adesso (OH-rah, ah-DEHS-soh)

number numero (m.) (NOO-meh-roh)

nurse infermiera (f.), nurse (f.) (een-fehr-MYEH-rah, nehrs)

nut noce (f.) (NOH-cheh)

O

obliged to, be essere grato (EHS-seh-reh GRAH-toh)

obtain ottenere (oht-teh-NEH-reh)

occupied occupato (ohk-koo-PAH-toh)

ocean oceano (m.) (oh-CHEH-ah-noh)

odd dispari (DEE-spah-ree)

of di (dee)

of course naturalmente (nah-too-rahl-MEHN-teh)

office ufficio (m.) (oof-FEE-choh)

often spesso (SPEHS-soh)

oil olio (m.) (OH-lyoh)

okay, it's va bene, d'accordo (vah BEH-neh, dahk-KOHR-doh)

old vecchio (VEHK-kyoh)

on su (soo)

once (one time) una volta (OO-nah VOHL-tah)

   at once subito (SOO-bee-toh)

one uno (OO-noh)

only solamente, soltanto (soh-lah-MEHN-teh, sohl-TAHN-toh)

open aperto (ah-PEHR-toh)

   to open aprire (ah-PREE-reh)

operator (phone) centralinista (m./f.) (chen-trah-lee-NEE-stah)

opportunity occasione (f.), opportunità (ohk-kah-ZYOH-neh, ohp-pohr-too-nee-TAH)

opposite contrario, opposto (kohn-TRAH-ryoh, ohp-POH-stoh)

   (across from) di fronte a (dee FROHN-teh ah)

or o (oh)

orange arancia (f.) (ah-RAHN-chah)

226

ENGLISH/ITALIAN

order ordine (m.) *(OHR-dee-neh)*

to order ordinare *(ohr-dee-NAH-reh)*

ordinary ordinario, comune *(ohr-dee-NAH-ryoh, koh-MOO-neh)*

oregano origano (m.) *(oh-REE-gah-noh)*

other altro *(AHL-troh)*

our; ours il nostro/la nostra/i nostri/le nostre *(eel NOH-stroh/lah NOH-strah/ee NOH-stree/leh NOH-streh)*

out fuori, all'aperto *(FWOH-ree, ahl-lah-PEHR-toh)*

outside fuori *(FWOH-ree)*

oven forno (m.) *(FOHR-noh)*

over sopra *(SOH-prah)*

it's over è finito *(eh fee-NEE-toh)*

overcoat cappotto (m.), soprabito (m.) *(kahp-POHT-toh, soh-PRAH-bee-toh)*

overnight (to stay) passare la notte *(pahs-SAH-reh lah NOHT-teh)*

owe dovere, essere debitore *(doh-VEH-reh, EHS-seh-reh deh-bee-TOH-reh)*

own possedere *(pohs-seh-DEH-reh)*

owner proprietario (m.) *(proh-pryeh-TAH-ryoh)*

P

pack (luggage) fare le valigie *(FAH-reh leh vah-LEE-jeh)*

package pacco (m.) *(PAHK-koh)*

page pagina (f.) *(PAH-jee-nah)*

pain dolore (m.) *(doh-LOH-reh)*

paint vernice (f.) *(vehr-NEE-cheh)*

painting pittura (f.), quadro (m.) *(peet-TOO-rah, KWAH-droh)*

pair paio (m.) *(PAH-yoh)*

palace palazzo (m.) *(pah-LAHT-tsoh)*

pants pantaloni (m.pl.) *(pahn-tah-LOH-nee)*

paper carta (f.) *(KAHR-tah)*

park parco (m.) *(PAHR-koh)*

parking parcheggio (m.) *(pahr-KEHD-joh)*

parsley prezzemolo (m.) *(preht-TSEH-moh-loh)*

part parte (f.) *(PAHR-teh)*

(separate) dividere, separare *(dee-VEE-deh-reh, seh-pah-RAH-reh)*

to pass passare *(pahs-SAH-reh)*

passage passaggio (m.) *(pahs-SAHD-joh)*

passenger passeggero (m.) *(pahs-sehd-JEH-roh)*

passport passaporto (m.) *(pahs-sah-POHR-toh)*

past passato (m.) *(pahs-SAH-toh)*

pastry paste (f.pl.) *(PAH-steh)*

(shop) pasticceria (f.) *(pah-steet-cheh-REE-ah)*

pay pagare *(pah-GAH-reh)*

pedestrian pedone (m.) *(peh-DOH-neh)*

pen penna (f.) *(PEHN-nah)*

pencil matita (f.) *(mah-TEE-tah)*

people gente (f.) *(JEHN-teh)*

pepper pepe (m.) *(PEH-peh)*

perfect perfetto *(pehr-FEHT-toh)*

performance rappresentazione (f.) *(rahp-preh-zehn-tah-TSYOH-neh)*

perfume profumo (m.) *(proh-FOO-moh)*

perhaps forse *(FOHR-seh)*

period periodo (m.) *(peh-REE-oh-doh)*

permit permesso (m.) *(pehr-MEHS-soh)*

   to permit permettere *(pehr-MEHT-teh-reh)*

person persona (f.) *(pehr-SOH-nah)*

photograph fotografia (f.) *(foh-toh-grah-FEE-ah)*

picnic picnic (m.), scampagnata (f.) *(peek-NEEK, skahm-pah-NYAH-tah)*

picture (art) quadro (m.) *(KWAH-droh)*

pie torta (f.) *(TOHR-tah)*

piece pezzo (m.) *(PEHT-tsoh)*

pill pillola (f.) *(PEEL-loh-lah)*

pillow cuscino (m.) *(koo-SHEE-noh)*

pity!, what a che peccato! *(keh pehk-KAH-toh!)*

place posto (m.) *(POH-stoh)*

   to place mettere, posare *(MEHT-teh-reh, poh-ZAH-reh)*

plate piatto (m.) *(PYAHT-toh)*

platform binario (m.), piattaforma (f.) *(bee-NAH-ryoh, pyaht-tah-FOHR-mah)*

play commedia (f.) *(kohm-MEH-dyah)*

   to play (game) giocare *(joh-KAH-reh)*

   to play (instrument) suonare *(swoh-NAH-reh)*

   to play (role) recitare *(reh-chee-TAH-reh)*

playground campo (m.) *(KAHM-poh)*

please per piacere, per favore *(pehr pyah-CHEH-reh, pehr fah-VOH-reh)*

pleasure piacere (m.) *(pyah-CHEH-reh)*

pocket tasca (f.) *(TAH-skah)*

pocketbook portafoglio (m.) *(pohr-tah-FOH-lyoh)*

point punto (m.) *(POON-toh)*

police polizia (f.) *(poh-lee-TSEE-ah)*

   (station) posto di polizia (f.) *(POH-stoh dee poh-lee-TSEE-ah)*

policeman poliziotto (m.) *(poh-lee-TSYOHT-toh)*

polite cortese, gentile *(kohr-TEH-zeh, jehn-TEE-leh)*

pool piscina (f.) *(pee-SHEE-nah)*

poor povero *(POH-veh-roh)*

pork porco (m.), maiale (m.) *(POHR-koh, mah-YAH-leh)*

port porto (m.) *(POHR-toh)*

porter portabagagli (m.) *(pohr-tah-bah-GAH-lyee)*

possess possedere *(pohs-seh-DEH-reh)*

possible possibile *(pohs-SEE-bee-leh)*

postage affrancatura (f.) *(ahf-frahn-kah-TOO-rah)*

post office ufficio postale (m.) *(oof-FEE-choh poh-STAH-leh)*

postcard cartolina (f.) *(kahr-toh-LEE-nah)*

practical pratico *(PRAH-tee-koh)*

prefer preferire *(preh-feh-REE-reh)*

pregnant incinta *(een-CHEEN-tah)*

prepare preparare *(preh-pah-RAH-reh)*

prescription ricetta (f.) *(ree-CHEHT-tah)*

present regalo (m.) *(reh-GAH-loh)*

   to present presentare *(preh-zehn-TAH-reh)*

pretty carino *(kah-REE-noh)*

price prezzo (m.) *(PREHT-tsoh)*

priest prete (m.), sacerdote (m.) *(PREH-teh, sah-chehr-DOH-teh)*

print (photo) copia (f.) *(KOH-pyah)*

private privato *(pree-VAH-toh)*

profession professione (f.), lavoro (m.) *(proh-fehs-SYOH-neh, lah-VOH-roh)*

prohibit proibire *(proh-ee-BEE-reh)*

promise promettere *(proh-MEHT-teh-reh)*

protect proteggere *(proh-TEHD-jeh-reh)*

public pubblico *(POOB-blee-koh)*

purchase acquisto (m.) *(ahk-KWEE-stoh)*

purple viola *(VYOH-lah)*

push spingere *(SPEEN-jeh-reh)*

put mettere *(MEHT-teh-reh)*

Q

quality qualità (f.) *(kwah-lee-TAH)*

quarter quarto (m.) *(KWAHR-toh)*

question domanda (f.) *(doh-MAHN-dah)*

quick veloce *(veh-LOH-cheh)*

quiet silenzioso *(see-lehn-TSYOH-zoh)*

quite abbastanza *(ahb-bah-STAHN-tsah)*

R

radio radio (f.) *(RAH-dyoh)*

railroad ferrovia (f.) *(fehr-roh-VEE-ah)*

   railroad crossing passaggio a livello (m.) *(pahs-SAHD-joh ah lee-VEHL-loh)*

   railroad station stazione ferroviaria (f.) *(stah-TSYOH-neh fehr-roh-VYAH-ryah)*

rain pioggia (f.) *(PYOHD-jah)*

   it's raining piove *(PYOH-veh)*

raincoat impermeabile (m.) *(eem-pehr-meh-AH-bee-leh)*

rapid rapido, veloce *(RAH-pee-doh, veh-LOH-cheh)*

rare (meat) al sangue *(ahl SAHN-gweh)*

raspberry lampone (m.) *(lahm-POH-neh)*

rather piuttosto *(pyoot-TOH-stoh)*

raw vegetables verdura cruda (f.) *(vehr-DOO-rah KROO-dah)*

razor rasoio (m.) *(rah-ZOH-yoh)*

razor blade lametta (f.) *(lah-MEHT-tah)*

read leggere *(LEHD-jeh-reh)*

ready pronto *(PROHN-toh)*

real vero *(VEH-roh)*

really veramente *(veh-rah-MEHN-teh)*

reason ragione (f.) *(rah-JOH-neh)*

reasonable ragionevole *(rah-joh-NEH-voh-leh)*

receipt ricevuta (f.) *(ree-cheh-VOO-tah)*

receive ricevere *(ree-CHEH-veh-reh)*

recent recente *(reh-CHEHN-teh)*

recommend raccomandare *(rahk-koh-mahn-DAH-reh)*

red rosso *(ROHS-soh)*

reduction riduzione (f.) *(ree-doo-TSYOH-neh)*

refund rimborso (m.) *(reem-BOHR-soh)*

refuse rifiutare *(ree-fyoo-TAH-reh)*

regards saluti (m.pl.) *(sah-LOO-tee)*

register (check) registrare *(reh-jee-STRAH-reh)*

regret rimpiangere *(reem-PYAHN-jeh-reh)*

regular regolare *(reh-goh-LAH-reh)*

remain rimanere *(ree-mah-NEH-reh)*

remember ricordare *(ree-kohr-DAH-reh)*

to rent (car) noleggiare *(noh-lehd-JAH-reh)*

to rent (house) affittare *(ahf-feet-TAH-reh)*

repair riparare *(ree-pah-RAH-reh)*

repeat ripetere *(ree-PEH-teh-reh)*

reservation prenotazione (f.) *(preh-noh-tah-TSYOH-neh)*

reserve prenotare *(preh-noh-TAH-reh)*

reserved seat posto riservato (m.) *(POH-stoh ree-zehr-VAH-toh)*

responsible responsabile *(reh-spohn-SAH-bee-leh)*

rest riposo (m.) *(ree-POH-zoh)*

to rest riposare *(ree-poh-ZAH-reh)*

restroom toelette (f.) *(toh-eh-LEHT)*

restaurant ristorante (m.) *(ree-stoh-RAHN-teh)*

result risultato (m.) *(ree-zool-TAH-toh)*

return (give back) restituire *(reh-stee-too-EE-reh)*

(go back) ritornare *(ree-tohr-NAH-reh)*

rice riso (m.) *(REE-zoh)*

rich ricco *(REEK-koh)*

ride giro (m.) *(JEE-roh)*

right (direction) destra *(DEH-strah)*

all right d'accordo *(dahk-KOHR-doh)*

right now subito *(SOO-bee-toh)*

to be right avere ragione *(ah-VEH-reh rah-JOH-neh)*

ring anello (m.) *(ah-NEHL-loh)*

river fiume (m.) *(FYOO-meh)*

road strada (f.) *(STRAH-dah)*

  (highway) autostrada (f.) *(ow-toh-STRAH-dah)*

  road map carta stradale (f.) *(KAHR-tah strah-DAH-leh)*

roast arrosto (m.) *(ahr-ROH-stoh)*

roll (bread) panino (m.) *(pah-NEE-noh)*

  (film) rullino (m.) *(rool-LEE-noh)*

roof tetto (m.) *(TEHT-toh)*

room camera (f.), stanza (f.) *(KAH-meh-rah, STAHN-tsah)*

  (bedroom) camera da letto (f.) *(KAH meh-rah dah LEHT-toh)*

  room service servizio in camera (m.) *(sehr-VEE-tsyoh een KAH-meh-rah)*

  room with all meals pensione completa (f.) *(pehn-SYOH-neh kohm-PLEH-tah)*

round-trip viaggio d'andata e ritorno (m.) *(VYAHD-joh dahn-DAH-tah eh ree-TOHR-noh)*

row (theatre) fila (f.) *(FEE-lah)*

rubber gomma (f.) *(GOHM-mah)*

rug tappeto (m.) *(tahp-PEH-toh)*

ruins rovine (f. pl.) *(roh-VEE-neh)*

rule regola (f.) *(REH-goh-lah)*

run correre *(KOH-reh-reh)*

S

sad triste *(TREE-steh)*

safe cassaforte (f.) *(kahs-sah-FOHR-teh)*

  (adj.) sicuro *(see-KOO-roh)*

sale vendita (f.) *(VEHN-dee-tah)*

salesman commesso (m.) *(kohm-MEHS-soh)*

salt sale (m.) *(SAH-leh)*

same stesso *(STEHS-soh)*

sand sabbia (f.) *(SAHB-byah)*

sandals sandali (m.pl.) *(SAHN-dah-lee)*

sandwich panino (m.), sandwich (m.) *(pah-NEE-noh, SEHND-weech)*

sanitary napkins assorbenti igienici (m.pl.) *(ahs-sohr-BEHN-tee ee-JEH-nee-chee)*

sauce salsa (f.) *(SAHL-sah)*

sausage salsiccia (f.) *(sahl-SEET-chah)*

say dire *(DEE-reh)*

scarf (wool) sciarpa (f.) *(SHAR-pah)*

  (silk) foulard (m.) *(foo-LAHR)*

schedule orario (m.) *(oh-RAH-ryoh)*

school scuola (f.) *(SKWOH-lah)*

scissors forbici (f.pl.) *(FOHR-bee-chee)*

sculpture scultura (f.) *(skool-TOO-rah)*

231

ENGLISH-ITALIAN

sea mare (m.) *(MAH-reh)*
seafood pesce (m.), frutti di mare (m.pl.) *(PEH-sheh, FROOT-tee dee MAH-reh)*
season stagione (f.) *(stah-JOH-neh)*
seat posto (m.) *(POH-stoh)*
 to seat sedersi (refl.) *(seh-DEHR-see)*
second secondo *(seh-KOHN-doh)*
section sezione (f.), zona (f.) *(seh-TSYOH-neh, DZOH-nah)*
see vedere *(veh-DEH-reh)*
seem sembrare *(sehm-BRAH-reh)*
sell vendere *(VEHN-deh-reh)*
send mandare *(mahn-DAH-reh)*
senior citizens anziani (m.pl.) *(ahn-TSYAH-nee)*
sentence (grammatical) frase (f.) *(FRAH-zeh)*
serious serio *(SEH-ryoh)*
serve servire *(sehr-VEE-reh)*
service servizio (m.) *(sehr-VEE-tsyoh)*
shampoo shampoo (m.) *(SHAHM-poh)*
share dividere *(dee-VEE-deh-reh)*
shave farsi la barba (refl.), radersi (refl.) *(FAHR-see lah BAHR-bah, RAH-dehr-see)*
she lei *(lay)*
sheet (bed) lenzuolo (m.) *(lehn-TSWOH-loh)*
ship nave (f.) *(NAH-veh)*
shirt camicia (f.) *(kah-MEE-chah)*

shoe scarpa (f.) *(SKAHR-pah)*
shoe size misura (f.) *(mee-ZOO-rah)*
shopping, go (grocery) andare a fare la spesa *(ahn-DAH-reh ah FAH-reh lah SPEH-zah)*
 (general) andare a fare compere *(ahn-DAH-reh ah FAH-reh KOHM-peh-reh)*
shopping center centro commerciale (m.) *(CHEHN-troh kom-mehr-CHAH-leh)*
short corto, basso *(KOHR-toh, BAHS-soh)*
shoulder spalla (f.) *(SPAHL-lah)*
show (art) mostra (f.) *(MOH-strah)*
 (performance) spettacolo (m.) *(speht-TAH-koh-loh)*
shower doccia (f.) *(DOHT-chah)*
sick malato *(mah-LAH-toh)*
sickness malattia (f.) *(mah-laht-TEE-ah)*
side lato (m.) *(LAH-toh)*
sidewalk marciapiede (m.) *(mahr-chah-PYEH-deh)*
sign (traffic) segnale (m.) *(seh-NYAH-leh)*
 to sign firmare *(feer-MAH-reh)*
silk seta (f.) *(SEH-tah)*
silver argento (m.) *(ahr-JEHN-toh)*
since da *(dah)*
 since when? da quando? *(dah KWAHN-doh?)*
sing cantare *(kahn-TAH-reh)*

232

single (unmarried, man)
celibe, single *(CHEH-lee-beh, SEEN-gol)*
(woman) nubile *(NOO-bee-leh)*
sister sorella (f.) *(soh-REHL-lah)*
sit down sedersi (refl.) *(seh-DEHR-see)*
site posizione (f.) *(poh-zee-TSYOH-neh)*
size misura (f.), taglia (f.) *(mee-ZOO-rah, TAH-lyah)*
skating rink pista di pattinaggio (f.) *(PEE-stah dee paht-tee-NAHD-joh)*
ski sci (m.) *(shee)*
to ski sciare *(shee-AH-reh)*
skin pelle (f.) *(PEHL-leh)*
skirt gonna (f.) *(GOHN-nah)*
sky cielo (m.) *(CHEH-loh)*
sleep dormire *(dohr-MEE-reh)*
sleeping berth cuccetta (f.) *(koot-CHEHT-tah)*
sleeping car vagone letto (m.) *(vah-GOH-neh LEHT-toh)*
sleepy, to be avere sonno *(ah-VEH-reh SOHN-noh)*
slice fetta (f.) *(FEHT-tah)*
slide (photo) diapositiva (f.) *(dyah-poh-zee-TEE-vah)*
slippery scivoloso *(shee-voh-LOH-zoh)*
slow lento *(LEHN-toh)*
slow down rallentare *(rahl-lehn-TAH-reh)*
slowly lentamente *(lehn-tah-MEHN-teh)*
small piccolo *(PEEK-koh-loh)*
to smoke fumare *(foo-MAH-reh)*

smoked affumicato *(ahf-foo-mee-KAH-toh)*
snack bar tavola calda (f.), snack bar (m.) *(TAH-voh-lah KAHL-dah, "snack bar")*
snow neve (f.) *(NEH-veh)*
to snow nevicare *(neh-vee-KAH-reh)*
so così *(koh-ZEE)*
so many tanti(-e) *(TAHN-tee) (-teh)*
so much tanto(-a) *(TAHN-toh) (-tah)*
soap sapone (m.), saponetta (f.) *(sah-POH-neh, sah-poh-NEHT-tah)*
soccer calcio (m.) *(KAHL-choh)*
socks calzini (m.pl.) *(kahl-TSEE-nee)*
soft soffice *(SOHF-fee-cheh)*
some qualche *(KWAHL-keh)*
someone qualcuno *(kwahl-KOO-noh)*
something qualcosa *(kwahl-KOH-zah)*
sometimes a volte, qualche volta *(ah VOHL-teh, KWAHL-keh VOHL-tah)*
somewhere da qualche parte *(dah KWAHL-keh PAHR-teh)*
son figlio (m.) *(FEE-lyoh)*
song canzone (f.) *(kahn-TSOH-neh)*
soon presto *(PREH-stoh)*
sore throat mal di gola (m.) *(mahl dee GOH-lah)*
sorry, to be dispiacere *(dee-spyah-CHEH-reh)*
I'm sorry mi dispiace *(mee dee-SPYAH-cheh)*

233

soup zuppa (f.), minestra in brodo (f.) *(TSOOP-pah, mee-NEH-strah een BROH-doh)*

south sud (m.) *(sood)*

souvenir souvenir (m.), ricordo (m.) *(soo-veh-NEER, ree-KOHR-doh)*

speak parlare *(pahr-LAH-reh)*

specialty specialità (f.) *(speh-chah-lee-TAH)*

speed velocità (f.) *(veh-loh-chee-TAH)*

spend (money) spendere *(SPEHN-deh-reh)*
(time) passare *(pahs-SAH-reh)*

spice spezie (f.pl.) *(SPEH-tsyeh)*

spicy (hot) piccante *(peek-KAHN-teh)*

spoon cucchiaio (m.) *(kook-KYAH-yoh)*

spring (season) primavera (f.) *(pree-mah-VEH-rah)*

square (town) piazza (f.) *(PYAHT-tsah)*

stadium stadio (m.) *(STAH-dyoh)*

stairs scale (f.pl.) *(SKAH-leh)*

stamp (postage) francobollo (m.) *(frahn-koh-BOHL-loh)*

start cominciare *(koh-meen-CHAH-reh)*

station stazione (f.) *(stah-TSYOH-neh)*

stationery carta da lettere (f.) *(KAHR-tah dah LEHT-teh-reh)*

stationery store cartoleria (f.) *(kahr-toh-leh-REE-ah)*

statue statua (f.) *(STAH-twah)*

stay soggiorno (m.) *(sohd-JOHR-noh)*
to stay rimanere *(ree-mah-NEH-reh)*

steal rubare *(roo-BAH-reh)*

steward(-ess) assistente di volo (m./f.) *(ahs-see-STEHN-teh dee VOH-loh)*

still (again) ancora *(ahn-KOH-rah)*

stock exchange borsa (f.) *(BOHR-sah)*

stockings calze (f.pl.) *(KAHL-tseh)*

stomach stomaco (m.) *(STOH-mah-koh)*

strong forte *(FOHR-teh)*

subway metropolitana (f.) *(meh-troh-poh-lee-TAH-nah)*

sudden improvviso *(eem-prohv-VEE-zoh)*

suede camoscio (m.) *(kah-MOH-shoh)*

sugar zucchero (m.) *(TSOOK-keh-roh)*

suit abito (m.) completo (m.) *(AH-bee-toh, kohm-PLEH-toh)*

suitcase valigia (f.) *(vah-LEE-jah)*

summer estate (f.) *(eh-STAH-teh)*

sun sole (m.) *(SOH-leh)*

sunglasses occhiali da sole (m.pl.) *(ohk-KYAH-lee dah SOH-leh)*

sunny soleggiato *(soh-lehd-JAH-toh)*

suntan lotion abbronzante (m.) *(ahb-brohn-DZAHN-teh)*

supermarket supermercato (m.) *(soo-pehr-mehr-KAH-toh)*

supper cena (f.) *(CHEH-nah)*

sure sicuro *(see-KOO-roh)*

sweater pullover (m.) *(pool-LOH-vehr)*

sweet dolce *(DOHL-cheh)*

swim nuotare *(nwoh-TAH-reh)*

swimming pool piscina (f.) *(pee-SHEE-nah)*

switch (electric) interruttore (m.) *(een-tehr-root-TOH-reh)*

T

table tavola (f.), tavolo (m.) *(TAH-voh-lah, TAH-voh-loh)*

tailor sarto (m.) *(SAHR-toh)*

take prendere *(PREHN-deh-reh)*

  (carry) portare *(pohr-TAH-reh)*

taste assaggiare *(ahs-sahd-JAH-reh)*

tavern taverna (f.) *(tah-VEHR-nah)*

tax tassa (f.) *(TAHS-sah)*

taxi taxi (m.) *(TAHK-see)*

tea tè (m.) *(teh)*

teach insegnare *(een-seh-NYAH-reh)*

telegram telegramma (m.) *(teh-leh-GRAHM-mah)*

telephone telefono (m.) *(teh-LEH-foh-noh)*

tell dire *(DEE-reh)*

teller (window) sportello (m.) *(spohr-TEHL-loh)*

tennis tennis (m.) *(TEHN-nees)*

terrace terrazza (f.) *(tehr-RAHT-tsah)*

thank ringraziare *(reen-grah-TSYAH-reh)*

  thank you grazie *(GRAH-tsyeh)*

that quello *(KWEHL-loh)*

  (thing) ciò *(choh)*

  (which) che *(keh)*

the il, lo, la, i, gli, le *(eel, loh, lah, ee, lyee, leh)*

theater teatro (m.) *(teh-AH-troh)*

their il/la/i/le loro *(eel/lah/ee/leh LOH-roh)*

them loro *(LOH-roh)*

then allora *(ahl-LOH-rah)*

there là *(lah)*

  there is c'è *(cheh)*

  there are ci sono *(chee SOH-noh)*

therefore quindi *(KWEEN-dee)*

these questi *(KWEH-stee)*

they loro *(LOH-roh)*

thick spesso, denso *(SPEHS-soh, DEHN-soh)*

thief ladro *(LAH-droh)*

thin magro *(MAH-groh)*

thing cosa (f.) *(KOH-zah)*

think pensare *(pehn-SAH-reh)*

thirsty, to be aver sete *(ah-VEHR SEH-teh)*

this questo *(KWEH-stoh)*

those quelli *(KWEHL-lee)*

through attraverso *(aht-trah-VEHR-soh)*

ticket biglietto (m.) *(bee-LYEHT-toh)*

  ticket window biglietteria (f.) *(bee-lyeh-teh-REE-ah)*

tie (neck-) cravatta (f.) *(krah-VAHT-tah)*

time tempo (m.) *(TEHM-poh)*

tip mancia (f.) *(MAHN-chah)*

tired, to be essere stanco *(EHS-seh-reh STAHN-koh)*

tissues fazzolettini di carta (m.pl.), kleenex (m.pl.) *(faht-tsoh-leht-TEE-nee dee KAHR-tah, KLEE-nehks)*

to a *(ah)*

toast (bread) pane tostato (m.), toast (m.) *(PAH-neh toh-STAH-toh, tohst)*

(drink) brindisi (m.) *(BREEN-dee-zee)*

tobacco tobacco (m.) *(tah-BAHK-koh)*

today oggi *(OHD-jee)*

together insieme *(een-SYEH-meh)*

toilet toilette (f.) *(twah-LEHT)*

toilet paper carta igienica (f.) *(KAHR-tah ee-JEH-nee-kah)*

token gettone (m.) *(jeht-TOH-neh)*

toll pedaggio (m.) *(peh-DAHD-joh)*

tomato pomodoro (m.) *(poh-moh-DOH-roh)*

tomorrow domani *(doh-MAH-nee)*

tongue lingua (f.) *(LEEN-gwah)*

too anche *(AHN-keh)*

too much troppo *(TROHP-poh)*

tooth dente (m.) *(DEHN-teh)*

toothbrush spazzolino da denti (m.) *(spaht-tsoh-LEE-noh dah DEHN-tee)*

toothpaste dentifricio (m.) *(dehn-tee-FREE-choh)*

touch toccare *(tohk-KAH-reh)*

to touch up ritoccare *(ree-tohk-KAH-reh)*

tour giro (m.), gita (f.) *(JEE-roh, JEE-tah)*

tourist turista (m./f.) *(too-REE-stah)*

toward verso *(VEHR-soh)*

towel asciugamano (m.) *(ah-shoo-gah-MAH-noh)*

town città (f.) *(cheet-TAH)*

traffic light semaforo (m.) *(seh-MAH-foh-roh)*

train treno (m.) *(TREH-noh)*

translate tradurre *(trah-DOOR-reh)*

to travel viaggiare *(vyahd-JAH-reh)*

travel agency agenzia viaggi (f.) *(ah-jehn-TSEE-ah VYAHD-jee)*

traveler's check travellers cheques (m.pl.) *(TREH-vehl-ler check)*

tree albero (m.) *(AHL-beh-roh)*

trip viaggio (m.) *(VYAHD-joh)*

trouble disturbo (m.) *(dee-STOOR-boh)*

trout trota (f.) *(TROH-tah)*

truck camion (m.) *(KAH-myohn)*

true vero *(VEH-roh)*

truth verità (f.) *(veh-ree-TAH)*

try provare *(proh-VAH-reh)*

turn girare, voltare *(jee-RAH-reh, vohl-TAH-reh)*

TV set televisore (m.) *(teh-leh-vee-ZOH-reh)*

type tipo (m.), genere (m.) *(TEE-poh, JEH-neh-reh)*

typical tipico *(TEE-pee-koh)*

U

ugly brutto *(BROOT-toh)*

umbrella ombrello (m.) *(ohm-BREHL-loh)*

unbelievable incredibile *(een-kreh-DEE-bee-leh)*

uncle zio (m.) *(TSEE-oh)*

uncomfortable scomodo *(SKOH-moh-doh)*

under sotto *(SOHT-toh)*

underpants mutande (f.pl.) *(moo-TAHN-deh)*

understand capire *(kah-PEE-reh)*

underwear biancheria intima (f.) *(byahn-keh-REE-ah EEN-tee-mah)*

unhappy scontento *(skohn-TEHN-toh)*

unique unico *(OO-nee-koh)*

United States Stati Uniti (m.pl.) *(STAH-tee oo-NEE-tee)*

university università (f.) *(oo-nee-vehr-see-TAH)*

until fino a *(FEE-noh ah)*

up, upstairs sù *(soo)*

upon sopra *(SOH-prah)*

urgent urgente *(oor-JEHN-teh)*

us noi *(noy)*

use usare *(oo-ZAH-reh)*

useful utile *(OO-tee-leh)*

useless inutile *(ee-NOO-tee-leh)*

usher maschera (f.) *(MAH-skeh-rah)*

V

vacation vacanza (f.) *(vah-KAHN-tsah)*

valley valle (f.) *(VAHL-leh)*

value valore (m.) *(vah-LOH-reh)*

veal vitello (m.) *(vee-TEHL-loh)*

vegetables legumi (m.pl.), verdura (f.) *(leh-GOO-mee, vehr-DOO-rah)*

very molto *(MOHL-toh)*

view vista (f.) *(VEE-stah)*

villa villa (f.) *(VEEL-lah)*

village paese (m.) *(pah-EH-zeh)*

vinegar aceto (m.) *(ah-CHEH-toh)*

vineyard vigna (f.) *(VEE-nyah)*

to visit visitare *(vee-zee-TAH-reh)*

W

waist (size) cintura (f.), vita (f.) *(cheen-TOO-rah, VEE-tah)*

wait attesa (f.) *(aht-TEH-zah)*

   to wait for aspettare *(ah-speht-TAH-reh)*

waiter cameriere (m.) *(kah-meh-RYEH-reh)*

waiting room sala d'attesa, . . . d'aspetto (f.) *(SAH-lah daht-TEH-zah, . . . dah-SPEHT-toh)*

waitress cameriera (f.) *(kah-meh-RYEH-rah)*

wake up svegliarsi (refl.) *(zveh-LYAHR-see)*

walk passeggiata (f.) *(pahs-sehd-JAH-tah)*

   to walk camminare *(kahm-mee-NAH-reh)*

237

wall muro (m.), parete (f.) *(MOO-roh, pah-REH-teh)*

wallet portafoglio (m.) *(pohr-tah-FOH-lyoh)*

want volere *(voh-LEH-reh)*

war guerra (f.) *(GWEHR-rah)*

warm caldo *(KAHL-doh)*

wash lavare *(lah-VAH-reh)*
  (oneself) lavarsi (refl.) *(lah-VAHR-see)*

watch orologio (m.) *(oh-roh-LOH-joh)*
  to watch guardare, osservare *(gwahr-DAH-reh, ohs-sehr-VAH-reh)*

water acqua (f.) *(AHK-kwah)*

way (manner) maniera (f.), modo (m.) *(mah-NYEH-rah, MOH-doh)*

we noi *(noy)*

wear indossare, portare *(een-dohs-SAH-reh, pohr-TAH-reh)*

weather tempo (m.) *(TEHM-poh)*
  (forecast) previsioni del tempo (f.pl.) *(preh-vee-ZYOH-nee dehl TEHM-poh)*

wedding matrimonio (m.) *(mah-tree-MOH-nyoh)*

week settimana (f.) *(seht-tee-MAH-nah)*

weight peso (m.) *(PEH-zoh)*

welcome benvenuto *(behn-veh-NOO-toh)*
  you're welcome prego *(PREH-goh)*

well bene *(BEH-neh)*
  (then) allora, dunque *(ahl-LOH-rah, DOON-kweh)*

well-done (meat) ben cotto *(behn KOHT-toh)*

west ovest (m.) *(OH-vehst)*

wet bagnato *(bah-NYAH-toh)*

what? che cosa?, quale? *(keh KOH-zah?, KWAH-leh?)*

when? quando? *(KWAHN-doh?)*

where? dove? *(DOH-veh?)*

which? quale? *(KWAH-leh?)*

white bianco *(BYAHN-koh)*

who che *(keh)*
  who? chi? *(kee?)*

whole intero *(een-TEH-roh)*

why? perché? *(pehr-KEH?)*

wide ampio *(AHM-pyoh)*

wife moglie (f.) *(MOH-lyeh)*

wild selvaggio *(sehl-VAHD-joh)*

win vincere *(VEEN-cheh-reh)*

window finestra (f.) *(fee-NEH-strah)*

wine vino (m.) *(VEE-noh)*

winter inverno (m.) *(een-VEHR-noh)*

wish desiderio (m.) *(deh-zee-DEH-ryoh)*

with con *(kohn)*

without senza *(SEHN-tsah)*

woman donna (f.) *(DOHN-nah)*

wonderful meraviglioso *(meh-rah-vee-LYOH-zoh)*

wood legno (m.) *(LEH-nyoh)*

wool lana (f.) *(LAH-nah)*

word parola (f.) *(pah-ROH-lah)*

work lavoro (m.) *(lah-VOH-roh)*
  to work lavorare *(lah-voh-RAH-reh)*

world mondo (m.) *(MOHN-doh)*

worse peggio *(PEHD-joh)*

worst peggiore *(pehd-JOH-reh)*

worth, be valere *(vah-LEH-reh)*

write scrivere *(SKREE-veh-reh)*

wrong, be aver torto *(ah-VEHR TOHR-toh)*

X

X-ray raggi x (m.pl.), radiografia (f.) *(RAHD-jee eeks, rah-dyoh-grah-FEE-ah)*

Y

year anno (m.) *(AHN-noh)*

yellow giallo *(JAHL-loh)*

yes sì *(see)*

yesterday ieri *(YEH-ree)*

yet ancora *(ahn-KOH-rah)*

yogurt yogurt (m.) *(YOH-goort)*

you (familiar sing.) tu/te/ti *(too/teh/tee)*

  (familiar pl.) voi/vi *(voy/vee)*

  (polite sing.) Lei/La/Le *(lay/lah/leh)*

  (polite pl.) Loro *(LOH-roh)*

young giovane *(JOH-vah-neh)*

younger (age) minore *(mee-NOH-reh)*

your (fam. s.) il tuo/la tua/i tuoi/le tue *(eel TOO-oh/lah TOO-ah/ee TWOH-ee/leh TOO-eh)*

  (fam. pl.) il vostro/la vostra/i vostri/le vostre *(eel VOH-stroh/lah VOH-strah/ee VOH-stree/leh VOH-streh)*

  (pol. s.) il Suo/la Sua/i Suoi/le Sue *(eel SOO-oh/lah SOO-ah/ee SWOH-ee/leh SOO-eh)*

  (pol.pl.) il/la/i/le Loro *(eel/lah/ee/leh LOH-roh)*

youth hostel ostello per la gioventù (m.) *(oh-STEHL-loh pehr lah joh-vehn-TOO)*

Z

zero zero *(DZEH-roh)*

zipper lampo (f.) *(LAHM-poh)*

zoo zoo (m.) *(DZOH-oh)*

ENGLISH/ITALIAN

ITALIAN-ENGLISH DICTIONARY

See usage note under English-Italian Dictionary.

A

a *(ah)* to, at, in, by

abbastanza *(ahb-bah-STAHN-tsah)* enough

abbigliamento (m.) *(ahb-bee-lyah-MEHN-toh)* clothes, clothing

abbronzarsi (refl.) *(ahb-brohn-DZAHR-see)* to get tanned

abbronzato *(ahb-brohn-DZAH-toh)* tanned

abito (m.) *(AH-bee-toh)* man's suit

abito da sera (m.) *(AH-bee-toh dah SEH-rah)* evening suit; formal

accadere *(ahk-kah-DEH-reh)* to happen

accendere *(aht-CHEHN-deh-reh)* to light, to turn/switch on

accendino (m.) *(aht-chehn-DEE-noh)* lighter

accomodare *(ahk-koh-moh-DAH-reh)* to repair

accordo (m.) *(ahk-KOHR-doh)* agreement

accorgersi (refl.) *(ahk-KOHR-jehr-see)* to notice, to realize

acqua (f.) *(AHK-kwah)* water

acqua minerale *(. . . mee-neh-RAH-leh)* mineral water

acqua potabile *(. . . poh-TAH-bee-leh)* drinking water

acquistare *(ahk-kwee-STAH-reh)* to buy, to purchase

adagio *(ah-DAH-joh)* slowly

adesso *(ah-DEHS-soh)* now

aereo (m.) *(ah-EH-reh-oh)* airplane

aeroporto (m.) *(ah-eh-roh-POHR-toh)* airport

affare (m.) *(ahf-FAH-reh)* matter, business, bargain

affettato (m.) *(ahf-feht-TAH-toh)* cold cuts

affitto (m.) *(ahf-FEET-toh)* rent

affrancatura (f.) *(ahf-frahn-kah-TOO-rah)* postage

affrettarsi *(ahf-freht-TAHR-see)* to hurry up

agenzia (f.) *(ah-jehn-TSEE-ah)* agency

agenzia viaggi *(. . . VYAHD-jee)* travel agency

aggiustare *(ahd-joo-STAH-reh)* to repair, to adjust

aglio (m.) *(AH-lyoh)* garlic

aiutare *(ah-yoo-TAH-reh)* to help

aiuto (m.) *(ah-YOO-toh)* help

albergo (m.) *(ahl-BEHR-goh)* hotel

albero (m.) *(AHL-beh-roh)* tree

alcuno *(ahl-KOO-noh)* some, a few

alimentari (m.pl.) *(ah-lee-mehn-TAH-ree)* groceries

allegro *(ahl-LEH-groh)* merry, cheerful

allora *(ahl-LOH-rah)* then

alt *(ahlt)* stop

altezza (f.) *(ahl-TEHT-tsah)* height

alto *(AHL-toh)* high

altrettanto *(ahl-treht-TAHN-toh)* the same

altro *(AHL-troh)* other

alzarsi (refl.) *(ahl-TSAHR-see)* to get up

amare *(ah-MAH-reh)* to love

ambasciata (f.) *(ahm-bah-SHAH-tah)* embassy

americano(-a) *(ah-meh-ree-KAH-noh)(-nah)* American

amico (m.) *(ah-MEE-koh)* friend

ammobiliato *(ahm-moh-bee-LYAH-toh)* furnished

ampio *(AHM-pyoh)* wide

anche *(AHN-keh)* also, too

ancora *(ahn-KOH-rah)* still, yet

andare *(ahn-DAH-reh)* to go
  andarsene *(ahn-DAHR-seh-neh)* to go away, to leave

anello (m.) *(ah-NEHL-loh)* ring

angolo (m.) *(AHN-goh-loh)* corner

anno (m.) *(AHN-noh)* year

annullare *(ahn-nool-LAH-reh)* to annul, to cancel

antico *(ahn-TEE-koh)* old

antipasto (m.) *(ahn-tee-PAH-stoh)* appetizer, hors d'oeuvre

antipatico *(ahn-tee-PAH-tee-koh)* unpleasant, disagreeable

aperto *(ah-PEHR-toh)* open
  all'aperto *(ahl-lah-PEHR-toh)* in the open (air)

appartamento (m.) *(ahp-pahr-tah-MEHN-toh)* apartment

apprendere *(ahp-PREHN-deh-reh)* to learn

appuntamento (m.) *(ahp-poon-tah-MEHN-toh)* date, meeting

arancia (f.) *(ah-RAHN-chah)* orange

argento (m.) *(ahr-JEHN-toh)* silver

aria (f.) *(AH-ryah)* air

armadio (m.) *(ahr-MAH-dyoh)* closet

arrivare *(ahr-ree-VAH-reh)* to arrive

arrivederci *(ahr-ree-veh-DEHR-chee)* good-bye

arrivo (m.) *(ahr-REE-voh)* arrival

arte (f.) *(AHR-teh)* art

ascensore (m.) *(ah-shehn-SOH-reh)* elevator

asciugamano (m.) *(ah-shoo-gah-MAH-noh)* towel
  asciutto *(ah-SHOOT-toh)* dry, dried

ascoltare *(ah-skohl-TAH-reh)* to listen

aspettare *(ah-speht-TAH-reh)* to wait
  aspettarsi (refl.) *(ah-speht-TAHR-see)* to expect

aspetto (m.) *(ah-SPEHT-toh)* look, waiting
  sala d'aspetto (f.) *(SAH-lah dah-SPEHT-toh)* waiting room

aspirina (f.) *(ah-spee-REE-nah)* aspirin

assaggiare *(ahs-sahd-JAH-reh)* to taste

assegno (m.) *(ahs-SEH-nyoh)* check

assicurazione (f.) *(ahs-see-koo-rah-TSYOH-neh)* insurance (policy)

attenzione (f.) *(aht-ten-TSYOH-neh)* attention

    fare attenzione *(FAH-reh . . .)* to pay attention

atterrare *(aht-tehr-RAH-reh)* to land

attorno *(aht-TOHR-noh)* around

attraversare *(aht-trah-vehr-SAH-reh)* to cross

attraverso *(aht-trah-VEHR-soh)* across, through

augurare *(ow-goo-RAH-reh)* to wish

auguri! *(ow-GOO-ree!)* best wishes!

autista (m.) *(ow-TEE-stah)* driver

autobus (m.) *(OW-toh-boos)* bus

automobile (f.) *(ow-toh-MOH-bee-leh)* car

autostrada (f.) *(ow-toh-STRAH-dah)* highway

autunno (m.) *(ow-TOON-noh)* autumn, fall

avanti *(ah-VAHN-tee)* ahead

avere *(ah-VEH-reh)* to have

avvocato (m.) *(ahv-voh-KAH-toh)* lawyer

B

bacio (m.) *(BAH-choh)* kiss

bagaglio (m.) *(bah-GAH-lyoh)* luggage

    fare i bagagli *(FAH-reh ee bah-GAH-lyee)* to pack

bagnarsi (refl.) *(bah-NYAHR-see)* to bathe

bagnato *(bah-NYAH-toh)* wet

bagno (m.) *(BAH-nyoh)* bath

ballare *(bahl-LAH-reh)* to dance

bambinaia (f.) *(bahm-bee-NAH-yah)* babysitter, nanny

bambino (m.) *(bahm-BEE-noh)* child

banca (f.) *(BAHN-kah)* bank

banconota (f.) *(bahn-koh-NOH-tah)* banknote

barbiere (m.) *(bahr-BYEH-reh)* barber

barca (f.) *(BAHR-kah)* boat

basilico (m.) *(bah-ZEE-lee-koh)* basel

basso *(BAHS-soh)* low, short

basta! *(BAH-stah!)* enough!

bello *(BEHL-loh)* beautiful, handsome, lovely

benché *(ben-KEH)* although

bene *(BEH-neh)* well

bere *(BEH-reh)* to drink

bevanda (f.) *(beh-VAHN-dah)* drink

biancheria (f.) *(byahn-keh-REE-ah)* linen

    biancheria intima (f.) *(. . . EEN-tee-mah)* underwear

bianco *(BYAHN-koh)* white

biblioteca (f.) *(bee-blyoh-TEH-kah)* library

bicchiere (m.) *(beek-KYEH-reh)* drinking glass

bicicletta (f.) *(bee-chee-KLEHT-tah)* bicycle

bigliettaio (m.) *(bee-lyeht-TAH-yoh)* conductor

biglietteria (f.) *(bee-lyeht-teh-REE-ah)* ticket office, box office

biglietto (m.) *(bee-LYEHT-toh)* ticket

binario (m.) *(bee-NAH-ryoh)* track, platform

biondo *(BYOHN-doh)* blond, fair

birra (f.) *(BEER-rah)* beer

bisogno (m.) *(bee-ZOH-nyoh)* need

avere bisogno di *(ah-VEH-reh bee-SOH-nyoh dee)* to need

blu *(bloo)* blue

bocca (f.) *(BOHK-kah)* mouth

bollito *(bohl-LEE-toh)* boiled

borsa (f.) *(BOHR-sah)* bag

borsetta (f.) *(bohr-SEHT-tah)* handbag

bosco (m.) *(BOH-skoh)* wood

bottega (f.) *(boht-TEH-gah)* shop

bottiglia (f.) *(boht-TEE-lyah)* bottle

braccio (m.) *(BRAHT-choh)* arm

bravo *(BRAH-voh)* good, shout of approval

breve *(BREH-veh)* short

brillante *(breel-LAHN-teh)* sparkling, bright, brilliant

brindisi (m.) *(BREEN-dee-zee)* toast (to one's health)

bruciare *(broo-CHAH-reh)* to burn

bruciarsi (refl.) *(broo-CHAHR-see)* to burn oneself

bruno *(BROO-noh)* brown

brutto *(BROOT-toh)* ugly

buio (m.) *(BOO-yoh)* dark

buonanotte (buona notte) (f.) *(bwoh-nah-NOHT-teh)* good night

buonasera (buona sera) (f.) *(bwoh-nah-SEH-rah)* good evening

buongiorno (buon giorno) (m.) *(bwohn-JOHR-noh)* good morning, good day

buono *(BWOH-noh)* good

burro (m.) *(BOOR-roh)* butter

busta (f.) *(BOO-stah)* envelope

C

cabina (f.) *(kah-BEE-nah)* booth

caffè (m.) *(kahf-FEH)* coffee

calcio (m.) *(KAHL-choh)* kick, soccer

caldo *(KAHL-doh)* warm

calma (f.) *(KAHL-mah)* calm

calore (m.) *(kah-LOH-reh)* heat

calza (f.) *(KAHL-tsah)* stocking

calzatura (f.) *(kahl-tsah-TOO-rah)* footwear, shoe

calzino (m.) *(kahl-TSEE-noh)* sock

calzoleria (f.) *(kahl-tsoh-leh-REE-ah)* shoe store

calzoni (m.pl.) *(kahl-TSOH-nee)* pants

cambiare *(kahm-BYAH-reh)* to change

cambio (m.) *(KAHM-byoh)* change, auto clutch

camera (da letto) (f.) *(KAH-meh-rah dah LEHT-toh)* bedroom

cameriera (f.) *(kah-meh-RYEH-rah)* waitress, maid

cameriere (m.) *(kah-meh-RYEH-reh)* waiter

camicetta (f.) *(kah-mee-CHEHT-tah)* blouse

camicia (f.) *(kah-MEE-chah)* shirt

camion (m.) *(KAH-myohn)* truck

camminare *(kahm-mee-NAH-reh)* to walk

campagna (f.) *(kahm-PAH-nyah)* country, countryside

campana (f.) *(kahm-PAH-nah)* bell

campanile (m.) *(kahm-pah-NEE-leh)* bell tower

campo (m.) *(KAHM-poh)* field

cane (m.) *(KAH-neh)* dog

cantare *(kahn-TAH-reh)* to sing

cantina (f.) *(kahn-TEE-nah)* basement

canzone (f.) *(kahn-TSOH-neh)* song

capelli (m.pl.) *(kah-PEHL-lee)* hair

capire *(kah-PEE-reh)* to understand

capitare *(kah-pee-TAH-reh)* to happen

capo (m.) *(KAH-poh)* head

cappello (m.) *(kahp-PEHL-loh)* hat

cappotto (m.) *(kahp POHT-toh)* coat

carne (f.) *(KAHR-neh)* meat

caro *(KAH-roh)* dear, expensive

carta (f.) *(KAHR-tah)* paper

cartella (f.) *(kahr-TEHL-lah)* briefcase

cartoleria (f.) *(kahr-toh-leh-REE-ah)* stationery store

cartolina (f.) *(kahr-toh-LEE-nah)* postcard

casa (f.) *(KAH-zah)* house, home

casalingo *(kah-zah-LEEN-goh)* homemade

caso (m.) *(KAH-zoh)* chance, case

cassa (f.) *(KAHS-sah)* case, box

cassetta (f.) *(kahs-SEHT-tah)* box, audio-videocassette

cassetto (m.) *(kahs-SEHT-toh)* drawer

cassiere (m.) *(kahs-SYEH-reh)* cashier

castano *(kah-STAH-noh)* brown (hair)

castello (m.) *(kah-STEHL-loh)* castle

cattivo *(kaht-TEE-voh)* bad

cavallo (m.) *(kah-VAHL-loh)* horse

caviglia (f.) *(kah-VEE-lyah)* ankle

celebre *(CHEH-leh-breh)* famous

cena (f.) *(CHEH-nah)* dinner, supper

cenare *(cheh-NAH-reh)* to have dinner/supper

centrale *(chehn-TRAH-leh)* central

centralinista (m./f.) *(chehn-trah-lee-NEE-stah)* operator

centralino (m.) *(chehn-trah-LEE-noh)* switchboard

centro (m.) *(CHEHN-troh)* center

cercare *(chehr-KAH-reh)* to look for

certamente *(chehr-tah-MEHN-teh)* certainly

certo *(CHEHR-toh)* certain

che *(keh)* (who, that, which, whom, what

chi *(kee)* (he who, she who, whoever, anyone who, someone who, who, whom, which

chiamare *(kyah-MAH-reh)* to call

chiamarsi (refl.) *(kyah-MAHR-see)* to call oneself

chiaro *(KYAH-roh)* clear

chiave (f.) *(KYAH-veh)* key

chiedere *(KYEH-deh-reh)* to ask

chiesa (f.) *(KYEH-zah)* church

chiudere *(KYOO-deh-reh)* to close

chiudere a chiave (. . . ah KYAH-veh) to lock

chiuso *(KYOO-zoh)* closed

ciao *(chow)* hello, good-bye (familiar)

cibo (m.) *(CHEE-boh)* food

cielo (m.) *(CHEH-loh)* sky

cin cin *(cheen cheen)* cheers

cinema (m.) *(CHEE-neh-mah)* cinema, movies, movie theatre

cintura (f.) *(cheen-TOO-rah)* belt

cintura di sicurezza (. . . dee see-koo-REHT-tsah) safety belt

cioccolata(-o) (f.,m.) *(chohk-koh-LAH-tah)(-toh)* chocolate

cipolla (f.) *(chee-POHL-lah)* onion

circa *(CHEER-kah)* about

città (f.) *(cheet-TAH)* city

cittadino (m.) *(cheet-tah-DEE-noh)* citizen

cliente (m.) *(klee-EHN-teh)* customer

coda (f.) *(KOH-dah)* line

fare la coda *(FAH-reh lah . . .)* to stand on line

cognato (m.) *(koh-NYAH-toh)* brother-in-law

cognome (m.) *(koh-NYOH-meh)* surname, family name

colazione (f.) *(koh-lah-TSYOH-neh)* breakfast, lunch

collana (f.) *(kohl-LAH-nah)* necklace

collo (m.) *(KOHL-loh)* neck

colore (m.) *(koh-LOH-reh)* color

coltello (m.) *(kohl-TEHL-loh)* knife

come *(KOH-meh)* as, how

cominciare *(koh-meen-CHAH-reh)* to begin, to start

commedia (f.) *(kohm-MEH-dyah)* comedy, play

commessa(-o) (f., m.) *(kohm-MEHS-sah)(-soh)* shop assistant

commissariato (di polizia) (m.) *(kohm-mees-sah-RYAH-toh dee poh-lee-TSEE-ah)* police station

commissione (f.) *(kom-mees-SYOH-neh)* errand

comodo *(KOH-moh-doh)* convenient, comfortable

compagnia (f.) *(kohm-pah-NYEE-ah)* company

compartimento (m.) *(kohm-pahr-tee-MEHN-toh)* compartment

compera (f.) *(KOHM-peh-rah)* purchase

compleanno (m.) *(kohm-pleh-AHN-noh)* birthday

completo *(kohm-PLEH-toh)* full

comprare *(kohm-PRAH-reh)* to buy

comprendere *(kohm-PREHN-deh-reh)* to understand

compreso *(kohm-PREH-zoh)* included

con *(kohn)* with, by

concerto (m.) *(kohn-CHEHR-toh)* concert

conducente (m.) *(kohn-doo-CHEHN-teh)* driver

conferenza (f.) *(kohn-feh-REHN-tsah)* lecture, conference

confermare *(kohn-fehr-MAH-reh)* to confirm

confortevole *(kohn-fohr-TEH-voh-leh)* comfortable

confusione (f.) *(kohn-foo-ZYOH-neh)* noise

congratulazioni (f.pl.) *(kohn-grah-too-lah-TSYOH-nee)* congratulations

conoscere *(koh-NOH-sheh-reh)* to know, to meet

consegna (f.) *(kohn-SEH-nyah)* delivery

considerare *(kohn-see-deh-RAH-reh)* to consider, to think

consolato (m.) *(kohn-soh-LAH-toh)* consulate

contare *(kohn-TAH-reh)* to count

contento *(kohn-TEHN-toh)* happy, satisfied, glad

continuare *(kohn-tee-NWAH-reh)* to continue

conto (m.) *(KOHN-toh)* bill, check (restaurant, hotel)

contro *(KOHN-troh)* against

controllo (m.) *(kohn-TROHL-loh)* check, inspection, control

conveniente *(kohn-veh-NYEHN-teh)* convenient

coperta (f.) *(koh-PEHR-tah)* blanket, bedspread

coperto *(koh-PEHR-toh)* covered

corda (f.) *(KOHR-dah)* rope

corpo (m.) *(KOHR-poh)* body

correre *(KOHR-reh-reh)* to run

corsia (f.) *(kohr-SEE-ah)* lane (highway)

cortese *(kohr-TEH-zeh)* kind, polite

cortesia (f.) *(kohr-teh-ZEE-ah)* kindness, politeness

corto *(KOHR-toh)* short

cosa (f.) *(KOH-zah)* thing

che cosa? (keh . . . ?) what?

così (koh-ZEE) thus, this way

costare (koh-STAH-reh) to cost

costo (m.) (KOH-stoh) cost

costume (m.) (koh-STOO-meh) custom, habit

costume da bagno (m.) (. . . dah BAH-nyoh) bathing suit

cotone (m.) (koh-TOH-neh) cotton

cotto (KOHT-toh) cooked, done

cravatta (f.) (krah-VAHT-tah) necktie

credere (KREH-deh-reh) to believe, to think

crema (f.) (KREH-mah) cream

crescere (KREH-sheh-reh) to grow, to rise

crudo (KROO-doh) raw

cuccetta (f.) (koot-CHEHT-tah) berth, couchette

cucchiaino (m.) (kook-kyah-EE-noh) teaspoon

cucchiaio (m.) (kook-KYAH-yoh) spoon

cucina (f.) (koo-CHEE-nah) kitchen, cooking, cuisine, food

cucinare (koo-chee-NAH-reh) to cook

cuffia (f.) (KOOF-fyah) cap, headphones (radio/TV)

cuocere (KWOH-cheh-reh) to cook

cuoio (m.) (KWOH-yoh) leather

cuore (m.) (KWOH-reh) heart

cura (f.) (KOO-rah) care

cuscino (m.) (koo-SHEE-noh) cushion, pillow

D

da (dah) from, to, at, for, since

danno (m.) (DAHN-noh) damage, harm

dare (DAH-reh) to give

data (f.) (DAH-tah) date

davanti (dah-VAHN-tee) in front of, before

dazio (m.) (DAH-tsyoh) toll

debole (DEH-boh-leh) weak

decaffeinato (deh-kahf-fay-NAH-toh) decaffeinated

decidere (deh-CHEE-deh-reh) to decide

decisione (f.) (deh-chee-ZYOH-neh) decision

decollare (deh-kohl-LAH-reh) to take off

denaro (m.) (deh-NAH-roh) money

dente (m.) (DEHN-teh) tooth

dentifricio (m.) (dehn-tee-FREE-choh) toothpaste

dentista (m./f.) (dehn-TEE-stah) dentist

dentro (DEHN-troh) inside

deposito (m.) (deh-POH-zee-toh) deposit

deposito bagagli (m.) (. . . bah-GAH-lyee) baggage checkroom

desiderare (deh-zee-deh-RAH-reh) to wish

destinazione (f.) (deh-stee-nah-TSYOH-neh) destination

destra (f.) (DEH-strah) right

di (dee) of

247

dieta (f.) *(DYEH tah)* diet

dietro *(DYEH-truh)* behind

difficile *(deef-FEE-chee-leh)* difficult

difficoltà (f.) *(deef-fee-kohl-TAH)* difficulty

dimagrire *(dee-mah-GREE-reh)* to lose weight

dimenticare *(dee-mehn-tee-KAH-reh)* to forget

dire *(DEE-reh)* to say, to tell

direttore (m.) *(dee-reht-TOH-reh)* manager, director

diritto *(dee-REET-toh)* straight

diritto (m.) right (legal, moral)

discoteca (f.) *(dee-skoh-TEH-kah)* disco

disdire *(dee-ZDEE-reh)* to cancel, to discontinue

dispiacere *(dee-spyah-CHEH-reh)* to be sorry, to regret

mi dispiace *(mee dee-SPYAH-cheh)* I am sorry

distanza (f.) *(dee-STAHN-tsah)* distance

distare *(dee-STAH-reh)* to be far

quanto dista? *(KWAHN-toh DEE-stah?)* how far is it?

disturbare *(dee-stoor-BAH-reh)* to disturb, to bother

dito (m.) *(DEE-toh)* finger

diventare *(dee-vehn-TAH-reh)* to become

diverso *(dee-VEHR-soh)* different

divertimento (m.) *(dee-vehr-tee-MEHN-toh)* amusement

divertirsi (refl.) *(dee-vehr-TEER-see)* to have a good time

dividere *(dee-VEE-deh-reh)* to divide

divorziato *(dee-vohr-TSYAH-toh)* divorced

dizionario (m.) *(dee-tsyoh-NAH-ryoh)* dictionary

dogana (f.) *(doh-GAH-nah)* customs

passare la dogana *(pahs-SAH-reh la . . .)* to go through customs

dolce *(DOHL-cheh)* sweet

dolce (m.) cake, pie, pastry

dollaro (m.) *(DOHL-lah-roh)* dollar

dolore (m.) *(doh-LOH-reh)* pain

domanda (f.) *(doh-MAHN-dah)* question

domandare *(doh-mahn-DAH-reh)* to ask

domani *(doh-MAH-nee)* tomorrow

donna (f.) *(DOHN-nah)* woman

dono (m.) *(DOH-noh)* gift

dopo *(DOH-poh)* after

dopodomani *(doh-poh-doh-MAH-nee)* the day after tomorrow

dormire *(dohr-MEE-reh)* to sleep

dottore (m.) *(doht-TOH-reh)* doctor

dove *(DOH-veh)* where

dovere *(doh-VEH-reh)* must, to have to

dozzina (f.) *(dohd-DZEE-nah)* dozen

drogheria (f.) *(droh-geh-REE-ah)* grocery store
durare *(doo-RAH-reh)* to last
durata (f.) *(doo-RAH-tah)* length
duro *(DOO-roh)* hard

E

e *(eh)* and
eccellente *(eht-chehl-LEHN-teh)* excellent
ecco *(EHK-koh)* here
edicola (f.) *(eh-DEE-koh-lah)* newsstand
edificio (m.) *(eh-dee-FEE-choh)* building
elegante *(eh-leh-GAHN-teh)* elegant
elenco (m.) *(eh-LEHN-koh)* list
  elenco telefonico *(. . . teh-leh-FOH-nee-koh)* telephone book
elettrico *(eh-LEHT-tree-koh)* electric
entrambi *(ehn-TRAHM-bee)* both
entrare *(ehn-TRAH-reh)* to enter
entrata (f.) *(ehn-TRAH-tah)* entrance
entro *(EHN-troh)* within
epoca (f.) *(EH-poh-kah)* epoch, era
era (f.) *(EHR-bah)* grass
errore (m.) *(ehr-ROH-reh)* mistake, error
esatto *(eh-ZAHT-toh)* exact
esaurito *(eh-zow-REE-toh)* out of stock, sold out
escursione (f.) *(eh-skoor-ZYOH-neh)* excursion, trip

esempio (m.) *(eh-ZEHM-pyoh)* example, instance
  per esempio *(pehr . . .)* for instance
esente *(eh-ZEHN-teh)* exempt, free
  esente da imposta *(. . . dah eem-POH-stah)* duty-free
espresso *(eh-SPREHS-soh)* express, espresso coffee
essere *(EHS-seh-reh)* to be
  c'é *(cheh)* there is
  ci sono *(chee SOH-noh)* there are
estate (f.) *(eh-STAH-teh)* summer
esterno *(eh-STEHR-noh)* exterior, outside
estero *(EH-steh-roh)* foreign
estraneo (m.) *(eh-STRAH-neh-oh)* stranger
età (f.) *(eh-TAH)* age
etichetta (f.) *(eh-tee-KEHT-tah)* label
etto (m.) *(EHT-toh)* one hundred grams
evitare *(eh-vee-TAH-reh)* to avoid
evviva! *(ehv-VEE-vah!)* hooray!

F

fa *(fah)* ago
fabbricazione (f.) *(fahb-bree-kah-TSYOH-neh)* manufacture, make
facchino (m.) *(fahk-KEE-noh)* porter
faccia (f.) *(FAHT-chah)* face
facile *(FAH-chee-leh)* easy

fame (f.) *(FAH-meh)* hunger

famiglia (f.) *(fah-MEE-lyah)* family

famoso *(fah-MOH-zoh)* famous

fantastico *(fahn-TAH-stee-koh)* fantastic

fare *(FAH-reh)* to do, to make

farmacia (f.) *(fahr-mah-CHEE-ah)* drugstore, pharmacy

fari anteriori (m.pl.) *(FAH-ree ahn-teh-RYOH-ree)* headlights

fari posteriori *(. . . poh-steh-RYOH-ree)* taillights

fascia (f.) *(FAH-shah)* band

fastidio (m.) *(fah-STEE-dyoh)* trouble, annoyance

fatto *(FAHT-toh)* made

fatto a mano *(. . . ah MAH-noh)* handmade

fattorino (m.) *(faht-toh-REE-noh)* errand boy

favoloso *(fah-voh-LOH-zoh)* fabulous

favore (m.) *(fah-VOH-reh)* favor

per favore *(pehr . . .)* please

febbre (f.) *(FEHB-breh)* fever, temperature

felice *(feh-LEE-cheh)* happy

femmina (f.) *(FEHM-mee-nah)* female

ferita (f.) *(feh-REE-tah)* wound, injury

fermare *(fehr-MAH-reh)* to stop (something)

fermarsi (refl.) *(fehr-MAHR-see)* to stop

fermo *(FEHR-moh)* still, stationary

ferro (m.) *(FEHR-roh)* iron

ferrovia (f.) *(fehr-roh-VEE-ah)* railway

festa (f.) *(FEH-stah)* holiday, party

festivo *(feh-STEE-voh)* Sunday

giorno festivo *(JOHR-noh . . .)* Sunday, public holiday

fetta (f.) *(FEHT-tah)* slice

fiammifero (m.) *(fyahm-MEE-feh-roh)* match

fianco (m.) *(FYAHN-koh)* side

figlia (f.) *(FEE-lyah)* daughter

figlio (m.) *(FEE-lyoh)* son

fila (f.) *(FEE-lah)* row, line

film (m.) *(feelm)* film, movie

filo (m.) *(FEE-loh)* thread

fine (f.) *(FEE-neh)* end

finestra (f.) *(fee-NEH-strah)* window

finestrino (m.) *(fee-neh-STREE-noh)* window (vehicle)

finire *(fee-NEE-reh)* to finish, to end

finito *(fee-NEE-toh)* finished

fino (a) *(FEE-noh ah)* till, until, up to

finto *(FEEN-toh)* false

fiore (m.) *(FYOH-reh)* flower

firma (f.) *(FEER-mah)* signature

fiume (m.) *(FYOO-meh)* river

fontana (f.) *(fohn-TAH-nah)* fountain

forbici (f.pl.) *(FOHR-bee-chee)* scissors

forchetta (f.) *(fohr-KEHT-tah)* fork

formaggio (m.) *(fohr-MAHD-joh)* cheese

fornaio (m.) *(fohr-NAH-yoh)* baker

forno (m.) *(FOHR-noh)* oven

forse *(FOHR-seh)* perhaps

forte *(FOHR-teh)* strong

fortuna (f.) *(fohr-TOO-nah)* luck

forza (f.) *(FOHR-tsah)* strength

fotografare *(foh-toh-grah-FAH-reh)* to photograph

fotografia (f.) *(foh-toh-grah-FEE-ah)* photograph, picture

foulard (m.) *(foo-LAHR)* (silk) scarf

fra *(frah)* between, among; in (time)

fragile *(FRAH-jee-leh)* fragile

fragola (f.) *(FRAH-goh-lah)* strawberry

francobollo (m.) *(frahn-koh-BOHL-loh)* stamp

frase (f.) *(FRAH-zeh)* sentence

fratello (m.) *(frah-TEHL-loh)* brother

freddo *(FREHD-doh)* cold

freno (m.) *(FREH-noh)* brake

fresco *(FREH-skoh)* fresh

fretta (f.) *(FREHT-tah)* haste, hurry

friggere *(FREED-jeh-reh)* to fry

frigorifero (m.) *(free-goh-REE-feh-roh)* refrigerator

fronte (f.) *(FROHN-teh)* forehead, front

    di fronte a *(dee . . . ah)* in front of

frutta (f.) *(FROOT-tah)* fruit

frutti di mare (m.pl.) *(FROOT-tee dee MAH-reh)* seafood

fumare *(foo-MAH-reh)* to smoke

fumo (m.) *(FOO-moh)* smoke

fungo (m.) *(FOON-goh)* mushroom

fuoco (m.) *(FWOH-koh)* fire

fuori *(FWOH-ree)* out, outside, outdoors

furto (m.) *(FOOR-toh)* theft

futuro (m.) *(foo-TOO-roh)* future

G

gabinetto (m.) *(gah-bee-NEHT-toh)* lavatory, toilet

galleria (f.) *(gahl-leh-REE-ah)* tunnel (road), (art) gallery, balcony (theater)

gas (m.) *(gahs)* gas

gassare *(gahs-SAH-reh)* to carbonate

gatto (m.) *(GAHT-toh)* cat

gelateria (f.) *(jeh-lah-teh-REE-ah)* ice-cream parlor

gelato (m.) *(jeh-LAH-toh)* ice cream

genere (m.) *(JEH-neh-reh)* kind, sort

gentile *(jehn-TEE-leh)* kind

genuino *(jeh-noo-EE-noh)* genuine

gerente (m.) *(jeh-REHN-teh)* manager (store)

gettare *(jeht-TAH-reh)* to throw

gettone (m.) *(jeht-TOH-neh)* token

ghiacciato *(gyaht-CHAH-toh)* frozen

251

già *(jah)* already

giacca (f.) *(JAHK-kah)* coat, jacket

giallo *(JAHL-loh)* yellow

giardino (m.) *(jahr-DEE-noh)* garden

ginocchio (m.) *(jee-NOHK-kyoh)* knee

giocare *(joh-KAH-reh)* to play

gioielleria (f.) *(joh-yehl-leh-REE-ah)* jewelry store

giornale (m.) *(johr-NAH-leh)* newspaper

giorno (m.) *(JOHR-noh)* day

giovane *(JOH-vah-neh)* young

giovedì (m.) *(joh-veh-DEE)* Thursday

girare *(jee-RAH-reh)* to turn, to tour

giro (m.) *(JEE-roh)* turn, stroll, short walk
   fare un giro *(FAH-reh oon . . .)* to go for a walk

gita (f.) *(JEE-tah)* trip, excursion

giù *(joo)* down

giungere *(JOON-jeh-reh)* to arrive, to reach

giusto *(JOO-stoh)* right

godere *(goh-DEH-reh)* to enjoy

gola (f.) *(GOH-lah)* throat
   mal di gola *(mahl dee . . .)* sore throat

goloso *(goh-LOH-zoh)* greedy

gomma (f.) *(GOHM-mah)* rubber, gum

gonfiare *(gohn-FYAH-reh)* to swell

gonna (f.) *(GOHN-nah)* skirt

governo (m.) *(goh-VEHR-noh)* government

grande *(GRAHN-deh)* big, great

grano (m.) *(GRAH-noh)* grain (wheat, corn)

grasso *(GRAHS-soh)* fat

gridare *(gree-DAH-reh)* to shout

griglia (f.) *(GREE-lyah)* grill

grosso *(GROHS-soh)* big, large

gruccia (f.) *(GROOT-chah)* (clothes) hanger

guanto (m.) *(GWAHN-toh)* glove

guardare *(gwahr-DAH-reh)* to look at

guasto (m.) *(GWAH-stoh)* damage, breakdown

guida (f.) *(GWEE-dah)* guide, drive

guidare *(gwee-DAH-reh)* to drive, to lead

gustare *(goo-STAH-reh)* to taste

gusto (m.) *(GOO-stoh)* taste

H

hostess (f.) *(OH-stehs)* hostess, stewardess

hotel (m.) *(oh-TEHL)* hotel

I

idea (f.) *(ee-DEH-ah)* idea

idioma (m.) *(ee-DYOH-mah)* idiom, language

ieri *(YEH-ree)* yesterday
   ieri l'altro *(. . . LAHL-troh)* the day before yesterday

illuminato *(eel-loo-mee-NAH-toh)* lit up

imbarcarsi (refl.) *(eem-bahr-KAHR-see)* to embark, to sail

imparare *(eem-pah-RAH-reh)* to learn

impermeabile (m.) *(eem-pehr-meh-AH-bee-leh)* raincoat

impiegare *(eem-pyeh-GAH-reh)* to employ, to use

importante *(eem-pohr-TAHN-teh)* important

importanza (f.) *(eem-pohr-TAHN-tsah)* importance

importo (m.) *(eem-POHR-toh)* amount

impossibile *(eem-pohs-SEE bee-leh)* impossible

imposta (f.) *(eem-POH-stah)* tax, duty

improvviso *(eem-prohv-VEE-zoh)* sudden
  all'improvviso *(ahl-leem-prohv-VEE-zoh)* suddenly

in *(een)* in, at, to, on, by

incantevole *(een-kahn-TEH-voh-leh)* charming, wonderful

incendio (m.) *(een-CHEHN-dyoh)* fire

incidente (m.) *(een-chee-DEHN-teh)* accident

incontrare *(een-kohn-TRAH-reh)* to meet

incontro (m.) *(een-KOHN-troh)* meeting

incrocio (m.) *(een-KROH-choh)* crossing, crossroads

indicare *(een-dee-KAH-reh)* to show, to point at

indietro *(een-DYEH-troh)* back, backwards, behind

indigestione (f.) *(een-dee-jeh-STYOH-neh)* indigestion

indirizzo (m.) *(een-dee-REET-tsoh)* address

infatti *(een-FAHT-tee)* in fact, as a matter of fact

infermiere(-a) (m.,f.) *(een-fehr-MYEH-reh)(-rah)* nurse

informare *(een-fohr-MAH-reh)* to inform

informazione (f.) *(een-fohr-mah-TSYOH-neh)* information

inglese *(een-GLEH-zeh)* English

ingrandire *(een-grahn-DEE-reh)* to enlarge

ingrassare(-rsi) (refl.) *(een-grahs-SAH-reh)(-SAHR-see)* to gain/put on weight

ingresso (m.) *(een-GREHS-soh)* entry, entrance, admission

inizio (m.) *(ee-NEE-tsyoh)* beginning

inoltre *(ee-NOHL-treh)* besides

insalata (f.) *(een-sah-LAH-tah)* salad

insegnante (m./f.) *(een-seh-NYAHN-teh)* teacher

insegnare *(een-seh-NYAH-reh)* to teach

insieme *(een-SYEH-meh)* together

insipido *(een-SEE-pee-doh)* tasteless

interessante *(een-teh-rehs-SAHN-teh)* interesting

interessare *(een-teh-rehs-SAH-reh)* to interest

interessarsi di (refl.) *(een-teh-rehs-SAHR-see dee)* to be interested in

253

intero *(een-TEH-roh)* whole, all

invece *(een-VEH-cheh)* on the contrary, instead

inverno (m.) *(een-VEHR-noh)* winter

inviare *(een-VYAH-reh)* to send, to forward

invitare *(een-vee-TAH-reh)* to invite

io *(EE-oh)* I

isola (f.) *(EE-zoh-lah)* island

Italia (f.) *(ee-TAH-lyah)* Italy

italiano(-a) *(ee-tah-LYAH-noh) (-nah)* Italian

L

là *(lah)* there

labbro (m.) *(LAHB-broh)* lip

ladro (m.) *(LAH-droh)* thief, burglar

laggiù *(lahd-JOO)* down there

lago (m.) *(LAH-goh)* lake

lampada (f.) *(LAHM-pah-dah)* lamp

lampo (m.) *(LAHM-poh)* lightning

lana (f.) *(LAH-nah)* wool

lanciare *(lahn-CHAH-reh)* to throw

largo *(LAHR-goh)* wide

lasciapassare (m.) *(lah-shah-pahs-SAH-reh)* pass

lasciare *(lah-SHAH-reh)* to leave, to let

lato (m.) *(LAH-toh)* side

latte (m.) *(LAHT-teh)* milk

lattina (f.) *(laht-TEE-nah)* can (soft drinks, beer)

lattuga (f.) *(laht-TOO-gah)* lettuce

lavanderia (f.) *(lah-vahn-deh-REE-ah)* laundry

lavandino (m.) *(lah-vahn-DEE-noh)* sink

lavare *(lah-VAH-reh)* to wash

lavasecco (m.) *(lah-vah-SEHK-koh)* dry cleaner

lavorare *(lah-voh-RAH-reh)* to work

lavoro (m.) *(lah-VOH-roh)* work

legge (f.) *(LEHD-jeh)* law

leggere *(LEHD-jeh-reh)* to read

leggero *(lehd-JEH-roh)* light

legno (m.) *(LEH-nyoh)* wood

(legume (m.) *(leh-GOO-meh)* vegetable

lei *(lay)* she, her

lentamente *(lehn-tah-MEHN-teh)* slowly

lento *(LEHN-toh)* slow

lenzuolo (m.) *(lehn-TSWOH-loh)* bedsheet

lettera (f.) *(LEHT-teh-rah)* letter

letto (m.) *(LEHT-toh)* bed

letto matrimoniale *(. . . mah-tree-moh-NYAH-leh)* double bed

letti gemelli *(LEHT-tee jeh-MEHL-lee)* twin beds

lezione (f.) *(leh-TSYOH-neh)* lesson

lì *(lee)* there

libero *(LEE-beh-roh)* free

libreria (f.) *(lee-breh-REE-ah)* bookstore

libro (m.) *(LEE-broh)* book

lieto *(LYEH-toh)* happy, glad

limite (m.) *(LEE-mee-teh)* limit

limite di velocità (. . . dee veh-loh-chee-TAH) speed limit

limonata (f.) (lee-moh-NAH-tah) lemonade

limone (m.) (lee-MOH-neh) lemon

linea (f.) (LEE-neh-ah) line

lingua (f.) (LEEN-gwah) tongue, language

linguaggio (m.) (leen-GWAHD-joh) language

lino (m.) (LEE-noh) linen

liscio (LEE-shoh) smooth

lista (f.) (LEE-stah) list

lista dei vini (. . . day VEE-nee) wine list

litro (m.) (LEE-troh) liter

locale (loh-KAH-leh) local

locale (m.) room

locale notturno (m.) (. . . noht-TOOR-noh) nightclub

lontano (lohn-TAH-noh) far

loro (LOH-roh) they, them

luce (f.) (LOO-cheh) light

accendere la luce (aht-CHEHN-deh-reh lah . . .) to put/turn the light on

spegnere la luce (SPEH-nyeh-reh lah . . .) to put/turn the light off

lui (LOO-ee) he, him

luminoso (loo-mee-NOH-zoh) bright

luna (f.) (LOO-nah) moon

lungo (LOON-goh) long

luogo (m.) (LWOH-goh) place

lusso (m.) (LOOS-soh) luxury

M

ma (mah) but

macchiato (mahk-KYAH-toh) stained, spotted

macchina (f.) (MAHK-kee-nah) car, automobile, machine

macelleria (f.) (mah-chehl-leh-REE-ah) butcher's shop

madre (f.) (MAH-dreh) mother

maggiore (mahd-JOH-reh) older, the oldest (age)

maglietta (f.) (mah-LYEHT-tah) T-shirt

magnifico (mah-NYEE-fee-koh) magnificent

magro (MAH-groh) thin

mai (mahy) never

maiale (m.) (mah-YAH-leh) pig, pork

mais (m.) (MAH-ees) corn

malato (mah-LAH-toh) ill

malattia (f.) (mah-laht-TEE-ah) illness

male (m.) (MAH-leh) pain

mal di testa (. . . dee TEH-stah) headache

maleducato (mah-leh-doo-KAH-toh) rude

mamma (f.) (MAHM-mah) mom

mancare (mahn-KAH-reh) to lack, to miss

mancia (f.) (MAHN-chah) tip

dare la mancia (DAH-reh lah . . .) to tip

mandare (mahn-DAH-reh) to send

mangiare (mahn-JAH-reh) to eat

maniera (f.) (mah-NYEH-rah) manner, fashion, way

mano (f.) (MAH-noh) hand

mantenere *(mahn teh-NEH-reh)* to keep

manzo (m.) *(MAHN-dzoh)* beef

mappa (f.) *(MAHP-pah)* map

marciapiede (m.) *(mahr-chah-PYEH-deh)* sidewalk

mare (m.) *(MAH-reh)* sea

marito (m.) *(mah-REE-toh)* husband

marmo (m.) *(MAHR-moh)* marble

marrone *(mahr-ROH-neh)* brown

maschio (m.) *(MAH-skyoh)* male

massimo *(MAHS-see-moh)* greatest, maximum

materasso (m.) *(mah-teh-RAHS-soh)* mattress

matita (f.) *(mah-TEE-tah)* pencil

matrimonio (m.) *(mah-tree-MOH-nyoh)* marriage

mattina(-o) (m.,f.) *(maht-TEE-nah)(-noh)* morning

matto *(MAHT-toh)* mad, crazy

medicina (f.) *(meh-dee-CHEE-nah)* medicine

medico (m.) *(MEH-dee-koh)* doctor

meglio *(MEH-lyoh)* better

mela (f.) *(MEH-lah)* apple

memoria (f.) *(meh-MOH-ryah)* memory

meno *(MEH-noh)* less

mente (f.) *(MEHN-teh)* mind
  venire in mente *(veh-NEE-reh een . . .)* to remember, to come to mind

mentre *(MEHN-treh)* while

meraviglioso *(meh-rah-vee-LYOH-zoh)* wonderful

mercato (m.) *(mehr-KAH-toh)* market
  a buon mercato *(ah bwohn . . .)* cheap, low-priced

meridionale *(meh-ree-dyoh-NAH-leh)* southern

mescolare *(meh-skoh-LAH-reh)* to mix

mese (m.) *(MEH-zeh)* month

messa (f.) *(MEHS-sah)* (Catholic) mass

messaggio (m.) *(mehs-SAHD-joh)* message

metà (f.) *(meh-TAH)* half

metro (m.) *(MEH-troh)* meter

metropolitana (f.) *(meh-troh-poh-lee-TAH-nah)* subway

mettere *(MEHT-teh-reh)* to put, to put on, to wear

mezzanotte (f.) *(mehd-dzah-NOHT-teh)* midnight

mezzo *(MEHD-dzoh)* half

mezzogiorno (m.) *(mehd-dzoh-JOHR-noh)* noon

miele (m.) *(MYEH-leh)* honey

migliore *(mee-LYOH-reh)* better, the best

minestra in brodo (f.) *(mee-NEH-strah een BROH-doh)* soup

minimo *(MEE-nee-moh)* minimum, slightest, smallest

minore *(mee-NOH-reh)* younger, the youngest (age)

minuto (m.) *(mee-NOO-toh)* minute

misura (f.) *(mee-ZOO-rah)* measure, size

mobile (m.) *(MOH-bee-leh)* piece of furniture

moda (f.) *(MOH-dah)* fashion

modo (m.) *(MOH-doh)* way

moglie (f.) *(MOH-lyeh)* wife

molle *(MOHL-leh)* soft

molto *(MOHL-toh)* much, very

momento (m.) *(moh-MEHN-toh)* moment

mondo (m.) *(MOHN-doh)* world

moneta (f.) *(moh-NEH-tah)* coin

montagna (f.); monte (m.) *(mohn-TAH-nyah; MOHN-teh)* mountain

monumento (m.) *(moh-noo-MEHN-toh)* monument

morbido *(MOHR-bee-doh)* soft

morire *(moh-REE-reh)* to die

morto *(MOHR-toh)* dead

morso (m.) *(MOHR-soh)* bite

morte (f.) *(MOHR-teh)* death

mostra (f.) *(MOH-strah)* show, exhibition

mostrare *(moh-STRAH-reh)* to show

motocicletta (f.) *(moh-toh-chee-KLEHT-tah)* motorcycle

motore (m.) *(moh-TOH-reh)* motor

motorino (m.) *(moh-toh-REE-noh)* moped

motoscafo (m.) *(moh-toh-SKAH-foh)* motorboat

multa (f.) *(MOOL-tah)* fine, ticket

muoversi (refl.) *(MWOH-vehr-see)* to move

muoviti! *(MWOH-vee-tee!)* hurry up!

muro (m.) *(MOO-roh)* wall

museo (m.) *(moo-ZEH-oh)* museum

musica (f.) *(MOO-zee-kah)* music

mutande (f.pl.) *(moo-TAHN-deh)* underpants

N

nascere *(NAH-sheh-reh)* to be born

nato *(NAH-toh)* born

naso (m.) *(NAH-zoh)* nose

nativo *(nah-TEE-voh)* native

natura (f.) *(nah-TOO-rah)* nature

naturale *(nah-too-RAH-leh)* natural

naturalmente *(nah-too-rahl-MEHN-teh)* naturally

nausea (f.) *(NOW-zeh-ah)* nausea

nave (f.) *(NAH-veh)* ship

nazionale *(nah-tsyoh-NAH-leh)* national

necessario *(neh-chehs-SAH-ryoh)* necessary

necessità (f.) *(neh-chehs-see-TAH)* necessity, need

negativa (f.) *(neh-gah-TEE-vah)* negative (film)

negozio (m.) *(neh-GOH-tsyoh)* shop, store

nero *(NEH-roh)* black

nervoso *(nehr-VOH-zoh)* nervous

nessuno *(nehs-SOO-noh)* nobody, no one

neve (f.) *(NEH-veh)* snow

nevicare *(neh-vee-KAH-reh)* to snow

257

niente (NYEHN-teh) nothing

nipote (m./f.) (nee-POH-teh) nephew, niece, grandson, granddaughter

no (noh) no

noi (noy) we, us

noia (f.) (NOH-yah) boredom

noleggiare (noh-lehd-JAH-reh) to hire, to rent

nome (m.) (NOH-meh) name

non (nohn) not

nonna (f.) (NOHN-nah) grandmother

nonno (m.) (NOHN-noh) grandfather

nord (m.) (nohrd) north

normale (nohr-MAH-leh) normal

nostro (NOH-stroh) our, ours

nota (f.) (NOH-tah) note

notare (noh-TAH-reh) to note, to notice

notizia (f.) (noh-TEE-tsyah) news

noto (NOH-toh) well-known

notte (f.) (NOHT-teh) night

nozze (f.pl.) (NOHT-tseh) wedding

nube (f.) (NOO-beh) cloud

nubile (NOO-bee-leh) unmarried, single (woman)

nudo (NOO-doh) naked

numero (m.) (NOO-meh-roh) number

nuotare (nwoh-TAH-reh) to swim

nuovo (NWOH-voh) new

nuvoloso (noo-voh-LOH-zoh) cloudy

O

o (oh) or

òbbligo (m.) (OHB-blee-goh) obligation

occasione (f.) (ohk-kah-ZYOH-neh) occasion, opportunity, bargain

occhiali (m.pl.) (ohk-KYAH-lee) eyeglasses

occhiali da sole (. . . dah SOH-leh) sunglasses

occhio (m.) (OHK-kyoh) eye

occidentale (oht-chee-dehn-TAH-leh) western

occorrere (ohk-KOHR-reh-reh) to want, to need

occupare (ohk-koo-PAH-reh) to occupy

occupato (ohk-koo-PAH-toh) taken, busy

oculista (m./f.) (oh-koo-LEE-stah) eye doctor

odio (m.) (OH-dyoh) hate

odore (m.) (oh-DOH-reh) smell, scent

odori (m.pl.) (oh-DOH-ree) herbs

offerta (f.) (ohf-FEHR-tah) offer

offrire (ohf-FREE-reh) to offer

offerto (ohf-FEHR-toh) offered

oggi (OHD-jee) today

ogni (OH-nyee) every, each

ognuno (oh-NYOO-noh) everybody, everyone

olio (m.) (OH-lyoh) oil

oliva (f.) (oh-LEE-vah) olive

oltre (OHL-treh) beyond

ombra (f.) (OHM-brah) shade, shadow

ombrello (m.) (ohm-BREHL-loh) umbrella

onesto *(oh-NEH-stoh)* honest

opera (f.) *(OH-peh-rah)* work, opera

operaio (m.) *(oh-peh-RAH-yoh)* worker, workman

operare *(oh-peh-RAH-reh)* to operate

opinione (f.) *(oh-pee-NYOH-neh)* opinion

opposto *(ohp-POH-stoh)* opposite

oppure *(ohp-POO-reh)* or, otherwise

ora (f.) *(OH-rah)* hour
  ora *(adv.)* now

orario (m.) *(oh-RAH-ryoh)* timetable, schedule
  essere in orario *(EHS-seh-reh een . . .)* to be on time

orchestra (f.) *(ohr-KEH-strah)* orchestra

ordinare *(ohr-dee-NAH-reh)* to order

ordinario *(ohr-dee-NAH-ryoh)* ordinary, common

ordine (m.) *(OHR-dee-neh)* order

orecchino (m.) *(oh-rehk-KEE-noh)* earring

orecchio (m.) *(oh-REHK-kyoh)* ear

orientale *(oh-ryehn-TAH-leh)* eastern, oriental

orientarsi (refl.) *(oh-ryehn-TAHR-see)* to find one's way

originale *(oh-ree-jee-NAH-leh)* original

origine (f.) *(oh-REE-jee-neh)* origin, beginning

ormai *(ohr-MAHY)* by

ornare *(ohr-NAH-reh)* to adorn, to decorate

oro (m.) *(OH-roh)* gold

orologeria (f.) *(oh-roh-loh-jeh-REE-ah)* watchmaker's shop

orologio (m.) *(oh-roh-LOH-joh)* watch, klock
  orologio da polso (. . . dah POHL-soh) wristwatch

orribile *(ohr-REE-bee-leh)* horrible

orso (m.) *(OHR-soh)* bear

oscurità (f.) *(oh-skoo-ree-TAH)* darkness

ospedale (m.) *(oh-speh-DAH-leh)* hospital

ospite (m./f.) *(OH-spee-teh)* guest

osservare *(ohs-sehr-VAH-reh)* to observe

ostello (m.) *(oh-STEHL-loh)* youth hostel

osteria (f.) *(oh-steh-REE-ah)* tavern

ottico (m.) *(OHT-tee-koh)* optician

ottimo *(OHT-tee-moh)* very good, excellent

ovest (m.) *(OH-vehst)* west

P

pacchetto (m.) *(pahk-KEHT-toh)* pack, packet

pacco (m.) *(PAHK-koh)* parcel

padre (m.) *(PAH-dreh)* father

padrone (m.) *(pah-DROH-neh)* master, landlord, owner

paesaggio (m.) *(pah-eh-ZAHD-joh)* landscape

paese (m.) *(pah-EH-zeh)* country, land

259

pagare *(pah-GAH-reh)* to pay

pagina (f.) *(PAH-jee-nah)* page

paio (m.) *(PAH-yoh)* pair, couple

palazzo (m.) *(pah-LAHT-tsoh)* palace, building

palco (m.) *(PAHL-koh)* box

palestra (f.) *(pah-LEH-strah)* gym

palla (f.) *(PAHL-lah)* ball

pallido *(PAHL-lee-doh)* pale

pallone (m.) *(pahl-LOH-neh)* ball

pancetta (f.) *(pahn-CHEHT-tah)* bacon

pane (m.) *(PAH-neh)* bread

panificio (m.) *(pah-nee-FEE-choh)* bakery

panino (m.) *(pah-NEE-noh)* roll (bread)

panna (f.) *(PAHN-nah)* heavy cream

panne, in (f.) *(een-PAHN-neh)* breakdown (car)

pannolino (m.) *(pahn-noh-LEE-noh)* diaper

pantaloni (m.pl.) *(pahn-tah-LOH-nee)* trousers, pants

Papa (m.) *(PAH-pah)* pope

parabrezza (m.) *(pah-rah-BREHD-dzah)* windshield

paradiso (m.) *(pah-rah-DEE-zoh)* paradise

paragone (m.) *(pah-rah-GOH-neh)* comparison

parcheggio (m.) *(pahr-KEHD-joh)* parking lot

parchimetro (m.) *(pahr-KEE-meh-troh)* parking meter

parco (m.) *(PAHR-koh)* park

parere *(pah-REH-reh)* to seem, to look, to appear

parete (f.) *(pah-REH-teh)* wall

parlare *(pahr-LAH-reh)* to speak, to talk

parola (f.) *(pah-ROH-lah)* word

parte (f.) *(PAHR-teh)* part

partenza (f.) *(pahr-TEHN-tsah)* departure

particolare *(pahr-tee-koh-LAH-reh)* particular, special

partire *(pahr-TEE-reh)* to leave

partita (f.) *(pahr-TEE-tah)* game, match

Pasqua (f.) *(PAH-skwah)* Easter

passaggio (m.) *(pahs-SAHD-joh)* passage, passing, passageway

passare *(pahs-SAH-reh)* to pass

passato *(pahs-SAH-toh)* past

passeggiata (f.) *(pahs-sehd-JAH-tah)* walk, stroll

fare una passeggiata *(FAH-reh OO-nah . . .)* to go for a walk

pasta (f.) *(PAH-stah)* dough, pasta, pastry

pasticceria (f.) *(pah-steet-cheh-REE-ah)* pastry shop

pasticcino (m.) *(pah-steet-CHEE-noh)* pastry, cookie

pasto (m.) *(PAH-stoh)* meal

patente (f.) *(pah-TEHN-teh)* licence

patria (f.) *(PAH-tryah)* country

patto (m.) *(PAHT-toh)* pact, agreement

pattumiera (f.) *(paht-too-MYEH-rah)* garbage can

paura (f.) *(pah-OO-rah)* fear

pavimento (m.) *(pah-vee-MEHN-toh)* floor

pazienza (f.) *(pah-TSYEHN-tsah)* patience

pazzo *(PAHT-tsoh)* mad, crazy

peccato (m.) *(pehk-KAH-toh)* sin

  che peccato! *(keh . . . !)* what a pity!

pedaggio (m.) *(peh-DAHD-joh)* toll

pedone (m.) *(peh-DOH-neh)* pedestrian

peggio, peggiore *(PEHD-joh, pehd-JOH-reh)* worse, the worst

pelle (f.) *(PEHL-leh)* skin, complexion

pelliccia (f.) *(pehl-LEET-chah)* fur

pellicola (f.) *(pehl-LEE-koh-lah)* film

pelo (m.) *(PEH-loh)* hair (body)

pensare *(pehn-SAH-reh)* to think

pensiero (m.) *(pehn-SYEH-roh)* thought

pensione (f.) *(pehn-SYOH-neh)* pension, boarding house

  pensione completa *(. . . kohm-PLEH-tah)* full board

pepe (m.) *(PEH-peh)* pepper

per *(pehr)* for

perché *(pehr-KEH)* because, why

percorso (m.) *(pehr-KOHR-soh)* run, distance, way

perdere *(PEHR-deh-reh)* to lose

perduto, perso *(pehr-DOO-toh, PEHR-soh)* lost ·

perdita (f.) *(PEHR-dee-tah)* loss

perdonare *(pehr-doh-NAH-reh)* to forgive

perfetto *(pehr-FEHT-toh)* perfect

pericoloso *(peh-ree-koh-LOH-zoh)* dangerous

periferia (f.) *(peh-ree-feh-REE-ah)* suburbs

permanenza (f.) *(pehr-mah-NEHN-tsah)* stay, sojourn

permesso (m.) *(pehr-MEHS-soh)* permission

permettere *(pehr-MEHT-teh-reh)* to allow, to let, to permit

persona (f.) *(pehr-SOH-nah)* person

personale *(pehr-soh-NAH-leh)* personal

pesante *(peh-ZAHN-teh)* heavy

pesca (f.) *(PEH-skah)* peach, fishing

pesce (m.) *(PEH-sheh)* fish

peso (m.) *(PEH-zoh)* weight

pettine (m.) *(PEHT-tee-neh)* comb

petto (m.) *(PEHT-toh)* breast, chest

pezzo (m.) *(PEHT-tsoh)* piece

phon (m.) *(fohn)* hair dryer

piacere *(pyah-CHEH-reh)* to like

  mi piace/piacciono *(mee PYAH-cheh/PYAHT-choh-noh)* I like

  piacere (m.) pleasure

piangere *(PYAHN-jeh-reh)* to cry, to weep

piano (PYAH-noh) flat, even
  piano (m.) floor, plan
pianta (f.) (PYAHN-tah) plant
piatto (PYAHT-toh) flat
  piatto (m.) plate
piazza (f.) (PYAHT-tsah) square
piccante (peek-KAHN-teh) sharp, spicy, hot
piccolo (PEEK-koh-loh) small
piede (m.) (PYEH-deh) foot
  a piedi (ah PYEH-dee) on foot
pieno (PYEH-noh) full
pietanza (f.) (pyeh-TAHN-tsah) main course, dish
pietra (f.) (PYEH-trah) stone
pila (f.) (PEE-lah) pile, battery
pioggia (f.) (PYOHD-jah) rain
piovere (PYOH-veh-reh) to rain
  piove (PYOH-veh) it's raining
pittura (f.) (peet-TOO-rah) painting
più (pyoo) more, the most
piuttosto (pyoot-TOH-stoh) rather
platea (f.) (plah-TEH-ah) orchestra (theatre)
pneumatico (m.) (pneh-oo-MAH-tee-koh) tire
po'; poco (poh, POH-koh) little
  un po'; un poco (oon . . .) a little (of), some
poi (poy) then, afterwards, later
politica (f.) (poh-LEE-tee-kah) politics

polizia (f.) (poh-lee-TSEE-ah) police
pollo (m.) (POHL-loh) chicken
polmone (m.) (pohl-MOH-neh) lung
pomeriggio (m.) (poh-meh-REED-joh) afternoon
pomodoro (m.) (poh-moh-DOH-roh) tomato
ponte (m.) (POHN-teh) bridge
popolo (m.) (POH-poh-loh) people
porta (f.) (POHR-tah) door
portabagagli (m.) (pohr-tah-bah-GAH-lyee) porter, luggage rack (train, car)
portafoglio (m.) (pohr-tah-FOH-lyoh) wallet
portare (pohr-TAH-reh) to bring, to carry, to wear
portata (f.) (pohr-TAH-tah) course (meal)
porto (m.) (POHR-toh) harbor
posizione (f.) (poh-zee-TSYOH-neh) position
possibile (pohs-SEE-bee-leh) possible
posta (f.) (POH-stah) mail
  posta aerea (. . . ah-EH-reh-ah) airmail
posteggio (m.) (poh-STEHD-joh) parking lot/space
  posteggio taxi (. . . TAHK-see) taxi stand
posto (m.) (POH-stoh) place, job, position
potere (poh-TEH-reh) can, to be able
  potere (m.) power
povero (POH-veh-roh) poor

pranzo (m.) *(PRAHN-dzoh)* lunch

preciso *(preh-CHEE-zoh)* precise

preferire *(preh-feh-REE-reh)* to prefer

pregare *(preh-GAH-reh)* to pray

premio (m.) *(PREH-myoh)* prize

prendere *(PREHN-deh-reh)* to take

prenotazione (f.) *(preh-noh-tah-TSYOH-neh)* booking, reservation

preoccuparsi (refl.) *(preh-ohk-koo-PAHR-see)* to worry
  non si preoccupi *(nohn see preh-OHK-koo-pee)* don't worry (formal)

preparare *(preh-pah-RAH-reh)* to prepare

presentare *(preh-zehn-TAH-reh)* to present, to introduce

pressione (f.) *(prehs-SYOH-neh)* pressure

prestare *(preh-STAH-reh)* to lend

presto *(PREH-stoh)* soon

prezzo (m.) *(PREHT-tsoh)* price

prima *(PREE-mah)* before

primavera (f.) *(pree-mah-VEH-rah)* spring

primo *(PREE-moh)* first

probabile *(proh-BAH-bee-leh)* probable, likely

procedere *(proh-CHEH-deh-reh)* to proceed

procurare *(proh-koo-RAH-reh)* to get

produrre *(proh-DOOR-reh)* to produce

professione (f.) *(proh-fehs-SYOH-neh)* profession

professore (m.) *(proh-fehs-SOH-reh)* professor, teacher

profondo *(proh-FOHN-doh)* deep

profumo (m.) *(proh-FOO-moh)* perfume, scent

proibito *(proh-ee-BEE-toh)* forbidden

promessa (f.) *(proh-MEHS-sah)* promise

promettere *(proh-MEHT-teh-reh)* to promise

pronto *(PROHN-toh)* ready, hello (phone)

pronuncia (f.) *(proh-NOON-chah)* pronunciation

pronunciare *(proh-noon-CHAH-reh)* to pronounce

proprietà (f.) *(proh-pryeh-TAH)* property

proprietario (m.) *(proh-pryeh-TAH-ryoh)* owner

prossimo *(PROHS-see-moh)* next

protestante *(proh-teh-STAHN-teh)* Protestant

protezione (f.) *(proh-teh-TSYOH-neh)* protection

pugno (m.) *(POO-nyoh)* fist

pulire *(poo-LEE-reh)* to clean
  pulito *(poo-LEE-toh)* clean

punto (m.) *(POON-toh)* point, moment

puntuale *(poon-TWAH-leh)* punctual

puntura (f.) *(poon-TOO-rah)* injection, shot, sting

puro (POO-roh) pure
puzzare (poot-TSAH-reh) to stink, to smell bad

Q

qua (kwah) here
quadro (m.) (KWAH-droh) picture, painting
qualche (KWAHL-keh) some, a few
qualcosa (kwahl-KOH-zah) something
qualcuno (kwahl-KOO-noh) someone
quale (KWAH-leh) which, what
qualità (f.) (kwah-lee-TAH) quality
qualsiasi; qualunque (kwahl-SEE-ah-see, kwah-LOON-kweh) any, whatever
quando (KWAHN-doh) when
quantità (f.) (kwahn-tee-TAH) quantity
quanto (KWAHN-toh) how much, how many, as many as
quartiere (m.) (kwahr-TYEH-reh) neighborhood, section
quasi (KWAH-zee) almost
quello (KWEHL-loh) that
questione (f.) (kweh-STYOH-neh) matter
questo (KWEH-stoh) this
qui (kwee) here
quiete (f.) (kwee-EH-teh) calm
quieto (kwee-EH-toh) quiet, calm
quindi (KWEEN-dee) therefore
quotidiano (kwoh-tee-DYAH-noh) daily

quotidiano (m.) daily newspaper

R

raccomandare (rahk-koh-mahn-DAH-reh) to recommend
racconto (m.) (rahk-KOHN-toh) story, tale
radersi (refl.) (RAH-dehr-see) to shave
radio (f.) (RAH-dyoh) radio
radiografia (f.) (rah-dyoh-grah-FEE-ah) X-ray
raffreddore (m.) (rahf-frehd-DOH-reh) cold
ragazza (f.) (rah-GAHT-tsah) girl
ragazzo (m.) (rah-GAHT-tsoh) boy
raggiungere (rahd-JOON-jeh-reh) to reach, to arrive
ragione (f.) (rah-JOH-neh) reason
  aver ragione (ah-VEHR . . .) to be right
ragù (m.) (rah-GOO) meat sauce
rallentare (rahl-lehn-TAH-reh) to slow down
rapido (RAH-pee-doh) swift, quick
raro (RAH-roh) rare
rasarsi (refl.) (rah-ZAHR-see) to shave
rasoio (m.) (rah-ZOH-yoh) razor
razza (f.) (RAHT-tsah) race
re (m.) (reh) king
reale (reh-AH-leh) real, royal

realizzare *(reh-ah-leed-DZAH-reh)* to carry out, to achieve

recente *(reh-CHEHN-teh)* recent

recitare *(reh-chee-TAH-reh)* to act, to play

regalo (m.) *(reh-GAH-loh)* present, gift

reggia (f.) *(REHD-jah)* royal palace

reggipetto; reggiseno (m.) *(rehd-jee-PEHT-toh, rehd-jee-SEH-noh)* bra

regina (f.) *(reh-JEE-nah)* queen

regista (m./f.) *(reh-JEE-stah)* director (movie)

registrare *(reh-jee-STRAH-reh)* to record, to register

regola (f.) *(REH-goh-lah)* rule

regolare *(reh-goh-LAH-reh)* to adjust, to regulate

rendere *(REHN-deh-reh)* to give back, to return

reparto (m.) *(reh-PAHR-toh)* department

residenza (f.) *(reh-zee-DEHN-tsah)* residence

respirare *(reh-spee-RAH-reh)* to breathe

respiro (m.) *(reh-SPEE-roh)* breath

resto (m.) *(REH-stoh)* change (money)

rialzo (m.) *(ree-AHL-tsoh)* rise, increase

ribasso (m.) *(ree-BAHS-soh)* fall, drop

ricambio (m.) *(ree-KAHM-byoh)* replacement

ricchezza (f.) *(reek-KEHT-tsah)* wealth

riccio (m.) *(REET-choh)* curl, curly

ricco *(REEK-koh)* rich

ricetta (f.) *(ree-CHEHT-tah)* recipe, prescription

ricevere *(ree-CHEH-veh-reh)* to receive

ricevuta (f.) *(ree-cheh-VOO-tah)* receipt

ricezione (f.) *(ree-cheh-TSYOH-neh)* reception

richiedere *(ree-KYEH-deh-reh)* to ask for

richiesta (f.) *(ree-KYEH-stah)* request

riconoscere *(ree-koh-NOH-sheh-reh)* to recognize

ricordare *(ree-kohr-DAH-reh)* to remember

ricordo (m.) *(ree-KOHR-doh)* recollection, souvenir

ridere *(REE-deh-reh)* to laugh

ridotto *(ree-DOHT-toh)* reduced, discounted

riduzione (f.) *(ree-doo-TSYOH-neh)* reduction, discount

rientrare *(ryehn-TRAH-reh)* to reenter, to go back

rifare *(ree-FAH-reh)* to do/make again, to remake, to make (a bed)

riga (f.) *(REE-gah)* line

riguardo (m.) *(ree-GWAHR-doh)* regard, care, respect

rilassarsi (refl.) *(ree-lahs-SAHR-see)* to relax

rimanere *(ree-mah-NEH-reh)* to stay, to remain, to be left

265

rimborsare *(reem-bohr-SAH-reh)* to refund

rimborso (m.) *(reem-BOHR-soh)* refund

rimescolare *(ree-meh-skoh-LAH-reh)* to mix, to stir

rinfresco (m.) *(reen-FREH-skoh)* refreshments

ringraziamento (m.) *(reen-grah-tsyah-MEHN-toh)* thanks

ringraziare *(reen-grah-TSYAH-reh)* to thank

ripetere *(ree-PEH-teh-reh)* to repeat

riposare *(ree-poh-ZAH-reh)* to rest, to sleep

riscaldamento (m.) *(ree-skahl-dah-MEHN-toh)* heating

riscaldare *(ree-skahl-DAH-reh)* to warm up, to heat

riscuotere *(ree-SKWOH-teh-reh)* to cash, to collect

riso (m.) *(REE-zoh)* rice, laugh, laughter

risparmiare *(ree-spahr-MYAH-reh)* to save

rispetto (m.) *(ree-SPEHT-toh)* respect

rispondere *(ree-SPOHN-deh-reh)* to answer

risposta (f.) *(ree-SPOH-stah)* answer, reply

ristorante (m.) *(ree-stoh-RAHN-teh)* restaurant

ritardo (m.) *(ree-TAHR-doh)* delay

   essere in ritardo *(EHS-seh-reh een . . .)* to be late

ritornare *(ree-tohr-NAH-reh)* to return, to come back

ritratto (m.) *(ree-TRAHT-toh)* portrait

riuscire *(ryoo-SHEE-reh)* to succeed

rivista (f.) *(ree-VEE-stah)* magazine

rivolgere; rivolgersi (refl.) *(ree-VOHL-jeh-reh; ree-VOHL-jehr-see)* to turn around, to revolve; to address oneself

roba (f.) *(ROH-bah)* stuff

romanzo (m.) *(roh-MAHN-dzoh)* novel

rompere *(ROHM-peh-reh)* to break

rotto *(ROHT-toh)* broken

rosa *(ROH-zah)* pink

   rosa (f.) *(ROH-zah)* rose

rosso *(ROHS-soh)* red

rovina (f.) *(roh-VEE-nah)* ruin

rovinare *(roh-vee-NAH-reh)* to ruin, to spoil

   rovinato *(roh-vee-NAH-toh)* ruined

rubrica (f.) *(roo-BREE-kah)* address book

rullino (m.) *(rool-LEE-noh)* roll of film

rumore (m.) *(roo-MOH-reh)* noise

rumoroso *(roo-moh-ROH-zoh)* noisy

ruota (f.) *(RWOH-tah)* wheel

S

sabbia (f.) *(SAHB-byah)* sand

sacchetto (m.) *(sahk-KEHT-toh)* small bag

sala (f.) *(SAH-lah)* room

sale (m.) *(SAH-leh)* salt*

salire *(sah-LEE-reh)* to get on/into, to go up

salone (m.) *(sah-LOH-neh)* parlor, hall

salotto (m.) *(sah-LOHT-toh)* living room

salsa (f.) *(SAHL-sah)* sauce

saltare *(sahl-TAH-reh)* to jump

salutare *(sah-loo-TAH-reh)* to greet

salute (f.) *(sah-LOO-teh)* health
  salute! to your health! cheers!

saluto (m.) *(sah-LOO-toh)* greeting

salvietta (f.) *(sahl-VYEHT-tah)* (table) napkin, towel

sangue (m.) *(SAHN-gweh)* blood

sano *(SAH-noh)* healthy

sapere *(sah-PEH-reh)* to know

saponetta (f.) *(sah-poh-NEHT-tah)* soap

sapore (m.) *(sah-POH-reh)* taste

sbagliare *(zbah-LYAH-reh)* to make a mistake

sbaglio (m.) *(ZBAH-lyoh)* mistake, error

sbarcare *(zbahr-KAH-reh)* to land

sbrigarsi (refl.) *(zbree-GAHR-see)* to hurry up
  sbrigati! *(ZBREE-gah-tee)* hurry up! (familiar)

scala (f.) *(SKAH-lah)* staircase, stairs

scalare *(skah-LAH-reh)* to climb up

scalo (m.) *(SKAH-loh)* stop (airline)

scambio (m.) *(SKAHM-byoh)* exchange

scantinato (m.) *(skahn-tee-NAH-toh)* basement

scarpa (f.) *(SKAHR-pah)* shoe

scatola (f.) *(SKAH-toh-lah)* box

scegliere *(SHEH-lyeh-reh)* to choose

scelta (f.) *(SHEHL-tah)* choice

scendere *(SHEHN-deh-reh)* to go down, to get off

scherzo (m.) *(SKEHR-tsoh)* joke

schiena (f.) *(SKYEH-nah)* back

sci (m.pl.) *(shee)* ski

sciare *(shee-AH-reh)* to ski

sciarpa (f.) *(SHAHR-pah)* scarf

sciogliere *(SHOH-lyeh-reh)* to loosen, to undo, to melt

sciovia (f.) *(shee-oh-VEE-ah)* ski lift

scivolare *(shee-voh-LAH-reh)* to slide, to slip

scomodo *(SKOH-moh-doh)* uncomfortable

scomparire *(skohm-pah-REE-reh)* to disappear

scompartimento (m.) *(skohm-pahr-tee-MEHN-toh)* compartment

sconto (m.) *(SKOHN-toh)* discount

scontrino (m.) *(skohn-TREE-noh)* ticket, receipt

scontro (m.) *(SKOHN-troh)* clash, collision

scoprire *(skoh-PREE-reh)* to discover

scordare *(skohr-DAH-reh)* to forget

scorrere *(SKOHR-reh-reh)* to run, to flow

scorso *(SKOHR-soh)* last, past

scortese *(skohr-TEH-zeh)* rude, impolite

scottare *(skoht-TAH-reh)* to burn, to scald

scottatura (f.) *(skoht-tah-TOO-rah)* burn, sunburn

scotto *(SKOHT-toh)* overdone (of pasta)

scrittura (f.) *(skreet-TOO-rah)* writing

scrivere *(SKREE-veh-reh)* to write

scultura (f.) *(skool-TOO-rah)* sculpture

scuola (f.) *(SKWOH-lah)* school

scuro *(SKOO-roh)* dark

scusare *(skoo-ZAH-reh)* to excuse, to forgive

scusi! *(SKOO-zee!)* sorry!

scusarsi (refl.) *(skoo-ZAHR-see)* to apologize

se *(seh)* if

seccare *(sehk-KAH-reh)* to dry, to annoy, to bother

non mi seccare! *(nohn mee . . . !)* don't bother me!

secco *(SEHK-koh)* dry; skinny, thin

secolo (m.) *(SEH-koh-loh)* century

secondo (m.) *(seh-KOHN-doh)* second

secondo (prep.) according to

sedere *(seh-DEH-reh)* to sit down

sedia (f.) *(SEH-dyah)* chair

seggiola (f.) *(sehd-JOH-lah)* chair

segnale (m.) *(seh-NYAH-leh)* signal, sign

segnare *(seh-NYAH-reh)* to mark, to score

segno (m.) *(SEH-nyoh)* sign, mark

seguire *(seh-GWEE-reh)* to follow

semaforo (m.) *(seh-MAH-foh-roh)* traffic light

semplice *(SEHM-plee-cheh)* simple

sempre *(SEHM-preh)* always

senso (m.) *(SEHN-soh)* sense, meaning

sentire *(sehn-TEE-reh)* to hear, to feel

senza *(SEHN-tsah)* without

sera (f.); serata (f.) *(SEH-rah; seh-RAH-tah)* evening

serio *(SEH-ryoh)* serious

serratura (f.) *(sehr-rah-TOO-rah)* lock

servire *(sehr-VEE-reh)* to serve

servizio (m.) *(sehr-VEE-tsyoh)* service

seta (f.) *(SEH-tah)* silk

sete (f.) *(SEH-teh)* thirst

settentrione (m.) *(seht-tehn-TRYOH-neh)* north

settimana (f.) *(seht-tee-MAH-nah)* week

sezione (f.) *(seh-TSYOH-neh)* section, department

sfortuna (f.) *(sfohr-TOO-nah)* bad luck

sforzo (m.) *(SFOHR-tsoh)* effort

sguardo (m.) *(SGWAHR-doh)* look, glance

sì *(see)* yes

sicuro *(see-KOO-roh)* sure, certain

siesta (f.) *(SYEH-stah)* or **sonnellino (m.)** *(sohn-nehl-LEE-noh)* nap

significare *(see-nyee-fee-KAH-reh)* to mean

signora (f.) *(see-NYOH-rah)* lady, woman, madam

signore (m.) *(see-NYOH-reh)* gentleman, man, sir

signorina (f.) *(see-nyoh-REE-nah)* young lady, miss

silenzio (m.) *(see-LEHN-tsyoh)* silence

simile *(SEE-mee-leh)* like, similar, alike

simpatico *(seem-PAH-tee-koh)* likeable, pleasant

sindaco (m.) *(SEEN-dah-koh)* mayor

sinfonia (f.) *(seen-foh-NEE-ah)* symphony

sinistra (f.) *(see-NEE-strah)* left

sistema (m.) *(see-STEH-mah)* system

situazione (f.) *(see-twah-TSYOH-neh)* situation

slacciare *(zlaht-CHAH-reh)* to undo, to untie, to unbutton

slip (m.) *(zleep)* bathing suit, briefs

smalto (m.) *(ZMAHL-toh)* enamel, nail polish

smarrire *(zmahr-REE-reh)* to lose

smettere *(ZMEHT-teh-reh)* to stop

smoking (m.) *(ZMOH-keen)* tuxedo

snello *(ZNEHL-loh)* slim, slender

soccorso (m.) *(sohk-KOHR-soh)* help, aid
  pronto soccorso *(PROHN-toh . . .)* first aid

società (f.) *(soh-cheh-TAH)* society, company

soddisfare *(sohd-dee-SFAH-reh)* to satisfy, to please

sodo *(SOH-doh)* firm, hard

soffitto (m.) *(sohf-FEET-toh)* ceiling

soffrire *(sohf-FREE-reh)* to suffer

soggiorno (m.) *(sohd-JOHR-noh)* stay
  azienda di soggiorno (f.) *(ah-DZYEHN-dah dee . . .)* local tourist office

sogno (m.) *(SOH-nyoh)* dream

solaio (m.) *(soh-LAH-yoh)* attic

soldi (m.pl.) *(SOHL-dee)* money

sole (m.) *(SOH-leh)* sun

solito *(SOH-lee-toh)* usual, customary
  di solito *(dee . . .)* usually

solo; solamente; soltanto *(SOH-loh; soh-lah-MEHN-teh; sohl-TAHN-toh)* only (adv.)
  solo alone

somma (f.) *(SOHM-mah)* sum, addition

sonno (m.) *(SOHN-noh)* sleep

sopra *(SOH-prah)* on, upon, above

soprabito (m.) *(soh-PRAH-bee-toh)* overcoat

269

soprattutto *(soh-praht-TOOT-toh)* above all

sorella (f.) *(soh-REHL-lah)* sister

sorgere *(SOHR-jeh-reh)* to rise, to stand

sorpassare *(sohr-pahs-SAH-reh)* to go beyond, to exceed

sorridere *(sohr-REE-deh-reh)* to smile

sosta (f.) *(SOH-stah)* stop
  divieto di sosta *(dee-VYEH-toh dee . . .)* no parking

sottile *(soht-TEE-leh)* thin

sotto *(SOHT-toh)* under, below

sovraffollato *(soh-vrahf-fohl-LAH-toh)* crowded, packed

spalla (f.) *(SPAHL-lah)* shoulder

spaventare *(spah-vehn-TAH-reh)* to frighten, to scare

spazzatura (f.) *(spaht-tsah-TOO-rah)* garbage

spazzola (f.) *(SPAHT-tsoh-lah)* brush

specchio (m.) *(SPEHK-kyoh)* mirror

speciale *(speh-CHAH-leh)* special

specialità (m.) *(speh-chah-lee-TAH)* specialty

specie (f.) *(SPEH-cheh)* kind, sort

spedire *(speh-DEE-reh)* to send

spegnere *(SPEH-nyeh-reh)* to extinguish, to put out, to switch off

spendere *(SPEHN-deh-reh)* to spend

spesa (f.) *(SPEH-zah)* expense, shopping

spettatore (m.) *(speh-tah-TOH-reh)* spectator

spezie (f.pl.) *(SPEH-tsyeh)* spices

spiccioli (m.pl.) *(SPEET-choh-lee)* small change (money)

spiegare *(spyeh-GAH-reh)* to explain

spilla (f.) *(SPEEL-lah)* pin

spina (f.) *(SPEE-nah)* plug
  spina intermedia *(. . . een-tehr-MEH-dyah)* adapter

spingere *(SPEEN-jeh-reh)* to push

splendido *(SPLEHN-dee-doh)* splendid, wonderful

spogliarsi (refl.) *(spoh-LYAHR-see)* to get undressed

sporco *(SPOHR-koh)* dirty

sporgersi (refl.) *(SPOHR-jehr-see)* to lean out of

sportello (m.) *(spohr-TEHL-loh)* teller (bank)

sposa (f.) *(SPOH-zah)* bride

sposarsi (refl.) *(spoh-ZAHR-see)* to get married

sposo (m.) *(SPOH-zoh)* bridegroom

sprecare *(spreh-KAH-reh)* to waste

spuntino (m.) *(spoon-TEE-noh)* snack

squadra (f.) *(SKWAH-drah)* team

stadio (m.) *(STAH-dyoh)* stadium

stagione (f.) *(stah-JOH-neh)* season

stamattina (f.) *(stah-maht-TEE-nah)* this morning

stanco *(STAHN-koh)* tired

stanotte (f.) *(stah-NOHT-teh)* tonight

stanza (f.) *(STAHN-tsah)* room

stare *(STAH-reh)* to stay, to remain, to be (health)

stasera (f.) *(stah-SEH-rah)* this evening

stato (m.) *(STAH-toh)* state, condition

statua (f.) *(STAH-twah)* statue

stazione (f.) *(stah-TSYOH-neh)* station

stella (f.) *(STEHL-lah)* star

stesso *(STEHS-soh)* same, self

stile (m.) *(STEE-leh)* style

stirare *(stee-RAH-reh)* to iron

stivale (m.) *(stee-VAH-leh)* boot

stoffa (f.) *(STOHF-fah)* fabric, material

stomaco (m.) *(STOH-mah-koh)* stomach

storia (f.) *(STOH-ryah)* history, story

storto *(STOHR-toh)* crooked

strada (f.) *(STRAH-dah)* road, street, way

strano *(STRAH-noh)* strange

strappare *(strahp-PAH-reh)* to tear up

stringere *(STREEN-jeh-reh)* to tighten, to fasten

studente (m.); studentessa (f.) *(stoo-DEHN-teh; stoo-dehn-TEHS-sah)* student

studiare *(stoo-DYAH-reh)* to study

su *(soo)* on, upon, over, about

subacqueo *(soo-BAHK-kweh-oh)* underwater

subito *(SOO-bee-toh)* at once, immediately

succedere *(soot-CHEH-deh-reh)* to succeed, to happen

successo (m.) *(soot-CHEHS-soh)* success

succo (m.) *(SOOK-koh)* juice

sud (m.) *(sood)* south

sufficiente *(soof-fee-CHEHN-teh)* sufficient

suggestivo *(sood-jeh-STEE-voh)* impressive, evocative

superbo *(soo-PEHR-boh)* haughty, superb, excellent

superiore *(soo-peh-RYOH-reh)* superior

supermercato (m.) *(soo-pehr-mehr-KAH-toh)* supermarket

supporre *(soop-POHR-reh)* to assume, to suppose

surgelato *(soor-jeh-LAH-toh)* frozen (food)

sveglia (f.) *(ZVEH-lyah)* alarm clock

svegliarsi (refl.) *(zveh-LYAHR-see)* to wake up

svelto *(ZVEHL-toh)* quick

svoltare *(zvohl-TAH-reh)* to turn

  svoltare a destra *(. . . ah DEH-strah)* to turn right

T

tabaccheria (f.) *(tah-bahk-keh-REE-ah)* tobacco shop

taglia (f.) *(TAH-lyah)* size

tagliare *(tah-LYAH-reh)* to cut

271

tagliatelle (f.pl.) *(tah-lyah-TEHL-leh)* flat noodles

taglio (m.) *(TAH-lyoh)* cutting, cut

tallone (m.) *(tahl-LOH-neh)* heel

talvolta *(tahl-VOHL-tah)* sometimes

tamponare *(tahm-poh-NAH-reh)* to collide (car)

tanto *(TAHN-toh)* so, so much
  tanti *(TAHN-tee)* so many

tappeto (m.) *(tahp-PEH-toh)* carpet

tappo (m.) *(TAHP-poh)* cork

tardi *(TAHR-dee)* late
  a più tardi *(ah pyoo . . .)* see you later

targa (f.) *(TAHR-gah)* license plate

tariffa (f.) *(tah-REEF-fah)* rate

tartina (f.) *(tahr-TEE-nah)* small sandwich

tartufo (m.) *(tahr-TOO-foh)* truffle

tasca (f.) *(TAH-skah)* pocket

tassa (f.) *(TAHS-sah)* tax

tassista (m.) *(tahs-SEE-stah)* taxi driver

taverna (f.) *(tah-VEHR-nah)* inn

tavola(-o) (f./m.) *(TAH-voh-lah)(-loh)* table
  tavola calda/fredda *(. . . KAHL-dah/FREHD-dah)* snack bar

taxi (m.) *(TAHK-see)* taxi, cab

tazza (f.) *(TAHT-tsah)* cup

tazzina (f.) *(taht-TSEE-nah)* demitasse, small cup

tè (m.) *(teh)* tea

teatro (m.) *(teh-AH-troh)* theater

tela (f.) *(TEH-lah)* cloth

telefonare *(teh-leh-foh-NAH-reh)* to telephone

telefonico (adj.) *(teh-leh-FOH-nee-koh)* telephone
  cabina telefonica *(kah-BEE-nah . . .)* telephone booth
  elenco telefonico (m.) *(eh-LEHN-koh . . .)* telephone book

telefono (m.) *(teh-LEH-foh-noh)* telephone

telegramma (m.) *(teh-leh-GRAHM-mah)* telegram

televisione (f.) *(teh-leh-vee-ZYOH-neh)* television

televisore (m.) *(teh-leh-vee-ZOH-reh)* television set

temere *(teh-MEH-reh)* to fear

temperatura (f.) *(tehm-peh-rah-TOO-rah)* temperature

tempesta (f.) *(tehm-PEH-stah)* tempest, storm

tempo (m.) *(TEHM-poh)* time, weather

tenere *(teh-NEH-reh)* to keep, to hold

tennis (m.) *(TEHN-nees)* tennis

terme (f.pl.) *(TEHR-meh)* thermal baths

terminare *(tehr-mee-NAH-reh)* to end, to finish

termometro (m.) *(tehr-MOH-meh-troh)* thermometer

termosifone (m.) *(tehr-moh-see-FOH-neh)* radiator

terra (f.) *(TEHR-rah)* earth, soil, ground

terrazza(-o) (f./m.) *(tehr-RAHT-tsah)(-tsoh)* terrace

terreno (m.) *(tehr-REH-noh)* ground

terribile *(tehr-REE-bee-leh)* terrible

teso *(TEH-zoh)* tight

tesoro (m.) *(teh-ZOH-roh)* treasure

   tesoro! darling! honey!

tessera (f.) *(TEHS-seh-rah)* card (membership)

tessuto (m.) *(tehs-SOO-toh)* fabric, material

testa (f.) *(TEH-stah)* head

testardo *(teh-STAHR-doh)* stubborn

tetto (m.) *(TEHT-toh)* roof

timbro (m.) *(TEEM-broh)* stamp

tinello (m.) *(tee-NEHL-loh)* dining room (informal)

tinta (f.) *(TEEN-tah)* dye, color

tintarella (f.) *(teen-tah-REHL-lah)* suntan

tintoria (f.) *(teen-toh-REE-ah)* dry cleaner

tipico *(TEE-pee-koh)* typical

tipo (m.) *(TEE-poh)* type, guy

   che bel tipo! *(keh behl . . . !)* what a nice guy!

tirare *(tee-RAH-reh)* to pull, to draw

titolo (m.) *(TEE-toh-loh)* title

toccare *(tohk-KAH-reh)* to touch

toeletta (f.) *(toh-eh-LEHT-tah)* restroom [or, **toelette** *(toh-eh-LEHT) (s.)*; *(toh-eh-LEHT-teh) (pl.)*]

togliere *(TOH-lyeh-reh)* to take away, to take off

toilette (f.) *(twah-LEHT)* toilet, bathroom, lavatory

tondo *(TOHN-doh)* round

tonno (m.) *(TOHN-noh)* tunafish

tornare *(tohr-NAH-reh)* to return

torre (f.) *(TOHR-reh)* tower

torta (f.) *(TOHR-tah)* cake

tossire *(tohs-SEE-reh)* to cough

totale *(toh-TAH-leh)* total

tovaglia (f.) *(toh-VAH-lyah)* tablecloth

tovagliolo (m.) *(toh-vah-LYOH-loh)* napkin

tradurre *(trah-DOOR-reh)* to translate

traffico (m.) *(TRAHF-fee-koh)* traffic

traghetto (m.) *(trah-GEHT-toh)* ferryboat

tram (m.) *(trahm)* streetcar

tramezzino (m.) *(trah-mehd-DZEE-noh)* sandwich

tranquillo *(trahn-KWEEL-loh)* quiet, calm

traslocare *(trah-zloh-KAH-reh)* to move

trasmissione (f.) *(trah-zmees-SYOH-neh)* transmission, program, broadcast

trasparente *(trah-spah-REHN-teh)* transparent

trasportare *(trah-spohr-TAH-reh)* to carry, to convey

trattamento (m.) *(traht-tah-MEHN-toh)* treatment, service

trattoria (f.) *(traht-toh-REE-ah)* restaurant

273

traversa (f.) *(trah-VEHR-sah)* crossroad

treno (m.) *(TREH-noh)* train

tribunale (m.) *(tree-boo-NAH-leh)* court

triste *(TREE-steh)* sad

tristezza (f.) *(tree-STEHT-tsah)* sadness

troppo *(TROH-poh)* too much
  troppi *(TROHP-pee)* too many

trovare *(troh-VAH-reh)* to find

trucco (m.) *(TROOK-koh)* makeup

tuo *(TOO-oh)* your, yours

tuono (m.) *(TWOH-noh)* thunder

turismo (m.) *(too-REE-smoh)* tourism

turista (m./f.) *(too-REE-stah)* tourist

turistico *(too-REE-stee-koh)* tourist, touristic

turno (m.) *(TOOR-noh)* turn

tutto *(TOOT-toh)* all, every, everything

U

ubbidire *(oob-bee-DEE-reh)* to obey

ubriacarsi (refl.) *(oo-bryah-KAHR-see)* to get drunk
  ubriaco *(oo-bree-AH-koh)* drunk

uccello (m.) *(oot-CHEHL-loh)* bird

ufficio (m.) *(oof-FEE-choh)* office
  ufficio cambio *(. . . KAHM-byoh)* currency exchange office

ultimo *(OOL-tee-moh)* last, latest

umido *(OO-mee-doh)* damp, humid

umore (m.) *(oo-MOH-reh)* humor, mood

unghia (f.) *(OON-gyah)* nail (finger-/toe-)

unico *(OO-nee-koh)* unique, only

università (f.) *(oo-nee-vehr-see-TAH)* university

uno *(OO-noh)* one, a, an

uomo (m.) *(WOH-moh)* man
  uomini (m.pl.) *(WOH-mee-nee)* men

uovo (m.) *(WOH-voh)* egg
  uova (f.pl.) *(WOH-vah)* eggs

urbano *(oor-BAH-noh)* city, local

urlare *(oor-LAH-reh)* to shout, to yell

usare *(oo-ZAH-reh)* to use

uscio (m.) *(OO-shoh)* door

uscire *(oo-SHEE-reh)* to go out

uscita (f.) *(oo-SHEE-tah)* exit, way out

uso (m.) *(OO-zoh)* use

utensile (m.) *(oo-TEHN-see-leh)* tool

utile *(OO-tee-leh)* useful, helpful

uva (f.) *(OO-vah)* grapes

V

vacanza (f.) *(vah-KAHN-tsah)* holiday

vaglia (m.) *(VAH-lyah)* money order

vagone (m.) *(vah-GOH-neh)* car (train)

  vagone letto *(. . . LEHT-toh)* sleeping car

valere *(vah-LEH-reh)* to be worth

valido *(VAH-lee-doh)* valid, worth

valigia (f.) *(vah-LEE-jah)* suitcase

valle (f.) *(VAHL-leh)* valley

valore (m.) *(vah-LOH-reh)* value

valuta (f.) *(vah-LOO-tah)* currency, money

vantaggio (m.) *(vahn-TAHD-joh)* advantage, profit

vaporetto (m.) *(vah-poh-REHT-toh)* steamboat

varietà (m.) *(vah-ryeh-TAH)* variety; music hall

vario *(VAH-ryoh)* various, different

vaso (m.) *(VAH-zoh)* vase

vasto *(VAH-stoh)* vast, wide

vecchio *(VEHK-kyoh)* old, ancient

vedere *(veh-DEH-reh)* to see

  veduto, visto *(veh-DOO-toh, VEE-stoh)* seen

veduta (f.) *(veh-DOO-tah)* view

vegetable (m.) *(veh-jeh-TAH-leh)* vegetable

vela (f.) *(VEH-lah)* sail

veleno (m.) *(veh-LEH-noh)* poison

veloce *(veh-LOH-cheh)* quick, fast

velocità (f.) *(veh-loh-chee-TAH)* speed

limite di velocità (m.) *(LEE-mee-teh dee . . .)* speed limit

vendere *(VEHN-deh-reh)* to sell

vendita (f.) *(VEHN-dee-tah)* sale

venditore (m.) *(vehn-dee-TOH-reh)* seller, vendor

venire *(veh-NEE-reh)* to come

ventilatore (m.) *(vehn-tee-lah-TOH-reh)* fan

vento (m.) *(VEHN-toh)* wind

veramente *(veh-rah-MEHN-teh)* really, truly

verde *(VEHR-deh)* green

verdura (f.) *(vehr-DOO-rah)* vegetables

vergogna (f.) *(vehr-GOH-nyah)* shame

verità (f.) *(veh-ree-TAH)* truth

vernice (f.) *(vehr-NEE-cheh)* paint

vero *(VEH-roh)* true, real

versare *(vehr-SAH-reh)* to deposit, to pour, to spill

verso *(VEHR-soh)* toward

veste (f.) *(VEH-steh)* dress, clothes, garments

vestire *(veh-STEE-reh)* to dress, to wear

vestito (m.) *(veh-STEE-toh)* dress, outfit

vetrata (f.) *(veh-TRAH-tah)* glass window

vetrina (f.) *(veh-TREE-nah)* window (shop), showcase

vetro (m.) *(VEH-troh)* glass

via (f.) *(VEE-ah)* street, way, path

viaggiare *(vyahd-JAH-reh)* to travel

275

viaggio (m.) *(VYAHD-joh)* travel, journey

vicino *(vee-CHEE-noh)* near, close

vicolo (m.) *(VEE-koh-loh)* alley, lane

vietare *(vyeh-TAH-reh)* to forbid

vietato *(vyeh-TAH-toh)* forbidden

vigile (m.) *(VEE-jee-leh)* cop

  vigile del fuoco *(. . . dehl FWOH-koh)* firefighter

vigna (f.); vigneto (m.) *(VEE-nyah; vee-NYEH-toh)* vineyard

villa (f.) *(VEEL-lah)* villa

villaggio (m.) *(veel-LAHD-joh)* village

villeggiatura (f.) *(veel-lehd-jah-TOO-rah)* holiday, vacation

vincere *(VEEN-cheh-reh)* to win

  vinto *(VEEN-toh)* won

vino (m.) *(VEE-noh)* wine

visita (f.) *(VEE-zee-tah)* visit

visitare *(vee-zee-TAH-reh)* to visit

viso (m.) *(VEE-zoh)* face

vista (f.) *(VEE-stah)* sight

vita (f.) *(VEE-tah)* life, waist

vitello (m.) *(vee-TEHL-loh)* veal

viva! *(VEE-vah!)* hurrah!

vivere *(VEE-veh-reh)* to live

  vissuto *(vees-SOO-toh)* lived

vivo *(VEE-voh)* alive

vocabolario (m.) *(voh-kah-boh-LAH-ryoh)* dictionary

voce (f.) *(VOH-cheh)* voice

voglia (f.) *(VOH-lyah)* wish, desire

volante (m.) *(voh-LAHN-teh)* steering wheel

volare *(voh-LAH-reh)* to fly

volere *(voh-LEH-reh)* to want, to wish, to desire

volo (m.) *(VOH-loh)* flight

volta (f.) *(VOHL-tah)* time

  due volte *(DOO-eh VOHL-teh)* twice ·

voltare *(vohl-TAH-reh)* to turn

vuoto *(VWOH-toh)* empty

W

water-closet (m.) *(WOH-tah CLOH-zeht)* toilet, lavatory

Y

yogurt (m.) *(YOH-goort)* yoghurt

Z

zabaglione (m.) *(dzah-bah-LYOH-neh)* egg cream dessert

zaino (m.) *(DZAH-ee-noh)* backpack

zero (m.) *(DZEH-roh)* zero

zia (f.) *(TSEE-ah)* aunt

zio (m.) *(TSEE-oh)* uncle

zitto *(TSEET-toh)* silent

zolletta (f.) *(dzohl-LEHT-tah)* lump (sugar)

zona (f.) *(DZOH-nah)* zone

zoo (m.) *(DZOH-oh)* zoo

zucchero (m.) *(TSOOK-keh-roh)* sugar

zuppa (f.) *(TSOOP-pah)* soup